*f*P

AROUND
SARAH'S TABLE

*Ten Hasidic Women Share
Their Stories of Life, Faith,
and Tradition*

Rivka Zakutinsky
and
Yaffa Leba Gottlieb

The Free Press
New York   London   Toronto   Sydney   Singapore

*f*P
THE FREE PRESS
A Division of Simon & Schuster, Inc.
1230 Avenue of the Americas
New York, NY 10020

For information about special discounts for bulk purchases,
please contact Simon & Schuster Special Sales:
1-800-456-6798 or business@simonandschuster.com.

Designed by Deirdre C. Amthor

Manufactured in the United States of America

10   9   8   7   6   5   4   3   2   1

Library of Congress Cataloging-in-Publication Data
Zakutinsky, Rivka.
    Around Sarah's table: ten Hasidic women share their stories
of life, faith, and tradition/Rivka Zakutinsky and Yaffa Leba Gottlieb.
    p.   cm.
    1. Jewish women—New York (State)—New York—Biography. 2. Hasidim—
New York (State)—New York—Biography. 3. Jewish women—Religious life—
New York (State)—New York. 4. Bible O.T. Genesis—Commentaries.
5. Brooklyn (New York, N.Y.)—Biography. I. Gottlieb, Yaffa. II. Title.

BM753 .Z35 2001
296.8'3322'0820974723—dc21   2001033637

ISBN 0-684-87274-9

To all who join together around Sarah's table

Contents

Acknowledgments — ix

Authors' Note — xi

Prologue: Around Sarah's Table — 1

1 Shaina: Journey to the Other Side — 3
   Parshas Lech-Lecha
2 Reva: Achieving Revelations — 33
   Parshas Vayera
3 Tamar: Marrying Off the Next in Line — 58
   Parshas Chaye Sarah
4 Rachel: The Secrets of the *Mikvah* — 83
   Parshas Toldos
5 Glicka: Exile of the Body, Homecoming of the Soul — 112
   Parshas Vayeitzei
6 Levana: The Messenger of Peace — 135
   Parshas Vayishlach
7 Klara: Learning and Lawyering — 149
   Parshas Vayeshev
8 Erica: The Toil and the Oil — 171
   Parshas Mikeitz, Chanukah
9 Ora: Leadership with a Holy Vision — 194
   Parshas Vayigash
10 Sarah: The Ingathering, the Life, the Blessings — 212
   Parshas Vayechi

Contents

Afterword   235
Glossary of Hebrew and Yiddish Words   237
Suggested Reading   241

Acknowledgments

We are blessed with many to thank.

We want to thank Sarah and all our wonderful friends who gather around her table. From them we were inspired to write this book.

We want to thank our superagent, Gareth Esersky. We depended on her encouragement, guidance, know-how, and energy. We are very grateful.

We want to thank Alys Yablon for her extraordinary devotion, masterly editing, and astute sensitivity. No one else could have helped us shape this book so well. We are indebted to Alys.

We want to thank Liz Maguire for her interest in our manuscript and her pivotal role in getting the publishing under way. We want to thank Philip Rappaport, Beth Haymaker, Edith Lewis, and everyone else at The Free Press for their cheerful patience and expertise in seeing this project through.

Rivka wants to thank her husband, Rabbi Moshe Zakutinsky, O.B.M., who always took pride in joining her in their writing and publishing efforts; her parents, Hinda Alte and Chayim Yaakov Fedowitz, O.B.M., for their love and trust; her children, her son Yehudah and her daughter-in-law Adina, her son Yonason and her daughter-in-law Shulamith, her daughter Shoshana Malka and her son-in-law Yisroel Moshe, her son Yosef and her daughter-in-law Aliza, for being her pride and strength; and her grandchildren, who are the light of her eyes.

Yaffa wants to thank her encouraging friends-like-sisters Frumma Kulek and Tzvia Stern; and her enthusiastic sisters-in-law-like-sisters Etti, Chana Rivka, and Sarah Rivka Gottlieb; and her inspiring nieces and nephews; and her ever cheerful and ever helpful *machatonim*, Raizel and Levi Reiter.

Yaffa also wants to thank her wise teachers from Neve Yerushalayim, Beth Rivka and Machon Chana. She is particularly indebted and would like to express her *hakaras hatov* to Rabbi Moshe Chalkovsky, Rabbi Meir Shuster, and Rabbi Nissan Mangel.

She is grateful to her dear parents, Tzvi (Bud) and Sarah Malka (Mildred) Goldberg, for their love, support, and unswerving expectations.

She also wants to thank her children: Devorah Leah and her son-in-law, Yaakov, for their competence, their encouragement, and their energetic and unstinting helpfulness; Freidel for her *freid* in all areas, including writing; and Chaye Sara and Yanki, Yosef and Rachel, and Rebecca, for the joy they continue to bring; and her children's children, *kain yirbu*. May they all go from strength to strength and continue to bestow *chasidishe naches*.

And especially, her husband, Rabbi Yaakov Eliezer Gottlieb, for his patience and for his wisdom.

We are indebted to the Lubavitcher Rebbe, our mentor and guide, for his vision and blessings.

We humbly thank the Almighty for granting us health, life, strength, and insight to complete this book

—Rivka Zakutinsky, Borough Park
—Yaffa Leba Gottlieb, Crown Heights
The Tenth of Teves, 5761 (January 4, 2001)

Authors' Note

The women in *Around Sarah's Table* discuss some of the topics found in Beraishis (Genesis), the first of the five books of Moses. God gave these five books—collectively called the Torah—to Moses to teach to the Jewish people and through them, ultimately, to the world.

Parsha refers to a weekly Torah reading. The Torah is divided into weekly segments (*parshas*) that are read and studied in synagogues and shuls throughout the world. Because of the Divine nature of the Torah (which is also called the Tree of Life), the weekly *parsha* contains a timely message addressed to each individual and community. Hasidic masters explain that to "live with the times" one can look to the weekly *parsha* to direct and reflect upon one's life.

When a choice of spelling presented itself (for example, *Shabbat* or *Shabbos*), we selected the one most commonly used around Sarah's table.

Prologue:
Around Sarah's Table

We each have our own portion of the world, Hasidim say, a portion exclusively ours to elevate through our spiritual accomplishments. We are given three tools for this spiritual achievement: our thought, our speech, and our deeds. When well informed and directed, our thoughts, speech, and deeds can elevate our portion of the world to Godliness.

Of course, all kinds of obstacles and challenges obscure this goal. To accomplish despite challenges, a number of women meet together weekly at Sarah's table, to glean from the Torah teachings of the Lubavitcher Rebbe, Menachem Mendel Schneerson, using this as a springboard for other commentaries; and also to network, inform, direct, and redirect each other, make resolutions, find solutions, enjoy camaraderie, or just eat lunch. These women from the Ultraorthodox community include:

Shaina: a Ba'alas T'shuvah, one who has "returned" to Torah Judaism. Still haunted by the secular world she abandoned years ago, she is currently seeking the best for, and some relief from, her adopted, challenged two-and-a-half-year-olds.

Reva: author and publisher. Her vision is to popularize Torah insights through her books. But her husband's illness increasingly demanded her time.

Tamar: the homemaker. She is dedicated to her husband and
children, wholeheartedly devoted to making a home for
her family. None of her expertise, however, provides an
easy solution for marrying off her next in line "older"
daughter.

Rachel: Stretched beyond the limits of her community, she
now stretches beyond herself to do a *mitzvah*.

Glicka: She lost a fortune to gain a treasure.

Levana: Loyal wife, caring mother, devoted daughter, dutiful
rebbitzin, she is the buffer zone for all.

Klara: The successful professional, but she will not risk her
integrity, or her learning.

Erica: Vivacious wife of a world-renowned heart surgeon, she
turns her own heart to the perplexities of stepmotherhood.

Ora: Her life, once threatened, sings in endless thanksgiving.

And Sarah: Sarah is the facilitator, connector, informer, and
empowerer. She is the hostess, and her portion is her
table.

In *Around Sarah's Table* some names have been changed,
but the table is as Sarah has set it, for the Tuesday afternoon
lunch and learn.

The doors are open, and guests are always welcome.
Hasidic philosophy warns, however, that appetite comes with
eating.

1

Shaina: Journey to the Other Side
Parshas Lech-Lecha

The Lord said to Abram, "Go out, from your land, from your birthplace, and from your father's house, to the land that I will show you. I will make you into a great nation. I will bless you and make you great. You shall become a blessing. I will bless those who bless you and curse those who curse you. All the families of the earth will be blessed through you."
—Genesis 12:1, 2

Abraham's service, characterized by "proceeding beyond" his own limitations, set the standard for his descendants, the Jewish people. The secret of Abraham's strength was to go out of himself and to recognize and connect with the Creator. His connection was so strong that his very name was changed, from Abram to Abraham, adding the sacred letter that linked him with God. Standing alone in an era of idolatry, Abraham became known as the Ivri—the one on the other side.

Susan was recently divorced and acutely new to the "religious" Jewish lifestyle. Was she projecting the eroding boundaries of her personal life onto the universe at large? Her mother, Sylvia Gelfarb, thought so. Sylvia, a sensible native Midwesterner, was wary of a daughter more Jewish than the Reform temple or Conservative synagogue had educated her to be. Sylvia

absolutely allowed her children the choice of religious affilia-
tion, but Reform or Conservative should have been choice
enough.

So why wasn't it? Sylvia had been apprehensive about her
daughter's living arrangements ever since Susan, the birth
name that Sylvia had selected for her daughter two and a half
decades before, began signing her letters "Shaina." "Shaina," an
old-fashioned, grandmotherly name (the name, in fact, of
Sylvia's own departed grandmother), was a Hebrew school
name definitely not intended for general use.

Those "Shaina" letters came from Israel. After the unfor-
tunate divorce (in retrospect, Sylvia could find no fault with
her ex–son-in-law, a fine young mathematician) Susan had
flown to Israel, supposedly to prepare to teach a literature
course. At first she had great adventures. As soon as she
landed, she was invited to Beit Jala, as the guest of a Christian
Arab family. Susan wrote home about her hostess's multigen-
erational household, all living together within the thick stone
walls of their ancestral mountaintop villa. She mentioned
orchards, gardens, protective little "houses" that the farmers
built around each tomato plant, and the many marriage pro-
posals she received from young Arab boys longing for green
cards. It seemed that all was well.

But her later letters, the ones she began signing "Shaina,"
were different. Initially Sylvia conceded to Susan's logic, agree-
ing that a week among Christian Arabs might be balanced by
a weekend among religious Jews. But when that weekend led
to a change of convictions, Sylvia suspected brainwashing.
Clearly Susan, emotionally vulnerable as she must be at this
time, had become victim to a cult. Sylvia and her husband
flew to the Holy Land to set things straight.

Susan's cult was located in the Jerusalem suburb of Bayit
V'Gan (House and Garden), under the guise of a seminary for

young women called Neve Yerushalayim (Jerusalem Oasis). Sylvia combed the dorms but found only healthy and mentally sound young women. Puzzled, she inquired after the director. She was introduced to Rabbi Moshe Chalkovsky, a refined English scholar, so much a gentleman that Sylvia hardly noticed his yarmulke (head covering). Not that she would have objected; the rabbi's yarmulke, like the surgeon's scrubs, is a mark of the profession. Sylvia easily agreed with Rabbi Chalkovsky that girls often go to extremes when they first explore their Jewish heritage in depth. She could even concede that the synagogue's weekly postconfirmation class did not constitute depth. In time, the rabbi assured her, the girls adapt to the middle way. This pleased Sylvia. The Conservative synagogue, midway between Reform and Orthodox, always had made sense to her. So although Susan/Shaina was intent, just then, on brainwashing her mother, Sylvia looked forward to happier times.

They did not materialize. Shaina (Susan appeared lost and gone forever) confirmed Sylvia's worst fears and abandoned the university. She was even comparing a commitment to the study of English literature with a commitment to the study of Donald Duck! After a taste of what she called Torah, Shaina would not return to Shakespeare.

As time passed, Shaina compounded one incomprehensible act with another. Shaina did *not* settle onto a middle road; she became *religious*. Yet, as Sylvia explained to her friend Paula, even among the religious there must be some moderation, where, in spite of Torah, you lead a normal life. But not Shaina. She had to join the extremely religious, where Torah *is* one's life.

Even that situation might not have been hopeless. Sylvia explained to Paula that those who are extremely religious do not consider being extremely religious an extreme. In fact, among the extremely religious there can yet exist considerable normalcy! Among them are men with normal professions. Doctors, lawyers, businessmen, even professors—Shaina could have married one of these! But no. Shaina had to go to the extreme of the extreme and marry a rabbi. And not a fine, robust, school-directing, gentleman rabbi, like Rabbi Chalkovsky, which could be forgiven. Who Shaina married was a small man who stooped over a little desk writing *mezuzahs*. No, not the artist who designs the covers! There's supposed to be a little piece of paper *inside* the cover. How many people have heard of that? And not just any little piece of paper, but a special parchment one that had to be written *by hand* to be kosher! No, you can't buy them in the butcher store. You buy them from men who spend their days and nights writing them! Shaina *kisses mezuzahs* when she passes one. She says that nailing a *mezuzah* to the doorpost is a Divine commandment that identifies Jewish homes and helps protect them. The Jewish home, Shaina says, is a holy place, like a miniature Temple! So it's not enough to have one *mezuzah* on the front door, but *every* door that's not a bathroom door needs a *mezuzah*. And, according to Shaina, these *mezuzahs* need to be professionally checked at least twice in seven years to make sure their ink hasn't worn out. Well, who ever heard of such a thing? Sylvia had never bought a *mezuzah;* she had assumed that the one nailed to her front doorpost when she moved in twenty years earlier was sufficient. Paula's *mezuzah* had a similar history. So how many customers could Shaina's husband have?

But Sylvia had to accept that situation. She rationalized to Paula that Shaina's husband was not the only man in the world who wrote *mezuzahs*. There must be a number of such men, and among them exists normalcy. They eat and drink and have normal children. On the other hand, he and Shaina were not blessed with children. So what did they do? They fostered children. While this is going to extremes to obtain children, at least a middle road is possible. Take in average, normal, middle-of-the-road children.

But Shaina and her husband went beyond. The extreme of the extreme of the *extreme* until it's not worth discussing. They bought a house in the Hasidic community of Crown Heights. And they took in children who were "difficult," to say the least. And not one, but two, and not temporarily, but they adopted them. From this there was no solace, and even Paula had to admit that Shaina and her husband went forth beyond extremes, beyond understanding, and probably beyond return.

Going to the "other side" is a process, and Shaina, who had made the transition more than a decade ago, often felt caught in unfinished business. In retrospect, the initial, dramatic part—changing her diet, wardrobe, neighborhood, and name—was not so difficult or challenging as it had first appeared. Kosher food was plentiful and tasty; *tznius* (modest) clothing, covering elbows, knees, and collarbone, with trousers deleted and replaced with skirts, was comfortable and attractive. Her new neighborhood became familiar, her new name, after a pious great-grandmother whom she had never met, was strengthening. These seemingly major changes proved relatively minor. More difficult was reconciling parents, friends, and colleagues, who had cajoled, complained, and even condemned, urging her to return to them. Her insistence that she had not changed, but had only returned to her essence, perhaps even to her very source, convinced no one. "Essence" and "source" were not words that Susan would have used. Her protests only fueled the lamentations of her near and dear ones: Susan was theirs no more. What they didn't realize was that they seemed lost to her as well. The few cousins, the few friends who eventually made the same transition, she embraced as landsmen from a home far away. The others remained as close as a phone call—and as distant as a foreign world. Their absence left a vacancy, which remained over time, after her remarriage, and in spite of dear new friends. Yet the unbridged (but not unbridgeable, Shaina always hoped) gap between herself and her family was secondary to the chasm that lurked camouflaged between her old and new selves. Integrating self with self, extricating self from self, was an endless and ultimate challenge.

Years later, in October 1998, Shaina was facing a more mundane issue. She faced her closet. She was going out to meet Reva that afternoon. What did she have to go out in?

Shaina couldn't even remember the last time she had gone out. Three years ago, maybe, before she and her husband had adopted Chana and Dovid. Since then she had not had time to think about how she had not taken time to think about the consequences of that act. But suddenly this morning her little ones were gone to a playgroup for the very first time. This morning her vigilance wasn't necessary. The safety, amusement, health, progress, future, and well-being of her children need not be her immediate focus. This required some adjustment. Her mind groped, reaching back to that clouded era before Chana and Dovid entered—and upstaged—her life. Those early years of this marriage, years of fertility treatments interspersed with roller-coaster rides of foster parenting. Then came a winter's day when she and her husband were tossed a baby, a perfect newborn, who happened to have an extra twenty-first chromosome. Medically, this condition is called trisomy 21, which generally triggers what is gently called "developmental delays." Commonly, the condition is known as Down syndrome.

Her husband, Shloma, didn't call it anything at all. He was

gifted with an innate simplicity that enabled him to see the un-complicated side of complicated issues. Despite his constant study of Talmudic complexities, his simplicity remained intact. Thus he glanced at the angelic infant, eyed his longing wife, and concluded that the world erred. The child was not only salvageable, but desirable. Often unusually elevated souls choose to be recycled into such a body. Perhaps this soul needed to correct some minor spiritual flaw of its previous lifetime. Or, more likely, it wished to accomplish a mission of *ahavas Yisrael*, love of one's fellow, and selflessly elevate others. That was the exegesis of the matter. However, the simple inter-pretation—and Shloma identified with simple interpreta-tions—was that this infant, the documented child of a Jewish mother, was a Jewish child. A Jewish soul can only be nour-ished in a Torah environment, which the adoption agency's al-ternate parental possibilities could not provide. Here, therefore, was not a social, political, or religious issue, but a sit-uation clarified by Torah's simple truth. Shloma didn't elabo-rate on this, or on anything. For fifteen seconds he viewed the child, endured his wife's silent but incessant plea, lifted an eye-brow to signal approval, and disappeared into his study.

Shaina caught the sign and flew for the child, who flowed to her embrace like limp spaghetti. "No muscle tone," the caseworker commented. "But don't worry. Therapy will help. I've seen these children walk, talk, do everything." With that hope, Shaina and Shloma named the baby Chana so she would find *chein*, or favor, in the eyes of others. Shaina devoted herself to teaching Chana to drink from a bottle, hold up her head, tuck in her tongue. Chana responded with sweet charm, dogmatic perseverance, and twinkling eyes, a harbin-ger of lively times to follow. Greedy for more of a good thing, Shaina procured a blessing from the Lubavitcher Rebbe and brought home Dovid.

Dovid's main talent at four months was that he could hold his own bottle. Nine-month-old Chana looked once at this rival, then refused to acknowledge him for weeks. In time, however, she sensed a potential ally, and the relationship flourished. When the children began to walk, they gleefully scampered in opposite directions, skittering right up to the curb, to the horror of their frantic mother. Shaina continued to devote days and nights to feeding, grooming, and especially educating them that they might one day be included in a "normal" classroom. The children thrived. Shaina, however, was losing weight, color, and, her friend Reva Keter suspected, sanity. Reva's publishing house, Legacy Press, produced children's books, many authored by Shaina, until the adoptions took their toll. Since then there had been no books, and almost, almost, no Shaina. Reva urged Shaina to take a break.

"You need to get out of here," Reva pronounced, handing the youngsters a page of paper reinforcers as a peace offering. *"Gu"* (thank you), responded the well-mannered twosome, eager to plaster floor, table, windows, and mirror with ring-shaped stickers. Shaina, glassy-eyed, mumbled that manipulating stickers enhances fine motor coordination.

"You *must* get out," Reva repeated. "I know a great *shiur* (Torah class). Find a sitter for these two, and *leave your house!*"

"Uh-huh. Chana, it's dangerous to bang on the windows. Dovid, paper reinforcers are not for eating. . . ."

Reva nudged, until Shaina found Morah Mashie, a playgroup leader ready to take on the cause. Apprehensively, Shaina introduced Chana and Dovid to the wild-mannered denizens of Morah Mashie's Play Group. In Mashie's well-lit world of high-barred windows, padded floors, and sturdy toys, lively two-year-olds played and prayed to the music of cheerful audio tapes, such as "Uncle Moishy and the Mitzvah Men." Mashie, whose mother had pioneered the first playgroup in the neighborhood, was a teacher born and bred, her curly *sheitel* (wig) pinned firmly to her head, her markers, tape, and Elmer's glue peeking comfortably out of her duster pockets. Dovid grabbed a tom-tom, Chana began fingering the Lego. "They'll be fine," said Mashie, in the professional tone *morahs* use to escort mothers out the door.

Shaina stood blankly, her legs weak, her arms empty, and unbearably light. No Chana to retain. No Dovid to restrain. Was she floating? Where was gravity? She yearned to absorb the full impact of this shock. However, the Crown Heights–Borough Park shuttle bus would leave in twenty minutes, and Reva was expecting her to catch it. Shaina recovered sufficiently to dash home, face her closet, and extract a presentable skirt and blouse. She found keys, located a purse that was not a diaper bag, and took off down Crown Street for Kingston Avenue.

Sunlight, bright and glorious. She hadn't seen such a sparkling morning since her prebaby days. The energy was visible, and therefore a suitable backdrop for Crown Heights. Just as Jerusalem is the heart of the world, Crown Heights, thought Shaina, is its nerve center. Crown Heights! She remembered the elation she had felt when she first came here, in the 1980s, after she "graduated" from Neve. "Crown Heights," she realized, was actually the English translation of "Keter Elyon," a lofty spiritual world discussed in Kabbalah. It seemed to her then that Keter Elyon had grown from its supernal roots to form the streets, sidewalks, and houses of Crown Heights. After all, the streets carried prophetic names, and the addresses of the buildings tallied up to enlightening *gematrias* (number value combinations of Hebrew letters).

For example, the house of the Lubavitcher Rebbe, Menachem Mendel Schneerson, leader of the worldwide Lubavitch Hasidic movement, is, appropriately, on President Street. Another example, the *mikvah,* where women immerse themselves at the end of their menstrual cycle, before resuming marital relations with their husbands, is located on the corner of Union and Albany, *al beni* being Hebrew for "concerning my children." Another address of interest was that of the Lubavitch central house of worship. Here traditions of the Holy Land in the East are "parked" until the exile ends and all will relocate to Jerusalem—and this building was on a boulevard called Eastern Parkway. The address of the building, 770, also had mystical references.

Yes, it did seem to Shaina that Keter Elyon had found its physical counterpart here, and that chunks of spiritual enlightenment had in some way found housing on these few blocks of Brooklyn. After all, thought Shaina, the Hasid's constant goal is to elevate the physical and actualize the spiritual by making this physical world a Godly place. The Divine, mystical plan is that higher and lower realms are created to mingle. Mundane occupations, such as eating, drinking, sleeping, and housecleaning, encompass Godly potential, capable of bringing earth up to heaven, and heaven down to earth.

Shaina hurried down Crown Street, past bright-colored satin banners that hung from many of the houses. WELCOME MOSHIACH, the banners proclaimed. True, waiting for Moshiach's arrival has been a Jewish occupation for thousands of years. However, many Hasidim in Crown Heights felt that Moshiach was already backstage and we are all responsible to do every good deed possible to pull up the curtain. The energy of Crown Heights was charged with urgency.

Shaina reached the corner and was about to miss the bus.

"Stop! Stop!" shouted Shaina.

"Stop, stop!" the women in the bus called to Simon, the driver.

"I'm blind?" murmured Simon, pulling the bus back to

the curb, swinging open the door. Did any other driver have this double onus, to be dependably prompt but always available? Long ago he had complained to the boss.

"I have a schedule!" protested Simon. "Every lady and her baby carriage, running from three blocks away. I should wait?"

The boss looked squarely at the driver. "There are two," the boss replied. "Only two, who must be on time, yet leave no one behind: Moshiach and you."

Simon got the message. The schedule, that was up to God. That everyone got their ride, this was up to Simon. Thereafter, Simon steadfastly maneuvered the Crown Heights shuttle, contending with forces without and within. The careering cars on Empire Avenue. The multitude of baby carriages, all to be accommodated on the bus without fare. And disheveled passengers, like this one, who wave down the bus from blocks away, then hold things up even more, rummaging through bottomless shoulder bags for a dollar and change. It took all kinds, and all kinds rode the bus. When the lady finally sat down, Simon checked his rearview mirror, pulled away from the curb, and advanced up Kingston Avenue, until he'd have to stop again.

Shaina settled into her seat. Across the aisle black-hatted, bearded men stared into paperback versions of Talmudic tractates or pamphlets of Hasidic discourses. A few conversed in Hebrew or English on their cell phones. On the women's side, women and girls also learned Hasidic thought, or chatted easily, catching up on the latest news of family and friends. Some read from purse-sized psalm or prayer books.

In half an hour she'd be in Borough Park. Borough Park, the largest Orthodox community outside the Land of Israel, has a population of three hundred thousand. Covering an area of about one and a half square miles, Borough Park was

certainly a metropolis next to the seven scant square blocks of
Crown Heights. Despite its name, Borough Park was not a
park, and had hardly a place to park. Its cars, houses, and res-
idents all rubbed elbows. Five thousand children were born
every year in Borough Park's Maimonides Hospital, and
almost every block was home to at least one shul and yeshiva.
While most of the Hasidim in Crown Heights were Lubavitch,
Borough Park was home to Hasidim of many kinds, as well as
"black hatters"—strictly observant Jews whose customs were
not Hasidic at all. Shaina's mother had once summed up and
cut down both communities with a single term: Ultraorthodox.

Not Ultraorthodox to the people who live there, Shaina
had replied. Just a way of life.

At the time her mother had suspected, but had not yet
verified, that this way of life was becoming Shaina's.

The transition altered some of Shaina's lifelong assump-
tions. For example, before she came over to the other side,
Shaina had assumed that women were supposed to listen and
men were supposed to talk. So she had sought out young men
who had interesting, even brilliant, insights on elevated topics
like music, art, and science. Her listening was appreciated, but
these listening relationships lacked something. Looking back,
she wondered if she had listened herself into having no voice
at all.

Ironically Shloma, who belonged to the supposedly ultra-
patriarchy, fixed that. He, who was born into an Ultraorthodox home, and educated as a rabbi, not only listened to her,
but also respected her viewpoint. Their backgrounds were
vastly different. He was the first person she had ever met who
did not know who "Mary had a little lamb" was. He did not
watch television, listen to radio, or even buy newspapers, and
in his library were thousands of books on ancient topics,

mostly in Hebrew, Yiddish, or Talmudic Aramaic. Grounded as he was in the ancient code, he was prepared to accept literally the Torah dictum that "a man must love his wife as himself, and honor her more than himself" to the best of his ability.

After she and Shloma married, Shaina began to sense that although he listened, accepted, agreed, and when necessary, guided, their conversations did not have the charge of give and take. Their different backgrounds did make a temporary but substantial difference. In a marriage, Shaina realized, common ground is necessary. While she had unquestionably abandoned that side where she had been, she wasn't exactly native to the side that was his. It left a gap between them.

To close it, Shaina resorted to a favorite diversion of her former life. She wrote a children's story. But instead of whipping together a flashy, bubbling-over-the-edge-of-its-mug kind of tale, as she had once done, she now patiently listened for old, abandoned stories, to take them in, nurture them, and retell them from the depth of her being. The stories emerged alive, breathing. They were evidence of the Hasidic adage "The pen is a quill for the soul." Shaina sent them to Legacy Press, a small religious publishing house that specialized in children's books. She discovered that Legacy Press was Reva Keter.

As the shuttle reached the outskirts of Borough Park and turned onto Sixteenth Avenue, Shaina mused that Reva, like many of the small shops on this street, had not changed over time, but only became more firmly established. Reva had made her passage to the other side at the age of seven—under the inspiration and guidance of her best friend, whose father, Rabbi Maurice I. Hecht, was an emissary of the Lubavitcher Rebbe. An energetic and precocious child, Reva was soon rounding up the neighborhood youngsters for a *Shabbos* (sabbath) afternoon of songs, stories, and goodies. The Lubavitcher Rebbe himself sent Reva a weekly allowance to purchase these treats. Reva, in turn, supplied a weekly report of attendees, activities, and per item cost of refreshments.

"He wanted every detail," Reva commented, when she related the story to Shaina.

"Of course," Shaina responded. "It was his money."

"No!" Reva protested. "They were his souls! Everything is important to the *rebbe*. He always gave me such good advice."

"You were lucky to have good advice," said Shaina.

Shaina's good advice had come later in her life, in a very different form. She had by then discarded the religion of her temple. Even as a young child she wondered why her teachers never discussed God. The professional choir that sang for the children at assemblies always climaxed with the eerie proclamation, "The Lord is our God, the Lord is won!" Susan and her friends longed for the details of this thrilling battle, this war that won God. Good guys, bad guys, heroes, enemies, something worth fighting for would have given purpose to their colorless Sunday mornings. This battle tale, however, was not to be revealed, for the children's hopes were based on a misunderstanding of the text. What the choir was announcing was the universal Torah principle of God's unity: The Lord is One. One unique God, who has no divine family, relatives, assistants, or counterparts, as polytheistic doctrines throughout the ages have devised. One God who created all existence and who, as the Ba' al Shem Tov explains, constantly and caringly maintains His creation with creative energy so that it does not revert to its original nothingness. One God. To live by this principle, Jews have had to fight battles, physically and philosophically, resulting in a vivid and staggering history. Unfortunately, these action-packed details were also not related to Susan and her classmates. Instead the children listened to tales about "wise" men from Chelm who thought the moon could fall into a well. After this narrative, the young students were herded through spotless, spacious halls to their classrooms. Here they read of happy youngsters frolicking with small dogs and enjoying holidays that Susan and her classmates had never seen practiced in their homes. Young Susan concluded that the entire Sunday school experience was evolved from second-rate fiction.

Seeing that the Sunday school was not to Susan's taste, Sylvia enrolled her daughter in the Conservative synagogue. Perhaps that program would be more challenging and relevant to Susan. Indeed, Susan was one of only three students who continued to attend classes throughout high school. These serious youths were offered explanations, evaluations, and alterations, but something seemed missing. What held this all together? Susan wondered. Where did it begin, and where did it end? What could they learn today that wouldn't be changed tomorrow?

Inexplicably, Susan felt there must be more substance to Judaism. This compelled her, just before her high school graduation, to look into the quaint laws of Orthodoxy, which apparently never change. She visited a modest *shul* (synagogue) that featured a strange separation of men and women during prayer and a humble rabbi who wore no clerical dress. The rabbi did not announce page numbers. Everyone seemed enveloped in a private world, intoning Hebrew prayers without inhibition, and also without English translation. After praying, the aging congregants gathered in the back of the shul to converse in Yiddish or, at best, in thickly accented English. Shaina remembered her great-grandfather speaking similar warm garbled words, flavored with pickled herring and Manischevitz wine. Nothing to fault here. Shaina imagined that if she were fifty years older, she would like it.

She left for college, and subsequently met, married, and left a young mathematician who had taken enough graduate physics courses to expound upon how the universe was self-created from a big bang, and how it was also most likely self-destructive, although salvation may be at hand through zero population growth. As much as she admired him, she began feeling increasingly claustrophobic. How could she leave such an intelligent and talented person for no reason? Yet the walls of their spacious apartment seemed to be closing in on her. She finally moved out into a tiny rented room. It felt like a mansion, and she soared with contagious energy.

From here Susan found a world where all moral codes are created equal—where everything is right, where nothing is wrong, so long as you "don't hurt anyone"—and here no one admitted pain. Smiling faces masked tortured hearts, while dark nights of deep beating music catered to an embryonic consciousness.

Here in this tiny room, as she was contemplating life one day, Susan first heard the voice that gave advice. It came disguised as a thought of her own: She had been entertaining the possibility of staying in Ann Arbor to finish (i.e., start) her dissertation or, alternatively, to spend the summer preparing her course work in Israel. And the voice, which seemed to be herself thinking, but was clearly from elsewhere, answered her calmly, matter-of-factly, and totally without threat: *If you stay here, you will die.* Calmly, matter-of-factly, and totally unthreatened, she listened and agreed. She was even pleased to have an excuse to go somewhere. Of course the possibility of going over to the other side never occurred to her—she had never heard of, and would not have believed in, the other side.

Shaina glanced up. The shuttle had already reached the center of Borough Park—the "hub," as Reva gloried in calling it, the corner of Forty-ninth Street and Sixteenth Avenue.

Many of the passengers got out here, and Shaina did too, opting to walk and enjoy a few extra blocks of autumn. Borough Park was as crowded as ever, but the air was crisp, fresh, and plentiful. Shaina breathed deeply.

A different lifetime ago she had boarded a plane to Israel, breathing deeply, feeling weightless, free of all the past, and with a future as bright as the rising sun. What a thrill, to visit a foreign country where she knew no one! On the plane she met Maryn, a Christian Arab graduate student traveling with her two-year-old son. When Maryn invited Susan to her family's picturesque home in Beit Jala, Susan accepted, and enjoyed a week as an honored guest.

Beit Jala impressed her. She saw apricot, lemon, pomegranate, apple, and olive trees growing side by side on the hilltop; she saw an ancient stream drip from a hidden rock. She drank thick, sweet coffee out of thimble cups and began a collection of Arab nursery rhymes. The powerful sun could not penetrate the thick stone walls of the Beit Jala houses. Inside, on the cool stone floors, she watched the four generations of her hostess's family share a festive meal. The toothless grandmother was preparing portions of a traditional dish—her bony fingers deftly enclosing fistfuls of something in grape leaves. Susan watched, feeling that she had, with sound mind, stepped into one of those freshman anthropology texts that eavesdrop on unsuspecting natives.

She did not remember actually eating this offering. But just being there changed her, opened her mind. She could consider anything. Three weeks later, as she stood for the first time at the Kotel, the ancient Western Wall, a rabbi named Meir Shuster suggested that she spend *Shabbos* with a religious Jewish family in Kiryat Itri, a suburb of Jerusalem. She accepted.

There she met the red-bearded Hasid from Arkansas, five

foot three, with penetrating eyes. His three tiny sons, freshly bathed and diapered, danced behind him on the stone floor, while his wife, with an eye on the clock, pulled a sheet of chocolate cake from the oven. His wife lit candles. Shaina sat by the windowsill watching the trafficless street below fill with men, women, and children, all calm, all elegant as a picture she had once seen but had not believed in that childhood Sunday school textbook. The picture had been labeled *"Shabbos."*

Shabbos did exist. *Shabbos* existed here.

Shaina didn't need the voice to tell her. She felt *Shabbos*, its warmth, its radiance. In that moment, but with a lifetime behind her, she had come over to the other side.

And now she also stood on the other side—on the other side of the street from the stately mansion that corresponded to the address Reva had given her. Shaina followed the gracious walkway to a door that was slightly ajar. Inside she heard the low bustling of women, the clatter of china, the hush of heavy wooden chairs being pushed across varnished parquet floors. The lunch and learn group was here, but where was Reva? Shaina stood for a moment, her arms hanging awkwardly as she looked inside.

On this particular Tuesday afternoon, Tamar Edelman noticed an unfamiliar face at Sarah's door: pale, even gaunt, wearing no makeup, a touch of anxiety on her rounded shoulders. Hesitantly, the newcomer eyed the only vacant seat, next to Mrs. Blisme. Tamar rose to stop her, but too late.

"Oh, no!" Mabel Blisme guarded the empty chair vigilantly. "This place is for Ethel! She's coming soon!"

"What a welcome!" thought Tamar, as she rushed in to make amends. "Come over here," she said gently, as she opened a folding chair, pushed aside a salad bowl, and arranged another setting next to her own. "Come, have some carrot salad, it's good for the eyes." Cheerfully, Tamar piled grated carrots onto a plate. Something in Tamar's genes dictated that well-filled plates give strength. She had been raised like that.

The newcomer smiled but didn't make eye contact. Perhaps being served made her feel uncomfortable, thought Tamar. Some newcomers might feel that way, but Sarah's house was a place of give and take—one needed to cultivate the pleasures of both. "My name's Tamar," Tamar offered, attempting to put the new guest at ease.

"Shaina," the new guest volunteered, fidgeting with her shoulder bag,

"Your first time here, right?" Tamar continued to make conversation.

Shaina nodded. "But you've been here before."

"From the beginning," Tamar smiled. "I've been here since the days when Sarah had only one table, in the kitchen, with only her and me sitting there. Where are you coming from?"

"Coming from? Oh, Crown Heights."

"Interesting!" Tamar was amused. Sarah's material came from Crown Heights, where classes in Hasidic philosophy blossomed on every block. What had brought Shaina here?

"Uh-huh." Shaina missed Tamar's unasked question. She eyed the book half tucked under Tamar's plate. "What are you reading?"

"Oh, I just picked this up at a bookstore on Thirteenth Avenue," said Tamar, pleased at the prospect of a literary discussion. "It's Paysach Krohn's latest. Do you read him?"

"A little."

"Oh." Tamar had hoped for a more enthusiastic response to one of her favorite authors. "Well, his parables and stories here really reach you. . . . "

"Mmmm," said Shaina. "I guess it's been a long time since I've read anything."

"Oh." Tamar did not want to sound judgmental. However, she had raised nine children, some of them close in age, and had always found time to read. Finding time, Tamar always told her children, was simply a matter of organization and priority. She considered changing the subject, to suggest that Shaina wash her hands and enjoy the excellent home-baked challah rolls, when the newcomer's eyes lit up.

"Reva!"

Reva Keter, a short, blonde-*sheiteled* woman outfitted in a wake-you-up red plaid suit, was standing in the doorway, looking for Shaina. When their eyes met, Reva broke into her warm, gracious, all but gushing smile.

"I see you're in good hands!" Reva enthused to Shaina while nodding to Tamar. Reva had known that Tamar would find Shaina and welcome her, but get to know her? Probably not. Getting to know people was Reva's forte.

"Tamar," Reva began, "I want you to meet my friend Shaina Ore." Only Reva could turn an introduction into a proclamation. Her voice trumpeted that Shaina Ore was the best, most unique, dearest friend the world could offer. Publisher's hype, but also subliminal conditioning. Under Reva's tutelage, Shaina had become a better friend as well as a better writer. Reva could take the credit.

"Shaina *Ore?* Really!" Tamar would not have suspected that the author of those sweet children's books was a woman of pale face, unversed in Paysach Krohn. "We enjoy your books, Shaina. I read them to my kids, my grandkids. . . . "

"Grandchildren? You?" Shaina gawked.

Tamar smiled. "What's the title of your latest book, Shaina?"

Shaina's mind went blank. Reva hinted, *"The Cow . . . "*

"Uh-uh. *'Not Now, Said the Cow,'* about the cow that didn't work on *Shabbos,*" Shaina remembered.

"No work-y gobbled the turkey!" Tamar grinned at her favorite line. "My daughter teaches at a preschool—they made a play of it—all the parents came! We really enjoyed that barnyard scene!"

Shaina smiled, pleased that the little story had landed in someone's heart. But at the same time, being scrutinized as an author made her fumble for her shoulder strap.

"Let's wash for the meal," Reva suggested. "I want to have one of Tova Hersh's challah rolls before they disappear."

"Tova's rolls look professional, but they taste homemade," added Tamar. "Tova's over there, sitting at the front table."

Shaina looked and noted that Tova's soft, sincere smile revealed no hint of her talent. Reva guided Shaina into the kitchen. There Mira, Sarah's kitchen helper, was squeezing fresh lemon over a bowl of sliced beets. What is the secret of uncluttered counters? wondered Shaina. Her own kitchen seemed to house a live-in cyclone.

Reva was already at the sink, reaching for the double-handled washing cup that hung from a ceramic hook on the wall. She filled the cup with water, then poured three times on her right hand and three times on her left. She set the cup down, lifted her hands, and said the blessing, *al n'tilas yadayim,* "who commanded the uplifting of the hands," then headed back to the dining room to make the blessing over the bread. The action was washing, but the text of the blessing said "uplifting." The blessing was a reminder that hands can be used for lofty purposes, which could include eating, drinking, washing, and diaper changing, depending on the intent with which it is done. This complex concept flew through Shaina's mind as she, too, washed her hands and said the blessing. Here, on this other side, nothing was mundane. Even a seemingly banal act could further one's relationship with the Creator.

To understand the details of this process one had to learn the infinite sciences of Kabbalah and Hasidus, the mystical teachings of the Ba'al Shem Tov and his successors. No doubt something on this topic would follow this afternoon, during the "learn" portion of the session. Shaina replaced the cup on its hook and returned to the dining room to secure the last of the challah rolls.

"Aren't they special?" munched Reva. "You've got to meet Tova."

"Mmhmm," Shaina replied, still sitting at the edge of her seat, as if still on the alert for Chana and Dovid. Reva reached into her handbag for her book of *Tehillim* (book of psalms), and Shaina, noting her friend's poised tranquillity, did the same. No one would guess that only two weeks ago Reva's husband had undergone emergency quadruple-bypass surgery and was now convalescing at home. Shaina noticed that Reva now carried a cell phone. Having his wife available to him at all times was probably important to Moshe's healing, thought Shaina. Anyway, other than the phone, and perhaps her overly bright suit, Reva's life seemed to be flourishing.

"Ah, here's Sarah," said Reva.

Sarah was helping a latecomer find a seat as the *Tehillim* were being passed out. She appeared tasteful, efficient, focused. "Sarah's a connector, a facilitator par excellence," commented Reva.

Shaina had met other connectors, but Sarah seemed unusually intense. Merging the upper and lower worlds by infusing everything with Godliness, a uniquely human task, seemed Sarah's mission. "Every detail in Sarah's house," said Reva, "the hand-painted murals on the walls, these real linen tablecloths, these floral china place settings and glass stemware, that gorgeous chandelier—this is all Sarah's equipment for her personal service to the Creator. Watch."

"Time for psalms, ladies!" Sarah's voice, a little raspy, signaled above the crowd. "Does anyone have any names?"

The women began calling out names, firmly, affirmatively, as though that act in itself gave strength. Leah Esther *bas* Malka, Nechama *bas* Frumma, Aliza *bas* Zahava, Yitzchak *ben* Batya, on and on goes the list: first name in Hebrew or Yiddish, *ben* (son) or *bas* (daughter) of mother's first name. These names are highlighted for prayers for a *refuah shelaimah,* a complete recovery. When women gather to learn Torah, they often begin the session with *Tehillim,* along with adding a few coins to the *pushke,* the charity box. In this way they establish the three pillars the sages say hold up the world: Torah study, prayer, and kind deeds. In this way, too, the names of the needy quickly spread from gathering to gathering, often with an accompanying story. The little boy who fell into a coma after his house caught fire, the young girl with the unpronounceable illness, the mother of eight still in critical condition, the father of ten recovering from a car crash, and more—their names are called up and *Tehillim* recited en masse to give them healing and strength.

Some of the names Shaina recognized from before her involvement with Chana and Dovid. "After all our *Tehillim,* why are these names still on the list?" she wondered out loud to Reva.

"Because *Tehillim* gives them the strength to stay on the list," Reva responded. Then she added her husband's name, Moshe ben Chana.

Sarah asked Ora Bloom to lead the *Tehillim.*

"*Tehilla L'Dovid . . . ,*" Ora's voice was so resonant that her spoken word had perfect pitch.

"Incredible," whispered Shaina.

"Her son's a singer," Reva whispered back

Shaina nodded and began the *Tehillim,* which included verses written by Adam, Moses, King David, and other giants of Divine understanding. All prayer is effective, but here were unparalleled powerhouses. The first Lubavitcher Rebbe, Rabbi Shneur Zalman Schneerson, wrote that if we knew the true effect of reciting *Tehillim*, we would never stop saying them.

Shaina had been saying *Tehillim* daily, after her morning prayers, for many years. She recited them in the original *loshon hakodesh* (holy language) of ancient Hebrew. But she was still no speed reader, and the women here were zooming. Shaina lost the place, fell behind. How long would she have to live in this community to be good at it?

As the *Tehillim* continued, Shaina imagined herself born and bred in Crown Heights. As a young girl she would have been a serious student, excelling in the Beth Rivka girls' school system. She would have gone on to seminary, become knowledgeable in Torah, with the deep and wonderful elucidations of the classic scholars such as Rashi, Rambam, and Ramban (Rabbi Shlomo Yitzchaki, Maimonides, and Nachmonides), plus the Hasidic discourses laden with Torah secrets. At nineteen or twenty she would have married a brilliant boy who by now would be a rabbinic judge or perhaps the head of a yeshiva, who would secretly study the mystical teachings of Hasidus and Kabbalah deep into the night. She would teach their many children to be wise in the wisdom of Torah, to be kind, and to excel in Torah's commandments. And yes, she could even have become a seminary teacher! Now she knew what knowledge it was she had always craved! That temple library showcase—that window display that had perplexed her childhood soul, the one that pictured delighted young children, dancing around a towering volume, with the caption: We are the People of the Book. So she began to read, always reading, seeking that book of which we are the people. Had she only known from the beginning! She could now be teaching Torah, impressing her students with the magnificence of learning, the power of prayer, and the fundamental axiom that in prayer it's not how much you say, but rather your concentration and intention that counts.

The voice of perfect pitch stopped. The women closed their *Tehillim* and Shaina surfaced from her thoughts, realizing that she had not concentrated on one single word. Too late. Sarah was about to begin. "Listen for the quip and the controversy," Reva whispered to Shaina.

"Charity that begins at home ends at home," stated Sarah. Her words sounded large, coming from a deep place. "Don't wait to do good deeds in your spare time, because no woman *has* spare time. The question is, how much can you shave off?"

"*I* never have spare time, that's for sure," stated Mabel Blisme, from her station at the center table, near the food. Ethel had not shown up, and the seat next to Mabel was the only vacant one in the house.

"What about our children? Don't they come first?" asked Iyelet, a young woman holding an infant on her knee.

"The biggest kindness you can do for your children is to train them to help others," responded Sarah. "And preaching isn't teaching. A child may hear what we say, but they listen to what we do."

"Sarah herself is the best example of that!" interjected Esther Springer, a real estate agent. "The Inner Circle, the prestigious association of high school good-deed doers, is headed by—do you know who? Sarah's daughter, Chana Leah!"

Sarah had to raise her voice above the clamor of applause to change the subject. "Does everyone have a copy of today's study sheet? Okay, let's begin."

"This week's *parsha*, the Torah portion of the week, is 'Lech-Lecha.' Here we see firsthand what it means to have self-sacrifice for God's commandments. What's our life? Life is made up of time. Days, hours, minutes, seconds, all finite, all

limited. Our life is time, and when we use our precious time to
help others, especially when it seems that we don't have that
time to spare, this is self-sacrifice for God's commandments.
But that self-sacrifice doesn't deplete us. It strengthens us.
And this is what happens in Lech-Lecha. Abraham turns over
his life for *mitzvos,* and these *mitzvos* become his, and ultimately our, identity, energy, and actual life force. Esther, will
you read for us?"

As Esther read about how young Abraham rejected the
idolatry of the world to embrace the *mitzvos,* the commandments of the Creator, Shaina remembered how strange the
word "*mitzvah*" first seemed without a "*bar*" or "*bas*" attached
to it. A *bar* or *bas mitzvah,* when Shaina was growing up,
entailed a two-part type of birthday party. The first part was
on Friday night, when there would be a *kiddush* (refreshments) after services. The second, more major portion, was
on Sunday afternoon, when her Hebrew class would go bowl-
ing. Her Hebrew teacher mentioned holidays and history, but
the curriculum somehow overlooked this concept that God
designed, gave, and desires that Jews keep *mitzvos,* usually
translated as commandments, which were given in the Torah.

While studying in Israel, Shaina had come to understand
that there is no word in English to translate "*mitzvah*" accu-
rately. However, Rabbi Chalkovsky had explained the purpose
of a *mitzvah* with a parable. When you purchase a car, or any
valuable, complex piece of equipment, you read, and follow,
the instruction manual. Why? Not to limit your use of the car,
but to expand it. The instructions are included to help the
purchaser enjoy the best performance possible. Using the recommended gasoline and oil and arranging for tune-ups at
regular intervals all extend the life of the car and facilitate
happy riding. Similarly, when God put a Jewish soul in the
driver's seat of a body, He gave an instruction manual, the

Torah, prescribing how best to use that vehicle. Torah also provides a map, pointing out the roads that extend through life's varied terrain. So *mitzvah* is a command, yes, but one given by a caring Manufacturer.

Hasidus explains *mitzvah* even more deeply, pointing out that its root word means "connection." Through each *mitzvah* we connect to God and His infinity. Each time we do a positive *mitzvah,* or refrain from doing one of the *mitzvahs* that are prohibitions, our connection to God becomes stronger.

Esther continued reading: "'We are all familiar with the events in the early life of our forefather Abraham. He discovered God as a young boy and broke his father's idols. For this the despot King Nimrod sentenced him to death and threw him into a blazing furnace. Miraculously, God saved him.

"'These stories, which are handed down to us through the Midrashic, biblical literature, are not found in the Written Torah itself. The Torah tells us almost nothing about Abraham until the portion of "Lech-Lecha," which begins with God commanding Abraham: 'Go out from your land, from your birthplace, from your father's house, to a land that I will show you.'" (Genesis 12:5). Esther looked up. "It's a good question. In the midst of a society of idol worshipers, Abraham was the only one who worshiped the Creator of the universe. He stood alone against the whole world and was ready to give up his life for God. That's heroic. Why doesn't Torah mention it?"

Sarah smiled. "Read on."

Esther continued. "'While these early events in Abraham's life are inspiring and instructive, they focus only on his own personal striving to get closer to Godliness. A different and deeper relationship began when God commanded Abraham: "Go out from your land." As our sages tell us, a person who does a *mitzvah* because he was commanded to is greater than a person who does a *mitzvah* without having been commanded.'"

This led to some discussion. Wasn't it better to do an act out of your free will rather than because you were commanded to do it?

"We do have free will," said Sarah. "We can choose what we want to do, and we are responsible for our actions. But we have to remember that *mitzvah*s are not only commandments, but they are actually Godly acts. For example, it's nice to have dinner by candlelight. Your family and friends might appreciate it. But it's not a *mitzvah*. On *Shabbos,* however, God commanded us that eighteen minutes before sunset, Jewish women should light candles to bring in *Shabbos.* Here lighting candles becomes a *mitzvah* that connects us with God. If you do it on Wednesday night, it's the the same candles, the same table. But it's not a Godly act. Not a *mitzvah.* It may look the same, but it doesn't have the same effect. No Divinity, no infinity."

Esther continued. "'With the commandment to leave his home, Abraham was empowered to step beyond personal circumstances to establish an unlimited connection with God. The connection was fully actualized when God gave us the *mitzvos* of the Torah.'"

"Each *mitzvah* is a way to have an unlimited connection with God," Sarah added.

"I've been doing *mitzvos* for more than a year now," said Debra, a young woman who sat at Sarah's right. "I don't feel unlimited."

"It's a process," replied Sarah. "*Lech* means to proceed. *Lech-Lecha* means 'you go out,' but it also means, as Rashi, the great twelfth-century commentator explains, 'go out for your own benefit.' Go out of your present self and become something more. God is saying to Abraham: 'Go out. Leave everything behind. Do My *mitzvos*—and go to that land that *areka*

(I will show you). But *areka* can also mean 'I will reveal *you.*' *Mitzvos* lead to self-revelation. By following God's *mitzvos*, we 'Lech-Lecha.' We gain self-knowledge. We come to our essence."

> *Abram fell on his face; and God spoke with him further, "As for Me, this is My covenant with you: you shall be the father of a multitude of nations. And you shall no longer be called Abram, but your name shall be Abraham, for I have appointed you as the father of a multitude of nations. I will make you exceedingly fruitful, and make nations of you; and kings shall descend from you. I will maintain My covenant between Me and you, and between your offspring after you, as an everlasting covenant throughout the ages, to be God to you and to your offspring to come. I assign all the land of Canaan, as an everlasting holding, to you and to your descendants after you, and I will be a God to them." God said to Abraham: "As for you, you must preserve My covenant, you and your descendants after you throughout their generations." (Genesis 17:3–9)*

Esther continued: "'When Abraham did not follow his own will, but instead followed God's command, he connected directly to God. And he released an infinite potential. Every one of us is heir to this. For the essence of all of our spiritual journeys is to go beyond our usual way of thinking until we tap our Godly core.'"

As Esther sat down, Levana, who was sitting across the table from Sarah, had a comment. "We go on this spiritual journey, but sometimes the difficulties are more than we bargain for. Why?"

Sarah responded in a neutral voice, but Reva couldn't resist shooting Levana a knowing look of empathy, which Shaina didn't miss. Levana's translucent complexion, her ethereal highlights, must have come through tough processing. "All our lives," Sarah replied, "in all our spiritual travels, we struggle. Like an athlete. We have to put force against resistance to get stronger. We don't ask for tests, but if God sends them anyway, it's to bring out our hidden strengths."

"And what if instead of resisting the force, it crushes us?" someone asked.

Sarah nodded. "Our sages tell us that before we leap over something really big, we may have to take a few steps back, a descent for the purpose of ascent. Of course, we don't always understand. But we know that God runs the world, so the purpose of every experience is positive."

As Sarah concluded, steaming casseroles of eggplant Parmesan began arriving at the table. With no Chana or Dovid here to interrupt, Shaina settled back and relaxed into a dreamy, nicely humored smile.

"Ha!" Reva triumphed. "Okay, what do you think?"

"So, you were right," Shaina conceded. "I did need to get out. Do need to get out. Need to keep getting out. Maybe Morah Mashie will take them officially into the class."

"Mmhmm," Reva nodded, sipping tea, as though she knew nothing but leisure. No one would guess that she was gathering her strength for another round with Moshe. "The beauty of the King's daughter is within," and not everything is to share. Another sip of tea. Squeezed olives, Reva reminded herself, give sweet oil. But it's a private process. She knew, had always known, that part of going out was coming in.

"See you here next week?" she asked Shaina.

Shaina nodded. "Okay, next week."

2
Reva: Achieving Revelations
Parshas Vayera

God appeared to him [Abraham] in the groves of Mamrei, while he was sitting at the entrance of the tent in the hottest part of the day. Abraham lifted his eyes and saw three strangers . . . and ran to greet them, bowing down to the ground. He said, "Sir, if you would, do not go on without stopping by me."
—Genesis 18:1–3

Abraham was unique, worthy to be the physical and spiritual patriarch of the Jews, the Arabs, and all who believe in the oneness of the Creator. In this parsha, "Vayera," Abraham recently has elevated himself to a new spiritual rung through fulfilling the commandment of bris milah, *circumcision, which became an everlasting covenant between the Jewish people and God. On the third day since his* bris, *when the wound is most painful, God visits Abraham to show him honor.*

Who does God visit? Our sages tell us that God reveals himself to those who do great deeds. He is also present at the head of a sick person's bed. However, neither pain nor Divine presence could stop Abraham from spreading the knowledge of God to the world; he is sitting by his tent door, longing for guests. It was his practice to welcome visitors to his tent, where, amid gracious hospitality, he taught the world, person by person, to believe in and worship the Creator. For Abraham, having guests was more

than a kind deed. It was his vitality, his essential Divine service.
And so Abraham excused himself even from the Divine presence,
in order to welcome guests.

Tuesday. Tuesday is the day that good is doubled, for on the
first Tuesday of creation, God himself said twice, "Behold, it is
good." Tuesday is a day to be savored, a day second only to
Shabbos in its sweetness and blessing. Tuesday. The day of
Sarah's table.

Up and out, chick-chock, no time to lose. Seven-thirty, and
Reva was on her way to the beach. A *beach,* near Brooklyn, no
less! Who would have thought it—and a deserted beach, too.
A beach where golden sand and golden sun smile on one
woman who eagerly plunges into its exhilarating waters. Safe
from prying eyes and pointing fingers, here is a private par-
adise amid the heat and turmoil of New York and the greater
heat and turmoil of Reva's life. She reminded herself that this
sandy sanctuary was a gift, and her morning plunge almost a
mitzvah, really—her obligation to give a little time to herself,
to stay healthy, strong, better able to care for her work, her
children, and Moshe.
    Fighting the waves, even an unexpected big one with its
trailing undertow, Reva stayed calm. She was born in New
Haven, where she had always had a beach, had always known
the idiosyncrasies of the ocean. Thank God she had this spot
of beach in Brooklyn, too. No one else here now. It was hers.
    Hers, at least for a short time. Hers until onlookers, at the
far end of the beach, began their morning strolls, which signaled to Reva that it was time to leave. Reluctantly she swam
to shore and pulled on her robe. Soon the joggers would
come, embedding their sneaker prints on the untouched sand.

The little children would follow, tugging at their mothers'
sleeves, eager to spread their beach blankets and stake a claim.

Time to go. Time to check on Moshe. By now he must be
getting up.

Hurry, hurry. Time to be home. Time to serve breakfast,
time to measure portions of protein and carbohydrates. Line
up the whole grains and vegetables—all this wonderful medicine disguised as food. Witness, in her own kitchen, proof of
the Talmudic saying that before God sends the disease he pre-
pares the cure.

Years before, when her children were growing up, they
had a *Shabbos* guest named Mordecai, who liked to have sea
vegetables in his chicken soup. Her children found this more
than odd. "Not in *our* soup!" they had protested. "Seaweed
smells fishy! We don't want fishy smelling chicken soup."

"But Mordecai likes it," Reva had replied. "He even chews
sea vegetables raw, like gum!"

"Don't experiment on us!" Her oldest, Judah, was waxing
dramatic. "*Shabbos* food is s'posed to be a pleasure, remember!"

She had laughed and looked for ways to please both her
children and her guests. A sea vegetable known as kombu, she
discovered, dissolved in chicken soup with hardly trace or
taste. And that soybean curd, tofu, which Mordecai's roommate had a passion for, proved to be the secret ingredient for
a nondairy "cheese" cake. A good thing that tofu was the *secret*
ingredient; being discreet helped keep the peace. So Reva happily prepared those curiosities, sea vegetables and tofu, to
please health-conscious guests, little suspecting that these
recipes also prepared her for the time when Moshe would
need them. Moshe needed them now.

Moshe.

"Rev? You're here, Rev? What took so long?"

Gradually, very gradually, that simple-sounding illness,

diabetes, had become the tyrant that measured out their lives.
Tick, tock. Meals must be prompt to avoid an insulin reaction.
Tick, tock. Catch appointments with the specialists, be home
for the therapists, pick up the prescriptions, remember the
syringes, be prompt so you can bypass failing heart and
limbs . . .

"Rev, I was beginning to worry."

This was her life, now. Only God knew why.

"I was just parking, Moshe! Couldn't find a spot. I'll be
right with you with breakfast." She ducked into the shower.

A quick shower, of course. A quick splash of lavender
body wash for the perk, quick into the hot, stinging water.
Vibrant and energizing, these showers. Keeps the body and
mind limber. Now a bath sheet. Her fingers skimmed over the
hand grasp that she had installed for Moshe. He'd be strong
enough to use it soon, she kept telling herself. Meanwhile, he
was still taking those sponge baths—an attendant came several times a week to help. She wanted to help, of course, but
perhaps not in that way, if someone else could do it. She had
memories of sponge baths. Her mother would sit endlessly by
the bedside, dipping a sponge into tepid water, wringing the
water out, then dabbing, gently, gently, trying to bring down a
fever. She remembered the cooling sound the water made
dripping back into the bowl. She remembered the lumpy yellow sponge, cold, intruding, on sensitive, fevered skin. Her
mother also would bathe her bedridden grandmother. Warm
water. The sponge baths refreshed her, for a time.

At the bottom of the ocean, believe it or not, live animals
are created to be sponges. Gifted with the ability to absorb
warm water and refresh worn flesh, these creatures can comfort every stitch and scar without pity, compunction, or
regret.

She would not think about it. Would not.

She was becoming good at not thinking.

No. She was becoming good at thinking. Good at directing the mind. Good at recognizing those dark cranial crevices that attract mental energies, good at forbidding her mind to enter. She sensed what resided there. The sad scenarios, the fear of loss, the grip of loneliness that absorbs the thought, leaches the mind, and entwines the limbs. No. She'd turn her back on these soul traps. She had better things to do.

She didn't have to see everything the sponge would see; she already knew. "And they shall become one flesh." Of course she knew. His needles pricked her arm.

She knew everything. The diagnosis, the prognosis, the doctors explained so very well. But she also knew that doctors are not prophets. The Creator allows doctors to heal, not predict. She heard what the doctors said, but she didn't have to listen.

She did have to listen to Moshe's endless demands for pills, potions, and pampering. Of course a body assaulted by illness make demands as it seeks tranquillity, denying tranquillity to his wife.

"Rev?!"

"Coming!"

Better to focus on breakfast. Their breakfast was down to a science now, thanks to Goldie Newmark, herbal advocate, who, by Divine providence, had moved into the house across the street. Goldie coached Reva in how to replace sugar and ketchup with seasonings and herbs, and then encouraged her to untie her apron strings. "No chaining yourself to the kitchen!" commanded Goldie. "Fix four, freeze two—for next week. Think ahead, plan ahead, and keep a head!" Advice Reva aspired to follow.

"Oatmeal's ready, Moshe. Here, try some with blueberries!"

"Mhm." He would prefer brown sugar.

"What are your plans for today?" She offered orange juice, hoping to divert him.

"Well, I think I'll go over the accounts and take care of those delinquent payments. And maybe I'll call some stores for orders. You know, like I told you from the beginning, the account work is the hardest part of this business."

"You were very right. A good thing you're taking care of it." A very good thing. Thank God, this aspect of the business interested him now, occupied him, and gave him pleasure. Legacy Press was her baby, but he nurtured it and was with her as always. By profession Moshe was a *shochet*, a ritual slaughterer. Yet he was proud that her Legacy had grown, had succeeded. They had begun with one little children's book more than a decade ago. Since then Legacy had become a major Jewish publishing house, with new titles coming out every year. Who would have imagined it?

Well, maybe she had imagined it. She felt a big need, and felt something big had to fill it. And she had a very big love for books.

A big love for teaching, too. Her first baby, Judah, became her first live-in student. She was thrilled. Jewish parents are instructed *V'shinantam l'vanecha*, "teach [Torah] to your children." And a child is never too young to learn. The Gemara praises the mother of Rabbi Joshua, who placed her baby's crib by the door of the house of learning so he could hear the sound of Torah. Although Reva and her little family were then living in Bangor, Maine, a town that then had no rabbinic house of study, she was able to entertain little Judah with picture books. Even an infant could look at pictures. Those quiet, private moments of enjoying books together would create a wonderful bond between her and her baby, she was certain. She looked through her bookshelves for the appropriate literature.

By the time their second son, Yoni, was born, they had exhausted their home library. Reva, now with two youngsters in tow, eagerly set out for the public library. Secular books, after all, could demonstrate Torah values. Drawing upon the parental license that allows a mother to read however she pleases, Reva enthusiastically adapted texts. Her children listened to that engaging primer *Make Way for Ducklings,* a heart-rending story portraying the virtues of being kind to small animals. Judah and Yoni clamored for that model of brotherly love, *The Five Chinese Brothers.* And they thrilled to the inspiring tale of the courageous engineer who harnessed technology to enhance God's creation: *Mike Mulligan and His Steam Shovel.*

When Moshe's work relocated his growing young family to New Haven, Reva and the children continued combing libraries. Among their finds were books with Jewish content, including magnificently illustrated volumes about Chanukah and Passover, which required only a touch of Reva's supplemental text. Bible stories, such as *Joseph and the Coat of Many Colors* and *Noah and the Ark,* also found their way into the juvenile section, and into Reva's living room.

Judah, and Yoni, and later little Shoni, always assumed that their mother was reading the standard version, and Reva nearly forgot that she wasn't. However, young neighbors, visiting during story time, pounced on the difference. "Sal doesn't thank God for all the sweet delicious blueberries that grow on the hillside when *our* mom reads the story!"

No? Then something was lacking! When Reva supplemented a text, she packed it with essential nutrients. Any story could feed the mind, but well adapted it strengthened the soul.

There's a void! thought Reva. For herself it hardly mattered. She was fortunate to have a background steeped in Jewish education, and she knew countless stories from Torah sources to transmit to her children. But what about other parents? So many, who didn't have this background, must want children's books with basic Jewish values and traditions. They would search the libraries and bookstores—and find precious little for their efforts.

That void must be filled. Reva decided to attempt her first story.

Moshe came home, saw her writing, and noticed she hardly looked up.

"What's doing?" he asked.

"I'm writing. A book. For the kids."

"Book?" He knew she could teach. But write a book? A book was exalted.

"Yes." She added, "Debbie likes it." Debbie, a graduate student at Yale, carried weight in literary matters.

Debbie stopped in that evening. "Rev's book is great!" she confirmed. "Kids need books like this."

"Oh," said Moshe, considering, while Reva's imagination raced. Through her books, the deep well of Torah and Midrashic stories, spanning a history of over forty-seven hundred years, would be available to everyone. Now many parents could teach their children basic Jewish values and traditions. Reva's little classroom would expand to the world.

She submitted her manuscript to a small religious publishing house, and soon received a reply.

"Moshe! They like it!"

Moshe calculated. "But do you really want to give it to them? Why should they have it? Why not do it ourselves?"

Why not! Of course they could. Certainly one little book could be published on a shoestring. The main thing was to get it done—dive straight in!

More than a decade before PCs and desktops, Moshe and Reva plunged into the world of publishing.

"Do you remember, Moshe?" He was enduring his blueberries and needed to be rallied on. "Do you remember how we began Legacy, without a clue to what we were getting into?"

"It was all your idea," he recalled, chewing. "You wanted the books just so. You had to do them yourself."

That's how he remembered it, and she wasn't going to argue. At the time they hadn't known a font from a folio, but they were soon to meet typesetters, artists, graphic designers, color separators, and printers. Each had a price. Legacy clearly needed start-up money.

From where?

Reva considered using *ma'aser*, their tithe money. In accordance with Torah law, the first 10 percent of Moshe's paycheck was *ma'aser*, to be given directly to *tzedakah*, charity. They consulted with a rabbi, who assured them that using *ma'aser* money for educational purposes was permissible. Because Legacy's educational books would benefit the community, *ma'aser* money could be used.

They began. Once they put their plan into action, paths opened up. God seemed to be directing her to a cadre of graphic artists, writers, and illustrators, as one book led to another. An unexpected side benefit of publishing books was providing jobs, which according to Maimonides's *Golden Ladder of Tzedakah* was the highest rung of charity. Her search for talent led her to women as far away as Jerusalem. She forged friendships, encouraged her artists and writers in their creative quandaries, and launched careers. Shaina was one of her finds.

As a publisher she also wrestled with policy decisions. For example, how should she print the name of God? Jewish law prohibits defacing the name of God in any language. Considering that her books were for children, who might tear them, scribble on them, literally devour them or take them into an inappropriate place, God spelled G, dash, d, became Legacy's policy. As she explained in the note that prefaced her stories, this was also out of awe and respect for the Almighty, and symbolized all that is beyond our ability to express. "It's the dash," she quipped to Moshe, "which says it all."

Of course there were a few bumps on the road. One of Reva's favorite titles hit her market with a resounding thud; boxes of those books still lined her basement. Another little book would sell better, she had thought, with an accompanying T-shirt. That book had been a sellout, but the shirts were write-offs. Undaunted, she craved new angles. A new catalogue, "One Hundred Fifty Scents for Paper," declared that a page could now waft with anything from apples to zucchini. So she just *had* to do *God's Smelly World*. A book that smelled—oh dear, yes. So what? Costly errors and bloopers and oversights—such were the initiation rites of a young publisher. Legacy carried on, a vital link in an unbroken tradition, reaching ever further, ever stronger, Reva always liked to think.

Her doorbell rang.

Reva gulped the last of her juice. "Moshe, that must be Aidel. I totally forgot." The artist from Monsey was here to check out the proofs. "I'm dashing down. I'll be back in a few minutes."

Now where were those proofs? Where was the time she used to have to look them over herself, to plan, to plot, to organize and nurture every book? Now Legacy was running on automatic pilot—she would not think how long this could, or couldn't, go on.

Her caller downstairs was not Aidel, but the mailman. With her mail came the usual unsolicited manuscripts. Was there anything here she would really want to do, something that really *should* get out? Would she have time to do it now? She took her mail upstairs and dropped it on the kitchen table. "Probably either ditties, compositions, or sermons," she commented to her husband, almost oblivious to the sour grapes in her voice. "Everyone thinks it's so easy to write for children."

Moshe stirred Sweet'n Low into his coffee. "Eh. You can write yourself. You've got your own ideas." He had always thought that she was capable. But now, since his illness, he was drawing his little circle tighter and tighter around the two of them, always on guard, allowing less and less to come in.

A few minutes later the artist was at the door. "Always interruptions," muttered Moshe. Reva grabbed her proofs and ran downstairs.

Aidel Goldman, a small woman with a sharp eye for color and detail, was oblivious to the several publishing deadlines they had already missed.

"What do you think?" asked Reva, offering the proofs.

Aidel shrugged. "This is a summer scene. The leaves are supposed to be bright green, not brownish. And our fresh red apples came out dull orange. Not so good."

"We'll miss the Chanukah market." Again. Reva bit her lip, but feeling perturbed wouldn't help. This was beyond her control. Her mother would have called this *yenem's hent*—a matter in other people's hands. The book, like any newborn, would enter the world when God wanted, in its own time. She chatted with Aidel for a few minutes, catching up on news of the kids, husbands, and friends.

"Rev?"

Aidel reached for her portfolio case and nodded. Friends don't need explanations.

"Wonderful to see you, Aidel. When the proofs come back again, I'll call you, and you'll look them over?" So many details involved in publishing a book.

Breakfast was over. Now she would prepare lunch and

dinner, all homemade, of course. Take-out meals, loaded with salt or sugar or hidden who-knows-what, would never do for Moshe. She poured, she measured, she checked the calendar. Later this afternoon she would take him to the—which one this time? She found today's date. Cardiologist.

Suppose someone had told her that she, she who had no great love of kitchen work, she who felt queasy even opening a bandage, would be spending her middle years thus. The years when her children were grown and had children of their own, the years when she should be enjoying the companionship of her handsome husband, traveling to Hawaii perhaps, and Palm Beach, and especially to Israel! Could have been. And here she was, measuring proteins, carbohydrates, and milliliters of insulin—just as well that she had not been forewarned. A person is finite. We see what's in front, never what's up ahead.

And she had grown from this life. We can see only a fragment of the picture, of God's Divine plan. But we trust, grow, and learn. She was learning—she had to learn—how to navigate an altered life course. True, after the operation medical issues were increasing, not decreasing, but there was certainly hope that her husband would still get better, stronger. Of course there was hope. Meanwhile, as his strength ebbed, she had to strengthen her connection with God. *Me'ayin yovo ezri*—from where does my help come?

Well, suppose. Suppose her life had presented no greater challenges than strolling along a beach in Netanya. That would be pleasant. But in that very pleasantness, wouldn't there also have been a loss? On the Netanya beach she would never have seen how dependent we are on God—she would not have dared to imagine how dependent. The Brooklyn beach, not the Netanya beach, forced her to reach into herself, forced her to pluck the strength of her soul. She was often telling herself that, these days.

On the other hand, here in Brooklyn was Sarah's table. Here, at Sarah's, not in Netanya, was a highlight for her week, a Jerusalem for her consciousness. For Sarah's table alone, it was a pleasure to be in Brooklyn.

Lunch arranged. Dinner defrosting. Now was her time to get ready for Sarah's.

A comfortable, distracting ritual, to dress for Sarah's.

Let no one think that she had run out of the house without attending to her appearance. Her clothing never was chosen haphazardly. Today she would wear the black sweater with the silver necklace. Shiny, that silver. Makes whatever it reflects look good. Perfect for today. Last week she had chosen her red plaid suit. Chic. Red protected against the *ayin hara*, the evil eye, yes, but she had selected that suit because red gave her a lift. Colors are God's rainbow of visual perks, to cheer us on. Her red suit also spoke a second message: An Orthodox woman can be modest and still look good. And what a feeling it was when Shaina complimented, "Whew, you're hot today— fire engine red!"

Outfit chosen. Now. Which *sheitel?*

Over the years the wig had become a part of her. An organic extension, like her nails and her skin, as essential as her dress. Impossible to leave home without it now. How different she had felt when she first began wearing them! She smiled as she reached for her new honey-colored layered wig, remembering her talk with the Lubavitcher Rebbe years ago, just before her wedding. She and Moshe, a young and breathless couple, had gone to the *rebbe* to receive his blessing. Nervously, they had awaited his holy words. And what the *rebbe* said to her was, "Reva, are you going to cover your hair?"

Of course she was going to cover her hair.

"Mit vos?"

What did he mean "with what"? She heard the *rebbe*'s voice, strong and powerful. It mattered, with what?

"Oh, I have hats. I bought kerchiefs—"

But the *rebbe* shook his head. Did the *rebbe* want more details? Reva enumerated, "I had a special fall made for me, a beautiful custom hat, scarves. . . . "

The *rebbe* continued shaking his head. These weren't good enough, yet she had listed all possibilities. Except one. But no. Certainly the *rebbe* wasn't going to ask her to do *that!*

"I don't understand," Reva finally said. "I'm a religious woman, and of course I'm going to cover my hair. What—I mean, is there a problem with that?"

"*A tichel falt arup.*" The kerchief falls off.

"Mine won't," she had declared.

His silence unnerved her, until she blurted it out, "Not a wig! Please, not a wig!"

She explained herself, words tumbling out in justification. "Nobody wears a wig today, except women who are bald or bubbies like my grandmother. And hers has waves and a top-knot! Everyone will stare at me. Even *rebbitzins* don't wear wigs; they wear hats. My relatives in New Haven will laugh at me—they're already making comments, asking me if I'm going to shave my head! Even my own parents," she tried not to panic, "who are totally supportive, and really proud that I'm religious, just can't see that a young girl should ruin her beautiful tresses by sticking a *sheitel* on top!

"Isn't it enough that my hair is covered?"

The *rebbe* answered, his voice both firm and gentle. "Your parents want you to be happy. If they knew that this would make you happy. . . . "

Happy? Happy in a *wig?*

His eyes caring, penetrating, the *rebbe* continued. "I know that you will look the way a Jewish woman should look when she walks in the street. And in the *zechus*, the merit, of this *mitzvah*, I guarantee that you will have great *Yiddishe naches*."

Yiddish *naches*. He must have meant children. Good children. But who could think of children at this time? She was young, she felt almost like a child herself. Before her lay the *chuppah*, the bridal canopy, and all of the new laws she would soon be observing. And sharing her life with a man in new and exciting but also frightening ways. And running a household. Farthest from her mind were her own progeny and *their* distant marriages and spiritual development. But it was on the *rebbe*'s mind, and it was clear from the *rebbe*'s demeanor that this was the end of the discussion.

"Guarantee?" she pleaded.

He nodded. "Yes, I give you my guarantee." The *rebbe* gave his blessings before they left the room.

In the hallway, Moshe turned to her, his voice encouraging. "Don't worry. I'll pay for it."

"*Pay* for it?" she cried. "I have to *wear* it!" She ran out of the building, Moshe trying to keep up with her. "I should never have gone to the *rebbe* for this!" she moaned, "I thought we were going to get a blessing!"

Reva smiled, adjusting her *sheitel*, preparing for Sarah's. The blessing had definitely been there, although it hadn't felt like one at first. Determined not to dishonor the *rebbe*'s instructions, Reva had made an appointment with a wig maker for the following morning. "Blonde," murmured the wig maker disapprovingly. "Blonde is a very difficult color to match, especially your color. But I'll do my best. Sit still, I'll measure you." She wrapped a tape measure around Reva's head. It felt like a crown of thorns.

She looked at the young golden-haired girl in the mirror, with lustrous, bouncing, shoulder-length hair, her best, most identifying feature! Here was the end of herself as she knew herself! She couldn't hold back her tears. Soon, when she would look into the mirror, what would she see? She *wouldn't* look into the mirror! But the *rebbe* wanted the *sheitel*—and his blessing was contingent upon her meticulously following his directive. She *had* to follow through. She reached for a tissue. The future? The children she was to have—please God—they would have to become her crown.

She didn't, she couldn't, wear the *sheitel* right away.

At first she wore the custom-made hat. She even wore it to the *Purim farbrengen,* the special Purim holiday get-together that the *rebbe* held. How thrilled she was that one of her *sheva brachos* ceremonies, the special blessings recited for a bride and groom during the first week after their marriage, was held right there at the *farbrengen.* The *rebbe* sent up a piece of blessed honey cake, just for her, the bride. "And what's really wrong with the hat!" Reva thought to herself. "My head is still covered. Besides, no one can wear a wig all the time. You're sleeping, you take it off. You're in the shower, you take it off. You're putting your child in the playpen—you'd better take it off, or it'll fall off. After all, it isn't really part of you."

It wasn't part of her yet, but it became so, in Bangor, Maine, where Moshe had his first position. Shy and awkward, Reva sat next to Moshe. He was driving his blue Dodge, and she was wearing the new wig. When they pulled up to a traffic light, the driver of the car next to them waved hello. It was the president of their shul. "Rabbi, is this your new bride?" he asked.

Moshe nodded and introduced her. The man obviously was impressed. "Boy, I'm glad you didn't make her wear one of those awful bubby wigs!"

But he had to know the truth. Reva just couldn't let him drive away thinking that she wasn't covering her hair. She told him, and it set the tone for her self-perception for years afterward. "I *am* wearing a wig," she said.

His eyes widened. "No," he whistled softly. "You look terrific. Who could believe it!"

And that was that. The *rebbe*'s blessing would be fulfilled because the *sheitel* had set the tone and started her on her unique spiritual path: a committed Hasidic woman with knowledge of fashion and modernity. It wasn't her own hair, but that didn't matter. From then on she never questioned wearing the wig. She was a standard-bearer, a role model. She had a mission that went beyond herself, here in Bangor, and later in New Haven. At that time neither community was exactly a bastion of Jewish religious observance. She, and only she, would have to guide her children. She had to show them what an observant woman could be. She had to supply them not only with warmth, love, and understanding, but with Torah insights, ideas, and stories that they might not receive otherwise. She felt capable of steering her weighty household ship through the often turbulent waters of modern-day life.

The *sheitel*. Crown of gold.

As Reva walked to Sarah's she thought about her children. Wonderful children. Children who had fulfilled and even exceeded the *rebbe*'s blessing. Children who were themselves devout and committed, and who gave her support beyond her dreams. *Naches.*

Sarah's table: sparkling dishes; colorful linen cloth; warm, easy companionship; a hum of loving conversation. Reva opened the door to her Tuesday haven.

And here was Ora, greeting her with a plate piled high with tuna, challah roll, and Claremont cabbage vinaigrette. Ora, her good friend and former high school classmate. How had Ora known that Reva needed a little pampering, today, to get recharged. But reaching out to others came naturally to

Ora. Even in ninth-grade algebra class, Ora wore her party smile, as she offered sticks of gum to all her classmates. So now she was offering tuna fish. Reva, in the right place at the right time, received Ora's kindness and cheer.

Reva sighted an empty seat next to Shaina and settled in it just in time to hear Sarah comment, "Negative character traits? Huh! They have no hold over us if we are connected to the right thing!"

At that particular moment, Reva wanted to be connected to a cup of hot tea. Levana passed her one, and Reva found herself focusing on how tranquilly the tea released its steam.

"I made him his lunch," Reva mused to Shaina. "A sandwich and some soup. I set the table for him. Napkins, cutlery, place setting, even flowers. I took out the *pot* for him. And he said, 'What's this?' as though he never saw a pot before. I know he'll just leave everything untouched—without me, he just won't eat. He's like Abraham in this week's parsha, recuperating after surgery, sitting at his tent door, waiting. But Abraham is waiting for guests—and Moshe is waiting for me!"

Only I'm not a messenger of healing, she wanted to add. I can't heal him, or even take his pain away. I want to, but I can't. *Not a good place to be thinking,* she caught herself, and focused on the table conversation. The subject seemed to be the *mitzvah* of *hachnasas orchim,* welcoming guests.

"More than what the host does for his guest, the guest does for his host!" Faygi, Sarah's sister-in-law, quoted. Faygi, Reva always thought, was the epitome of the learned, well-dressed woman. This week she wore a light blue St. John suit with a crocheted matching shell. Stunning.

"Once you've been a *Shabbos* guest for a while, you appreciate being the hostess," added Shaina, pushing her glasses up the bridge of her nose. One of the lenses had fallen out. She had it, somewhere, and she could manage without it anyway. Yet several women, including Sarah herself, had recommended a glasses repair place, while a few other offered tips on how to make the repair herself. Impressed by their concern, Shaina resolved to fix the glasses.

"Don't you find that the kids behave better when there are guests?" Iyelet was commenting, her Eli contentedly sucking a bottle of orange juice. "With guests children get more attention—more people to show off for!"

"Depends on the guest. Some guests take over the show!" someone added.

"True," Reva allowed herself to be drawn into the conversation, "but so often guests broaden a child's outlook, and help them to practice what they've learned."

A guest such as Bliss, for example.

Reva remembered Bliss, a young woman, a single parent, who Reva had met in a writing class at Yale. While they were living in New Haven, Reva tried to take a class or two every semester, both to hone her skills and to meet people of the broader community. From this particular writing class, taught by a well-known author, Reva learned that good writers don't necessarily make good teachers. Yet the class was worthwhile because here she met Bliss. From time to time Bliss would mention her two-year-old son, Adam.

"I never had Adam circumsised," Bliss commented one day.

"Really?" replied Reva. "That's surprising, Bliss. Even non-Jews give cosmetic circumcisions."

"Didn't see any reason to change nature," Bliss stated definitively.

Reva, whose current backyard bordered on a thorn patch, saw good reason to change nature, when appropriate. But she certainly wouldn't discuss this issue bluntly with Bliss. Better to invite Bliss for *Shabbos,* where she could relate to *mitzvahs* in the context of a warm, accepting, sympathetic, nonjudgmental, Torah-true family. Her Judah was a manly fourteen,

Yoni a witty twelve, Shoni a charming eight, and Yosef an adorable four. On a cool November *Shabbos* evening, Bliss came. The parsha was "Vayera."

Reva's home-baked challahs were delicious, the gefilte fish just right, the chicken soup hot and golden, and Moshe's *d'var Torah, Shabbos* Torah thoughts, appropriate, impersonal, but stimulating and on target. "The baby's *bris* is a sign that he's a Jew," Moshe explained to Shoni.

"Oh, I never gave one to Adam," Bliss mentioned.

"Really? Why Bliss, I'm amazed," piped up Judah.

"Judah!" cautioned Reva. Had she been able to reach, she would have kicked him under the table.

"At what?" Bliss persisted.

"Well, think how embarrassed he'll be when he starts school," said Judah, reasonably.

"Yeah," seconded Yoni. "All the guys will say . . . "

Yoni was within reach.

"But they *will*, Ma!"

"It's a very basic *mitzvah*," said Judah in his best counseling voice. "I don't see how you could deprive your son of it." He showed off his vocabulary. "The *bris,* circumcision, is a spiritual refinement no man should be without."

"You are certainly sure of it," said Bliss.

"*I* wouldn't want to be Adam," said Yoni.

"You really should look into it more," suggested Judah. "Try to be open-minded."

"Oh, no," thought Reva, wondering what had happened to her sympathetic, nonjudgmental family.

Bliss laughed nervously. Nevertheless, she said she would look into it.

"You could speak with your neighbor, Rabbi Kahan." Judah wouldn't let up.

Bliss actually followed Judah's advice, and that year, to Reva's surprise, Adam was circumcised. When he grew older,

Bliss even enrolled him in a Jewish day school. You never know what can happen when you have guests.

"Having guests is not an easy *mitzvah*," Erica Fine, the doctor's wife, was saying. "We had a rare family evening planned when—ah! A guest. And a distraught guest at that. So we put our plans aside. Sometimes children have to learn that another's distress might come before their own enjoyment."

"But surely there have to be limits," said Klara Kirsh, tapping her pen on the yellow legal pad, which signaled her profession. "For years we had the same guest who invited himself every *Shabbos*. Perfect attendance. Now, for his own good, shouldn't he get to know other people? So I had other families invite him. But he never wanted to go! He preferred us!"

Shimona Lazelle, a former dancer, smiled. "He's welcome at our home. Please give me his number!"

"With you it's never a problem," smiled Tamar. "He'll just be lost in the crowd."

"And Shimona won't give up on him," added Ora. "She'll call him every week, until he feels that this poor family is so desperate to have him as a guest that he *must* show up."

"And when he does he'll find that half of Borough Park spends *Shabbos* at the Lazelles!"

"A happening place," said Levana, quoting her teenaged daughters. "Shimona always has an open house."

"The more you open your home, the more blessings come in," said Sarah. "Abraham and Sarah welcomed guests day and night to spread the word to the world that there is one, and only one, Creator."

"Our house was always full of guests," said Tamar. "I remember my grandmother saying, 'Your home is as big as your heart is.'"

"It works the other way, too," Sarah added. "The more you reach out, the more blessings flow into you. The bigger your home gets, the bigger your heart gets, too."

"That's right," Ora put in. "The bigger the home, the bigger the heart, the bigger the stretch. Like the Holy Temple, that stretched to fit in all the Jews who knelt in prayer. Elastic walls."

An elastic heart sounds good to me, thought Reva. If her own heart was elastic, it would be able to stretch endlessly to accommodate Moshe. "Every afternoon you have to go out?" were his parting words to her that morning, Well, she did need to get out. Even professional caretakers get some fresh air, don't they? Of course, she knew he wouldn't snap at her so much if he wasn't in pain. Yet if her heart was more elastic, his words might bounce off, instead of sinking in.

Sarah was talking about our patriarchs and matriarchs, our great forefathers and foremothers, who overcame their own negative traits, mastered their most difficult inner resistance, to serve God. Abraham's essential characteristic, for example, was kindness. He had to overcome his innate compassion when God commanded that he sacrifice his son Isaac. And he did. He was actually willing to give up his dear, beloved son. Such self-sacrifice dwarfed anything Reva could imagine.

Tamar chimed in, mentioning our matriarch Rachel and her self-sacrifice. "Today is Rachel's *yahrtzeit,* the anniversary of her passing," Tamar began. "Do you remember how Rachel was supposed to marry Jacob, and at the last minute, her father Laban substituted her sister Leah?" Everyone nodded, and Tamar continued. "The rabbis say that Rachel and Jacob were actually prepared for such a trick and had worked out secret signals to prevent it. Jacob was Rachel's soulmate; she had waited for him for seven years. But she gave the secret signs—and her husband—to her sister. Why? So that Leah wouldn't be embarrassed on her wedding night! Think of overcoming jealousy like that!"

"And Rachel's good deeds continue to affect all of us, right through until today," added Sarah. "From Rachel we inherit the strength to overcome our own negative traits. Our sages tell us that all souls are elevated on the day of their *yahrtzeit*. Why? Because the good deeds of their descendants and those they influenced give them elevation."

Just then Iyelet's baby started screaming. "Colic, again," she apologized, taking him from the room. The women around the table murmured sympathetically. Having babies was a *mitzvah*. Whatever came with the territory was a *mitzvah*, too. Reva remembered the many years of her own life when *davening* (prayer), learning, swimming, and especially sleeping, had to take second place to child care. There are priorities, and children come first. Why else were women not required to pray three times a day? Men must pray three times a day, but women are exempt from commandments that were linked to specific times—because God didn't need her prayers so much as her children needed her care.

Obviously, small children need constant care. And caring for them, while difficult, comes naturally.

To give that kind of care to a husband is not so natural.

She couldn't even get to shul on *Shabbos* these days. She had mentioned this to Judah, who had reminded her softly, "Like King Solomon says, there's a time for everything under the sun. Now God wants you to take care of Daddy."

Her eyes fell back on the study sheets. Wasn't caring as central a *mitzvah* as *davening*? Abraham left off communicating with God to take care of strangers. How much more so should she leave off *davening* to care for her own husband.

"Can you imagine an old lady and her husband having a baby?"

The question, and resulting chuckles, brought Reva's thoughts back to the table.

"Sarah was ninety years old when she and Abraham learned they would conceive a child!"

"See how we're all laughing over that one," observed

Faygi. "'God has made laughter for me,' is just what Sarah our matriarch said, and see—we are laughing!"

"Laughing now. But imagine how Abraham felt when God commanded him to sacrifice that very son. Yet Abraham was prepared to do it," said Tamar.

Sarah nodded. "And that is our strength and inheritance from Abraham—the power that we as a people have had through the ages, to sacrifice ourselves for God. Abraham *revealed* this to us. The Hebrew word for 'revealed' is from the same root as the name of the parsha—*vayera*. Abraham showed us real self-sacrifice."

"He had to give up his own self-definition," added Ora. "He saw himself as a compassionate person, and he had to override that compassion. He saw himself as teaching an advanced religion, which spurned human sacrifice, and he had to swallow those teachings. He saw himself as being a good father, but he had to overcome his paternal love and prepare to kill his own son. All that he had lived for, all that was to be perpetuated by his son, would be sacrificed as well. God demanded a total sacrifice of the ego, and Abraham complied."

Well, that's something to carry home, thought Reva. Abraham set aside all he thought precious, to do what God wanted. Of course, her husband and children were precious. Her *davening*, her writing, her publishing were also precious. Yet the purpose of her books was to "heighten the awareness of the Creator," or so she always claimed. And didn't a heightened awareness of the Creator lead you to do what He wanted, and not necessarily what you wanted?

Caring for her husband was clearly what the Creator was demanding of her now.

"We're here to engage in *tikkun*, repairing of the world," Sarah was saying. "In everything we touch and everything we do, there are hidden sparks. Every soul, every single one of us, is here to free those trapped sparks. Whenever we perform a *mitzvah* with a physical object, the holy sparks hidden in that object are freed and elevated."

"How does that work?" someone wanted to know.

"Take this tea, for example." Sarah held up the china cup. "Before drinking it, I said a blessing, to thank God for giving me the gift of this tea. I've freed the trapped spark in the teabag, in the water, and in the cup. I have made these physical objects holy."

"Does that work for people, too?" Levana asked.

Sarah nodded. "Every time you give of yourself, you are elevating the sparks in that moment of giving. You are calling forth the sparks in the person you're helping. And all those sparks together will ignite into a great fire that will light up the entire world."

Sparks. There was comfort in sparks. By conscientiously giving Moshe his prescribed medicine, who knew what sparks Reva could free . . .

Time to go home—to fulfill her destiny, the legacy of Abraham and Rachel. To serve her husband *b'seiver panim yafos*, graciously, with a smile. To free and elevate thousands of tiny, Divine sparks that would rise and join and bring more light into the world—Reva's contribution to illuminating the cosmic darkness and paving the way for Moshiach to come, she hoped.

3
Tamar: Marrying Off
the Next in Line
Parshas Chaye Sarah

Abraham was old, well advanced in years, and God had blessed Abraham with everything. Abraham said to the senior servant of his household, who was in charge of all that he owned, "Place your hand under my thigh. I will bind you by an oath to God, Lord of heaven and of earth, that you will not take a wife for my son from the daughters of the Canaanites among whom I live. Instead, you must go to my native land, to my birthplace, to obtain a wife for my son Isaac."
—Genesis 24:1–4

Parents begin their work by imprinting their deeds and ideals on the hearts and minds of their children. Then, to ensure the well-being of their child and the future of their people, parents help their child find his or her bashert, *their suitable, destined spouse. The search requires persistence, patience, fortitude, and faith.*

Tamar had much to say about matchmaking. On days of inner turbulence, such as this particular Tuesday, she would emphatically, in her mind, voice her opinions. Expounding from a mental podium gives emotional clarity and was in line with the Hasidic teaching that the mind must direct the heart. Often, while thinking, she would prepare one of her famous cakes, designed to delight family and friends at *simchahs,* happy events. Today, for example, she planned to bake a cake for the bar mitzvah of her neighbor's son. She envisioned a cake shaped like an open Torah scroll—a sheet cake in the middle, jelly rolls on either side, wooden "handles" made of pretzel sticks, all to be skillfully decorated to look like the real thing. And the topic of her mental discourse would be: preparing for an upcoming family crisis.

While flipping through a cookbook to find suitable recipes, a taunting thought kicked off her mental discussion: "With proper forethought might not this impending crisis have been waylaid? As our sages say, 'Who is wise? He who knows the end from the beginning.'"

But she *was* aware from the beginning, Tamar assured herself. She selected the recipe from page sixty-four, Bouffant Lemon Chiffon Cake, and arranged ingredients to double the recipe. She had known all along that two of her children, Abigail and Ephraim, close in age as they were, might one day face this situation. Abigail was less than a year old at her brother Ephraim's *bris.* And Tamar had minimized the risks as best she could. She had learned from her mother and grandmother that "joyful siblings shouldn't bump noses," which sometimes required deft maneuvering. Her mother and grandmother knew how. No matter how tight the living quarters had been, each child was assured some private place and emotional space. Tamar's grandmother seemed as familiar with emotional space as she was with the insides of a chicken.

Tamar watched waves of white powder settle delicately into her mixing bowl as she measured and sifted flour. At a similar kitchen table, her bubby would stand to *kosher* chickens. The red box of coarse kosher salt sat squarely on the table, next to trays of plucked chickens, freshly cleaned and quartered. Bubby would reach in for a fistful to toss over the chickens. The salt fell in graceful gusts, like pure white snow. Today this salting and koshering process is done by the kosher butchers, before the meat is sold. But Bubby always did her own. To properly draw out the blood, each piece had to be totally covered by salt, inside and out, and Bubby never missed a millimeter. With similar thoroughness she listened to her children and grandchildren, hearing them out, absorbing their unsettled energies, relaxing, refining, securing their emotional space. Her mother also knew how to listen, with the concern and trust that draws confidence. Tamar always had hoped she would do the same. When her children needed her, she put other things aside. Be there, and be aware, was her motto. She had always done her best to ward off problems before they occurred.

It's true, of course, that each child has unique needs, and each requires a unique piece of mother. This reality prompted questions. For example, a distant relative like cousin Jennifer, who married the statistician, might ask upon seeing that Tamar was expecting a baby *again:* "How can you bring yet *another* child into the world? Isn't your responsibility to the children you *already* have? You certainly don't want to take away from them!" Tamar agreed that she did not. The question had a point. The comment, based on finite math, was mathemetically flawless.

This particular cake, properly measured and baked, should also be flawless. Eggs should be at room temperature.

The point was, returning to cousin Jennifer, that unlike fine cakes, not all entities are measurement and temperature dependent. The theory that finite resources can't support unlimited children assumes that families are founded on math, which they are not. While successful cakes depend on measured ingredients and timed temperatures, children, and the families into which they enter, are founded on the supra-rational and the infinite. Each child, as Bubby would say, enters the world with blessings, and a breadbasket to catch them in. Mothers, who receive additional inner strength and outer resources with each successive child, are in tune with this.

"And how will you marry off all these children?" was cousin Jennifer's next question.

"They *will* all marry, please God," Tamar's grandmother, and later her mother, tranquilly replied. And apparently God was pleased, for they all did.

A lump in the baking powder. Meanwhile, another thought was clearing its voice to speak. According to Tamar's rules of mental discourse it should have its say. Expose the thought, then lay it to rest. This one whined, "Why isn't Abigail married already? Must she be the last in her class to find her *bashert?*"

Well. One needs the right one, at the right time. Abigail certainly merited a good match. She was a beautiful girl, and not only attractive, but kind, gracious, and *eidel*—that untranslatable word that bespoke refinement of character. And intelligent. Abigail was, in short, an *excellent* girl, and needed an excellent boy.

A boy, in other words, similar in caliber to her two older brothers, who had married outstanding girls. Baking powder lumps resolved, Tamar progressed to separating the eggs.

With her older sons, Tamar had to sort through a multi-tude of possibilities—no easy task. Ah, but finding one's *shid-duch* is as difficult as parting the Red Sea, our sages say. In short, each successful *shidduch* is a miracle, although some come easier than others. Looking back, marrying off her first son had gone as smoothly as dipping an apple into honey.

His was a *shidduch* hallowed in heaven and matched by

mothers. Tamar had had a special feeling when she first met Estie at a neighbor's house, seemingly by chance. Estie's mother had had a similar feeling when she heard of Tamar's Gershon. It was the first *shidduch* for both children. They met, liked each other, and have been good to and for each other ever since. A *mazeldik shidduch*, a fortunate match.

Most do not come so easily.

Tamar began beating the egg whites. A midrashic story about a Roman noblewoman demonstrates the complexity of the *shidduch*. This woman met the renowned sage, Rabbi Akiva, and asked him, "What does your God do all day?"

"He arranges marriages," Rabbi Akiva replied.

"I can arrange marriages," asserted the noblewoman. She called all her servants into the courtyard, lined the men servants up on one side, women servants on the other, and paired them off, two by two. After a glorious mass wedding, she sent everyone home for the night.

Complaints began before the crack of dawn: 'He hit me!' 'She insulted me.' 'Free me from this monster, before I go insane!'

"Great is the wisdom of the Jewish God," conceded the noblewoman.

Oh, it's all *bashert*, down to the tiniest detail, the sages say. How many offers one receives, how many times one must go out, and with whom, and how many meetings each person must endure before finding their destined "other half" is entirely *bashert*. Gershon had a special merit to succeed the first time.

Tamar watched as the egg whites became frothy, foamy, white, and thick. Then she began to beat the yolks. Yolks had a different consistency. They would foam up and become thick, but never stiff.

Levi, Tamar's second son, had been a more difficult case

than his brother, predictably. Levi was always her particular child, the one who fished the chickpeas out of his *cholent,* stew, that sort of thing. Levi nixed the first three girls he was offered, without explanation. Yet, any of the three, from Tamar's perspective, would have been a perfect selection.

"What," demanded Tamar, "was wrong with them?"

When he admitted the truth, Tamar almost wished he hadn't: His bride, Levi confessed, must have green eyes.

Green eyes! Tamar cringed. She should ask the *matchmaker* for green eyes? What would she think of her? What kind of a mother was she, to have raised a son who makes such a demand?! And what kind of a girl would they offer to such a boy? A green-eyed *what?*

But *shotkin* Nina Weinstein took the request in stride. "Green eyes, I've got," she said, evenly. "Green nails, green hair, *that's* a problem." True to her word, Nina found a green-eyed beauty who not only put Levi in seventh heaven, but also delighted Tamar and her husband. The girl with green eyes turned out to be more suitable, in all ways, than suggestions one, two, and three.

"Sometimes," Nina had explained to Tamar, "these unreasonable preferences, those peculiar requests, are actually the signposts that lead a young person to their *richtige zivvug*— their best destined mate."

"*Best?*" Tamar had questioned. "You mean there can be more than one?"

"Could be," said Nina. "Each person has a number of possible matches—the rabbis say three, or maybe ten—but there is always one who is the *richtige zivvug,* the optimal other half. He's there—we just have to find him. Kabbalah assures us that forty days before a child is conceived, a voice announces from the heavens that this child is the destined partner of so-and-so! And from what I've seen in making *shidduchim,* God

wants us to meet the right one—for *His* reasons, which are not
necessarily our own. Oh yes, we want a man who is handsome, loving, kind, learned, and successful, or a girl who is
beautiful, gentle, and charming. And with green eyes, straight
teeth, curly hair. Those, Tamar, are the wrappings on the package. But inside! Inside, we may see later, is a man with whom
we must learn patience, or boldness, or a woman who teaches
us to sometimes look the other way. The *zivvug* is the *ezer
k'negdo*—the helper, with whom God pairs us up to refine our
character and bolster our strengths, bringing us to our potential. Green eyes? Of course. I respect that. Green eyes may
mark his match. May he find the right one and have *simchahs!*"

"That makes me feel better," Tamar had said. "It sounded
like such a craziness."

"Not in this case," said Nina. "Of course, sometimes particular requests signal something else. Fear of marriage or of
world opinion, for example, may lead a young person to make
a request that is not really in their best interests. I remember
once a lovely girl who seemed suitable for a particular boy.
They both enjoyed their first date. But after the second, the
boy phoned to say he wasn't interested. I asked if he would
mind telling me why, and he replied that the girl was too
heavy.

"Well, this boy was a hefty kugel himself! And clearly he
had liked the girl's personality. So I asked him to think it over
for a day or two. Was this something *he* didn't like—or something he thought his *friends* wouldn't like! He, of course, not
his friends, would be enjoying the girl's company! So sometimes I've reminded a young person to think of their own
preferences and not try to second-guess their peers. I wouldn't
want anyone who comes to me to lose their rightly destined
partner through such a mistake."

Tamar often recommended Nina as a capable and caring *shotkin*, dedicated to the ideal that everyone deserves to be married to their destined partner, build everlasting houses, build a Torah nation, and hasten the Messianic era.

"And what does she charge?" someone had once asked, disdainfully.

Yes, some questioned whether the services of a *shotkin* should be compensated. They contended that making a *shidduch* was a *mitzvah*, and a *mitzvah*, our sages say, is its own reward. Does one need a professional? Aunts, cousins, friends, siblings sometimes put together a beautiful *shidduch*.

Tamar paused in her thoughts for a minute. The whites and yolks were all whipped up now. She began to alternately beat the liquid and dry ingredients together with the yolks, then continued, carefully, to fold in the egg whites. This cake needed delicate handling. Not every cake required such a light hand; for example, anyone could mix brownies. But a sensitive cake, over- or underbeaten, would not reach its delectable potential. Similarly a certain finesse also was involved in managing many *shidduchs*. A good *shidduch*, well executed, was priceless. Think how much wedding money is spent on flowers, which are thrown out the next day! But what the *shotkin* arranged should last forever. Any parent with a little gratitude would make sure the *shotkin* was well compensated.

How grateful Tamar would be to the *shotkin* who found the right match for Abigail. She had been "of marriageable age" for longer than Tamar liked to think.

There had been offers, of course, but so far Abigail had not met the right boy. Not that she was particular. She didn't demand a genius (although she had met some geniuses), and she wasn't asking for a millionaire (although she had met some millionaires also). She didn't even require a young man from a renowned rabbinic dynasty. Abigail simply sought a refined Torah-observant man, nice looking, understanding, someone she could feel comfortable with. But even with this modest list, she had not met Mr. Right. Already an "older" girl (older, in Tamar's circles, being any girl on the far side of twenty-two), Abigail seriously needed a *shidduch.*

Tamar always had advocated that girls marry young—young being the closer side of twenty-two. Most mothers and *shotkins* agreed with her. Of course, the girl must also have a certain basic maturity, understanding, and sensibility—yet, if she didn't have it earlier, what's to guarantee that she would acquire it later? As the years pile up the girl becomes more so-phisticated—and increasingly particular. She becomes more likely to overlook her *bashert,* her "destined" one, heaven for-bid. Also, as time marches on, the pickings get slimmer.

The cake batter had a lovely volume. Tamar delicately trans-ferred it to baking pans and arranged the pans in the oven.

Well, Tamar had put in every effort, searching for the right *shidduch.* But man plans and God laughs. Suitable boys were suggested, none was yet suitable enough.

How does one determine "suitability"? Compare the selection of a *shidduch* to the selection of a pair of shoes. Shoes must suit the eye, fit the foot, match the outfit, be appropriate for the occasion, and wear well. How often one checks a pair of shoes in the shoe store before actually buying them! And yet, this selection is not irreversible. With a receipt and within seven days, a mistaken purchase can be returned without consequence. A *shidduch,* however, must "fit" in infi-nitely more dimensions than a pair of shoes. Yet to a mistak-enly contracted *shidduch,* this inconsequential grace period does not apply. Therefore, Tamar, a discerning shoe shopper, became expert at "checking out" a boy. Discreetly, of course. Ask the principal of the boy's yeshiva, consult with the boy's roommates, his teachers, his neighbors, and listen. All will say he is a "wonderful" boy. But listen to how they say it. Listen for those little pauses, those tiny silences that speak what words may not.

Also, one can ask for concrete examples of his wonderfulness. Of the roommate inquire, Did this wonderful boy bring back lunch when his friend had the flu? Of a neighbor, discreetly request the name of the boy's mother's cleaning lady. Yes, for this cause, Tamar had interviewed women employed as domestics. A robust woman from Jamaica, a muscular blonde Polish lady, a Russian immigrant with gold teeth. Of these she asked: Does this boy speak respectfully to his parents? A boy who respects his parents, reasoned Tamar, is likely to respect his wife. So she asked: When no one but parents, siblings, and household help can hear—*how* does this boy speak? Teachers should also be consulted: Does this boy have a good head? Good heart? Good friends? Is he punctual in coming to class and going to shul? Promptness shows ability and responsibility. And is he generally nice looking and in good health? And what is the health and general situation of his family? Listen carefully. And if everything is suitable, then the boy and girl may meet to determine further suitability for themselves.

Some might ask: Doesn't this system restrict a young person's free choice? Don't they feel confined, receiving so slim a slice, selecting from what has already been selected?

That's one perspective. But another is that children allow their parents to pan for gold so that they themselves may select the nugget. Also, the possibilities in the *shotkin*'s files far outnumber the selections a young person would be likely to meet "on their own." Many were grateful to be spared those "singles evenings," where suitability takes a backseat to "chemistry." Chemistry certainly has a place, but not the first place.

Yes, unquestionably a *shidduch* requires chemistry, strong

chemistry, too. Imagine the young man, who, since his *up-sheren,* his first haircut at age three, lives in a society where boys and girls lead separate lives until they meet on a *shidduch.* Here they converse and discuss, and if there is no chemistry, there is no *shidduch.* One enters marriage with open eyes—and directs one's eyes properly ever after. Couples are advised to be like Adam and Eve. Regard each other as though she is the only woman in the world, and he the only man. For he is her other half, and she is his. Of course, one must have two whole halves to make a whole.

That first *shidduch,* Adam and Eve, also had a *shotkin*—God Himself, who, as Rabbi Akiva suggested, has been doing His best to arrange all marriages ever since. Yes, the sages say, if the boy is at this end of the world, and his destined partner is at the other end, then the One Above will find a way to put them together. Oh, it's a good system—countless marriages attest that the system is good, and it's based on character before chemistry. Yes, use the fine-toothed comb. Romance will come later. Look at this week's parsha, "Chaye Sarah"—Yitzchak married Rivka and *then* he loved her. The flame that blazes high dies quickly, Bubby would say. Slowly, gradually, stoke the engine. Ensure your fuel supply, then light the fire.

Well, even in the best of cases, time may pass and a girl or boy may still not have met the right one. As in Abigail's case. So? So. A girl like Abigail would not just sit around waiting for Mr. Right. After high school she went to seminary, of course. After seminary she trained as a bookkeeper, and then, little by little, she became a CPA. A bright girl will find something of interest to do. Why not? She squirreled away a little sum from it, too.

Meanwhile, she was going out. And recently she was introduced to a young man who seemed especially promising. Good family, good character, nicely honed intellect. Tamar had allowed herself to become quite hopeful. The boy liked

Abigail—why shouldn't he?—and they dated several times and enjoyed each other's company. Then he popped the question: *How* much did you say you make a year? *Past nisht!* Not suitable! Abigail dropped him, and Tamar had no regrets. A boy who figured the monetary too much into the matrimonial would not fit well with the family.

Out there, somewhere, was the right one.

So. When Nina had called that morning, Tamar was eager to hear her latest suggestion for Abigail.

The suggestion had been for Ephraim.

"But Nina," Tamar had reminded her, "our daughter Abigail . . . " She did not have to say more. Nina should understand that the Edelman family was not taking suggestions for Abigail's younger brother at this time. Any self-respecting *shotkin* would get the message.

But Nina persevered. "Abigail is a lovely girl," Nina had said, "and I wish I had a suggestion for her now. Believe me, Tamar, I'm looking out for her. I'm going to *sheva brachos* tonight at the Rosemans'—yes, that's right, Esther Malka's daughter married Lieberman's son. I understand a number of young men are coming from Lakewood for the *simchah*—and if I get any new names, you'll be the first to hear. And last night, after a *Hashiveynu* dinner I interviewed nine girls and ten boys! Yes, I know, Abigail wants only a yeshiva boy, but I did meet some fine young men. Anyway, everyone meets theirs at the right time, and I really feel, Tamar, that the right time for Ephraim could be now. He's quite ripe for a *shidduch*, and a particularly fine family has shown a certain interest. . . . "

And she said the name before Tamar had a chance not to hear it.

Bracha Milstein. Mutty Milstein's only daughter. A wonderful, beautiful girl. From a family with an open house and an open heart. Perfect for Ephraim. And Tamar's husband,

Natan, would be thrilled to have the Milsteins for *machatonim,* in-laws.

But the custom is, of course, to marry off the older before the younger. An exception might be made when a younger sister is ready for marriage before her slightly older brother. A girl at twenty, for instance, may be more ready than her brother aged twenty-one. But even in such a case, she should ask his consent before she marries first. Most likely he'll happily agree, enjoy his sister's wedding to the hilt, blush while his doting aunts assure him his single days are numbered, and then return to his yeshiva bachelorhood, shortly to meet his *bashert* and become engaged himself. All at the right time.

But for a younger sibling to marry before an older *sister* was a knish of a different filling. It was a *shanda,* embarrassment for the older sister. What's with the older one? people would want to know. What's wrong with her?

At Ephraim's *bris,* a flash of warning had swept over Tamar. Best marry off Abigail in a "timely" fashion, she remembered advising herself.

And now here was Nina, waiting for an answer.

"I'll, I'll speak it over with my husband, Nina. I'll let you know in the morning."

"If I don't hear from you, you'll hear from me."

Tamar had no doubts. "Thanks, Nina. I appreciate it."

The cake was baking beautifully. She would have to keep a watchful eye on it—a cake needs to be taken from the oven at exactly the right moment. Too soon, it tastes doughy. Too late, it would be tough, or even burned. Without proper timing, the most perfectly put together cake would not fulfill its function.

Tamar would never hurt Abigail. Nor could she deprive Ephraim. Every cake is on its own schedule, and should be baked one at a time. This cake should come out—yes, now. And now was also time to go to Sarah's.

Tamar arrived at Sarah's even earlier than usual, sat in her usual seat, and opened a book of *Tehillim*. She wanted the best for her son, yet she did not want to cause her daughter pain—or possibly resentment. Tamar certainly wanted to avoid resentment among her offspring. A mother's job was to avoid such collisions. What could she do? Natan might not be sensitive to what was transpiring here. Men did not always appreciate delicate issues. Better say *Tehillim*, which help for everything. Before she submerged herself she nodded at Reva and Shaina, who were making themselves comfortable at the other end of the table, apparently to hold a tête-à-tête before the *shiur* began.

"Look at this," Reva was saying, exhibiting her treasures. "A 1920 illustrated edition of *Aesop's Fables for Children!* And look at this one, from the same year, called *Jewish Aesop's Fables*. Well, you should know that *all* these fables are from us! Aesop took them from Talmudic and *midrashic* sources! Let's write a book and claim them back!"

"Yes, reclaim stories. Reclaim music, too," commented the familiar resonant voice.

"Ora!" Reva greeted her friend. "How are you? Come sit with us! You remember Shaina? She's back again. So tell us, what music?"

"Listen to this," Ora hummed a few bars of a haunting melody. "It's a *nigun*, melody, from the Ba'al Shem Tov. He discovered it one day when he was walking in the forest and heard a Russian peasant singing it. 'Would you sell me your melody?' the Ba'al Shem Tov asked. The peasant grabbed the chance to make a few easy kopeks, but once the coins were in his hand he could never recall that melody again. Meanwhile, the Ba'al Shem Tov brought the *nigun* home, taught it to his

Hasidim, and explained that this was an exiled *nigun* which had once been sung in the Holy Temple in Jerusalem!

"What is lost will be found," Ora concluded confidently.

"I wonder," said Reva, "why that *nigun* had to be lost in the first place?"

"*Nigunim* are not simple," said Ora. "By singing the *nigun* of a *tzaddik*, a righteous person, you can connect with his soul. Which shows us that we are closer to each other, in space, time, and in spirit, than we usually think."

"Well, with space it's obvious," said Esther joining the group. "A few computer clicks and I'm in touch with real estate directories all over the country. But closer in time?"

"Torah is above time," contended Ora. "Have you noticed that when you learn Torah in the morning, you have more time for your whole day? Also, Torah pulls us close to all previous generations. The way divine teachings were passed down to us, we are only seven eyewitness-teachers away from Adam, the first man."

"How do you figure that?" asked Reva.

"I'll show you exactly," said Ora, as she rummaged through her generously sized black tote. "Here they are. I ran them off for my class with the Russian ladies last night, and I have a few left. Since Sarah isn't here yet, why not start!" She passed out copies entitled "Seven Eyewitness-Teachers."

"Counting from the first day of creation," her resonant voice began, "the exact age of the earth on January 1, 2000, C.E. will be 5760 years, three months, four weeks, and six days old. This lengthy history, however, is spanned by an eyewitness chain of only seven people who connect us with our very origins. Adam, of course, is the first link. He was created with an innate understanding of divine wisdom, and of man's purpose in creation. During the 930 years of his life, Adam passed down this wisdom to many of his descendants, including his great-grandson Methuselah, who lived for 969 years, until a week before the flood. Methuselah taught the history and knowledge of his fathers to his great-grandson, Noah's son, Shem. Shem, the third link in our chain, got off of the ark, set up a school of divine wisdom, and taught, among other descendants, Abraham's grandson, Jacob, the fourth link. Jacob taught his grandson, Amram, the father of Moses. Amram is our fifth link. Amram transmitted his knowledge to the prophet Achia HaShiloni, link six, who taught the prophet Elijah. Elijah, one of a select few who never died, is the seventh and last link in the chain. He lives forever, the sages say, to help those in dire need, to tutor the worthy in sacred wisdom, and to announce the arrival of Moshiach. Thus, a chain of seven eyewitnesses, Elijah, Achia HaShiloni, Amram, Jacob, Shem, Methuselah, and Adam, links us to the beginning of time."

"That's great if you happen to know Elijah the prophet," said Shaina. "But my past is pretty murky. My mother remembers her grandmother, who told her some stories about *her* grandmother. And that's it. Beyond what my mother remembers of what my grandmother remembered, I have no clue who was out there. Just a gap. A clouded era of unknown bubbies, lost throughout centuries of exile."

"And common to us all," put in Shifra Birnstein, founder and executive director of the Leah Birnstein Women's Torah Tape Library, efficiently run from her laundry room. "But you should know that beyond this hiatus of unknown bubbies, millennia beyond, we reach a time where all is known and recorded—in the Torah and *midrashic* literature. Think of all the details Torah tells us about the lives of our matriarchs, beginning with our mother Sarah. Sarah our matriarch, our foremother. Whose daughters are we, anyway? We know her name, we can nurture from her deeds, and we can feel quite

close to her. I quote: 'She who married Abraham and became
the first Jewish woman, we are her daughters. She comforts us
for the grandmothers whose names we never knew. Her life,
character, and deeds fill our genealogical gaps and enhance
our pride in our common genetics.' Unquote. Do you like
that, ladies? I'm quoting one of the tapes in my library. I forgot who said it, but it was someone good. Please remember,
14992 Fourteenth Avenue, open Sundays, one to five. Free
Torah tapes, on loan, in memory of my daughter, may her
memory be blessed. She loved tapes—used to listen to them
while she helped me in the kitchen. May learning in her memory hasten the redemption, which will be followed by *t'chias
hameisim*, resurrection of the dead, when all our loved ones
will be returned to us."

"Amen," the women replied, Tamar among them. Leah
Birnstein, of blessed memory, had been Abigail's good friend.
Her mother had kept that library open and going strong in her
memory for the past ten years. Tamar closed her *Tehillim*, feeling ashamed for being overly emmeshed in a situation that involved, thank God, her children's *lives*. By now her mind felt
clear and ready to listen to Sarah. Here she is, finally. This week's
discussion would be about "Chaye Sarah," the weekly parsha,
which begins with praises of our foremother Sarah, then continues with the famous *shidduch* story of Isaac and Rebecca.

After the usual *Tehillim*, Sarah began talking about our
matriarch Sarah. "After all, every Jew has our mother Sarah's
genes," Sarah addressed her typically packed dining room. She
paused to look at her guests. Shaina had joined them again,
looking more relaxed than on her first visit. Reva looked
bright and chipper—hopefully her husband was getting better. Erica Fine was sitting near the portico where she had been
speaking with Esther Springer, the real estate agent. Was
Glicka here? Yes, again she had found a seat in the back corner.

Nearby is Tamar, still holding a *Tehillim*. Levana is at the center table, helping Mrs. Blisme to her place, or to be more exact, places. And look at that! Here comes Rachel Rosenberg from Williamsburg, and she's bringing friends with her. Excellent! Sarah waved to Rachel, who had missed the past few weeks. And there was Faygi. Sarah nodded to her sister-in-law, who looked stunning, as usual. Yehudit Sears, Sarah's neighbor, was in her usual seat near the front table. She had already passed out her colorful copies of *Miracles*, a newsletter filled with stories of personal encounters with the Lubavitcher Rebbe. A newcomer, looking over *Miracles* now, was raising her eyebrows. However, *Miracles* was well documented, and anyone who wished to verify these accounts of the Lubavitcher Rebbe's inexplicable insights, counsel, and blessings could easily do so. The stories rivaled those of the Ba'al Shem Tov. Well, Jews themselves are miracles. After so many enemies, and so many years, yet we survive and continue to learn our Torah—Sarah felt that that was the biggest miracle of all. She looked around for the women from Israel, who had come to raise money for orphaned young brides. Good, they had found comfortable seats and were enjoying refreshments. Sarah continued.

"We all really do have our mother Sarah's genes," she said. "Now think of how that works. One child gets the mother's hair, another her eyes, another her voice, still another her patience. So. Since we are all Sarah's daughters—let me ask you, ladies—which of her traits did you get?"

The women laughed, and the question was well received. However, most of the women found it easier to point out the fine traits of their friends than to boast of their own inheritance.

"Sarah taught the women she met—just like you do, Sarah!"

"I bet Tova got our mother Sarah's challah recipe!"

"Sarah was the world's most beautiful woman, next to Eve, say our sages—so physically we *all* take after her!" This remark was roundly approved.

Tova spoke up. "Sarah was also an excellent *akeres habayis*," she said. "And I'm sure we all try to take after her in that way, too."

"*Akeres habayis* means the foundation of the home," put in Tamar. This was one of her favorite topics when she didn't have *shidduchim* on her mind. "The *akeres habayis* is more than a champion housekeeper who serves nutritious meals in a spotless kitchen with all the laundry done!"

"Some of us would be happy to achieve that level," someone murmured from the back of the room.

"I'm not denying that it's an accomplishment," said Tamar. "But if *akeres habayis* meant only a housekeeper, then a finely cut diamond is only a stone. And to see diamond but perceive stone misses all the diamond's facets, its masterful beauty, its outer flame, its inner fire."

The women applauded. Good talking.

"Yes, think of the facets of the *akeres habayis*," Tamar continued. "She develops an ever deepening relationship with her husband. She raises, educates, and sets a guiding example for her children and grandchildren. And she elevates her home and extends it to become an integral part of the larger community. She is the foundation. By infusing her marriage, family, and community with Torah values, she directs her inner fire, releases her flame, and shines!"

"That's true," said Faygi, leaning forward as she cuffed the sleeve of her hunter green felt jacket. "And I would also like to comment on housekeeping. Many of the things a religious woman does are considered 'menial' by the rest of the world— diapering babies, preparing dinner, and so on. But we're not going to buy into that. 'Menial' literally means 'handwork,' which is the ideal occupation, our sages say. For while the hands work, the mind is free. This means that when a woman washes dishes, or sorts laundry, she can listen to a Torah tape, or otherwise direct her thoughts toward spiritually elevating her home. Through her every action, the *akeres habayis* is not only the crown of her husband, but the secret of Jewish survival."

"Beautifully expressed," said Sarah. "And if you will look at our copies, ladies, we'll see how a woman can indeed wield her power through her tent."

Sarah turned to the paper she had passed out. "Here we will see how the threefold blessing of Sarah's tent corresponds to the three *mitzvahs* given especially to women," she said, and nodded to Levana to begin: "The first blessing," Levana read, "was that Sarah's *Shabbos* candles never went out—they burned from one *Shabbos* to the next. In the same way, when a woman inaugurates the *Shabbos* into her home by lighting *Shabbos* candles, she elevates her home with sacred purpose, not only for the day of *Shabbos,* but for the entire week. Our sages tell us that the light of *Shabbos* should be useful light— light that will bring peace into the home, light that will prevent stumbling in the darkness. Of course, what is true physically is also true spiritually. The privilege and responsibility of a woman is to bring into her home the light that guides her family on their spiritual journey.

"The second blessing," Levana continued, "is the blessing in Sarah's challah. Her challahs stayed fresh an entire week, and even a small portion satisfied like a full meal. In the time of the Holy Temple women were required to give a small portion of their challah dough to the *kohanim,* the priests. Today women still have the *mitzvah* to separate a piece of challah dough."

"Tova, are you reading this?" commented Tamar. "Your challah rolls are really the best, the only ones worth eating!"

Tova turned pink as all eyes fell upon her.

"Do you still teach women to bake challahs?" asked Ora. "I know some young women who would like to learn."

"Tova taught me how to bake challah," said Faygi, "and it is an experience. You should see the honor Tova gives this *mitzvah*. She actually wears a special challah-baking robe and turban, as though she were baking challahs for the Holy Temple. When you are baking with her, that's how you feel, too. Tova gives you your own mixing bowl, measuring cups, and apron to take home with you, not to mention her own goof-proof challah recipe. She shows you exactly how to do everything, including what *kavanah*, what intent, to have in mind each step of the way. The mental ingredients, she calls them. She tells you what your thoughts should be when you give charity before you knead the challah dough. And what to think while you are kneading the dough. She explains how the seven ingredients of challah—flour, water, salt, oil, yeast, eggs, and sugar—correspond to *Shabbos*, the seventh day of the week. And when she comes to the *mitzvah* of separating a portion of the challah dough, she explains that, too. The actual *mitzvah* was to separate some of the dough to give to the *kohanim*, the priests of the Holy Temple in Jerusalem. Since we don't have the Holy Temple now, we can't give part of our challah dough to them. However, we can still separate a small portion of the dough, and then burn it. Tova explains that when we separate the dough, we should have in mind that a part of our efforts to nourish our household are to be given away to others, extended toward the community at large, according to our means, abilities and talents. And of course, throughout the entire process, whether she's measuring the ingredients, kneading the dough, braiding the dough, or putting the braided challahs in the oven, she is saying 'in honor of the holy *Shabbos*,' or 'in honor of the *mitzvah* of challah.' I've never seen anyone bake or teach like that. No wonder Tova's challahs taste the way they do!"

Tova blushed. "Everyone is welcome to come and learn," she said. "I just hope that other women will begin to observe the *mitzvah* of baking challahs. It's one of the special *mitzvah*s given to women, and it certainly brings a warm atmosphere and delicious fragrance into the house. The whole family becomes proud to have homemade challahs on *Shabbos*."

Several women took Tova's phone number before Levana continued to read. "A third blessing was that clouds of glory surrounded Sarah's tent, uniquely exalting it. A woman's tent also symbolizes her relationship with her husband, which she builds and beautifies through the laws of family purity.

"A woman can wield great power through her tent," Levana concluded, "because our mother Sarah bequeathed all these blessings to us, her daughters."

Nina Weinstein spoke up. "To make that power perpetual," she added, "we have to marry off our children. Ladies, parshas 'Chaye Sarah' is our famous *shidduch* chapter, where Rivka becomes the bride of Isaac, and we have a few topics here worth mentioning!"

Matchmaking was a favorite subject at Sarah's table. Nina particularly identified with the occupation, but most of the women had had their hands in matchmaking, at least occasionally.

"You know," said Shifra, "some young people are trying to meet through these 'singles' nights.'"

"Butcher-shop *shidduchim*," someone commented disdainfully.

"We must marry them young," said another woman, "before they think that shopping around is a good idea."

"I don't know. I always get better buys when I shop around!"

"Who shops for a *shidduch*? A *shidduch* is *bashert*! A parcel all wrapped up with your name and address on the wrapper."

"That got lost in the mail!" interjected Faygi. "The *rebbe* has written many times that we have to diligently search for a *shidduch,* just as we would search for something precious that we have lost."

"Yes," agreed Nina, "a diligent search is very important. On the other hand, you can't hurry a *shidduch*. You can only *daven* that the child will meet the right one at the right time. Look at Isaac. He had to wait until he was thirty-seven years old. Why? Because Rebecca wasn't even born until he was thirty-four!"

"We all hope that the *bashert* of all our marriageable children has been at least born!" said Tamar.

"Another problem is the career disease. Dis-ease, I call it," continued Nina. "Careers have a place, but that place should not *re*place a marriage. Girls who postpone marriage for a career are putting themselves at risk."

"It's not so easy to be simultaneously mommy, wife, and student," said a grad student who was visiting the *shiur.*

"The best thing is for young mothers to stay home with their children," stated Mrs. Blisme.

"A part-time job is good—get out a little bit," ventured Levana.

"Sarah never left her tent," said Shaina.

"Sarah always had company!" smiled Shimona.

"Talk about planning weddings, when my niece planned hers, she had to set a date that wouldn't conflict with when her mother was due to give birth! Our biggest problems should always be scheduling our *simchahs!*" said Ora, smiling.

"Talking about scheduling," said Faygi, "we recently had

this predicament in our family. Two of my sisters-in-law have daughters very close in age. And in both cases, the younger sister was ready to go out before the older one was married. So each younger girl had to ask her older sister for permission to begin dating.

"One gave permission right away. She knew what it was like to wait and wanted to spare her younger sister that pain. The other older cousin, however, was insulted. Her younger sister marry first? She wouldn't hear of it. She was waiting, and her younger sister would have to wait, too!

"As it happened, the first of the younger cousins went out, and soon afterwards became engaged to a fine boy—whose fine friend turned out to be just right for his intended's older sister! In the merit of setting her feelings aside for her sister, the older girl met her destined partner. And, in fact, they worked it out so that the older sister's wedding was first!"

"Look at that!" said Nina. "See how we pay the consequences if we act according to what we fear others will say instead of listening to what is generous and right."

"It's hard to believe that everyone really has their *bashert*," commented Nesha, a slim, long-haired woman who had just turned thirty-five and was not yet married.

"If I bring half a cake to the table," replied Sarah, "do you doubt that there is another half?"

The women began to discuss the kabbalistic concept that God initially created Adam as a duplex being. "Afterwards," Sarah explained, "God divided Adam into a male and a female half. On the spiritual level this doubleness continues. Every soul, in the spiritual realms, has a male and female dimension, and when the soul is about to enter the physical world, these halves are split apart. Each half enters a separate body, and each lives a separate life, until the time when the halves are given the opportunity to meet and marry. So you see that people who call their spouse their 'other half' are speaking kabbal-istic truth. Each person is part of a preexisting combo, and, as guaranteed as socks are paired, is this essential, although per-haps not yet revealed, match."

"Well," said Nesha, "I don't know about you, but I have a drawer filled with odd socks!"

"Me, too," agreed Iyelet. "In my house socks hide, under the couch, behind the piano—who knows how they get there!"

"Exactly!" said Nesha. "Some socks are harder to pair up than others!"

Sarah nodded. "So let's look at this parsha a little more—the scene with Rebecca at the well. God arranged that Eliezer should meet her there. But what did Rebecca do that proved to Eliezer that she was the right one? She drew water for his camels. Now imagine how much a camel drinks! Does anyone know how many gallons per camel? And although Eliezer had a whole caravan of camels, Rebecca *ran* to draw enough water so every camel could drink as much as it liked! That was the greatness of her kindness. And immediately after, please note, she became engaged. Acts of kindness are a known *s'gulah*, facilitator, for a good *shidduch*."

Tamar looked up. Maybe this was it. For Abigail to let her younger brother precede her would certainly be an act of kindness. Not an easy one, but knowing Abigail, she, like Rebecca, would run to help. More than dwelling on her own situation, she would be happy for her brother. As to what would others would say, well, the wise would only comment that in the merit of letting her brother precede her, this won-derful girl should find her own *bashert!*

With help from above, and with some activity below, thought Tamar, she certainly would.

4
Rachel: The Secrets of the *Mikvah*
Parshas Toldos

Isaac called Jacob and blessed him: "May the Almighty, God, bless you, make you fruitful, and multiply you, May you become an assembly of peoples. May He give you the blessing of Abraham, to you and to your descendants with you. . . . "
—Genesis 28:1, 3–4

Each person has a unique function, but with a common goal: to serve God totally and fully. To have children and teach them this message is an essential part of our divine service. To have a child, our sages tell us, depends on three partners: the mother, the father, and the Almighty. The father provides a seed, the mother nurtures the embryo, and the Almighty adds the soul. To sensitize the body to the mission of the Jewish soul, Torah gives us the laws of mikvah, *family purity.*

One of Rachel Rosenberg's many pleasures was to savor her many blessings. Her husband, their productive, dynamic, marital harmony, their children, her *shiurim,* and other pleasant occupations, all of these thoughts bolstered her usual mood of *simchah,* that satisfying internal harmony that makes life so enjoyable. Her generally tranquil state of mind also enabled her to rise above a certain apprehension the Williamsburg community might have had about her family.

Of course the Rosenberg family was well respected, but they were a bit different, somewhat radical, and Rachel took this all in stride. In time she hoped to augment her neighbors' understanding. Meanwhile, she continued to expand her good works and deeds. In general, these seemed so compatible with her personality that she could take them on easily and genuinely, enjoying with each one a new harmonious depth. Just now, however, the action she was facing required a radical change in herself.

Rachel had spent all her life in Williamsburg, the oldest Hasidic neighborhood of Brooklyn. Here dark-brick row houses tower sternly above the pavement, which stretches tightly from the building's foundation until the curb. A few blades of grass sometimes peek through a sidewalk crack, and spindly trees erupt sporadically. Trees, however, seem superfluous as the buildings themselves band together to shield their streets from the sun. Inside, homes are bright, shining, often elegant, and astutely managed by the woman of the house.

The women of Williamsburg have professionalized their role of *akeres habayis.* Their cooking and baking, sewing and tailoring, child rearing and educating are crafted to meet the exacting standards of their firmly knit community. In fact, the Hasidim here, predominantly Satmar Hasidim of Hungarian descent, have exacting standards in many areas, including character refinement. This refinement extends also to one's clothing, especially on *Shabbos,* when many of the men, sporting long, curled *peyos,* sidelocks, don embroidered silk frock coats, white socks, and slip-on shoes. Some have mistaken these refinements for an easy target. The fact, however, is to the contrary. Should a Williamsburg Hasid be provoked, he need only shout *"Khops em"* (grab him!). Immediately, swarms of Hasidim, *peyos* flying, would descend upon the foe. The streets of Williamsburg have become the safest in Brooklyn.

So on Ross or Hewes or Rutledge streets young mothers wheel their carriages, strollers, and double strollers unprovoked. They coo to their babies, toddlers, and slightly older children who might be hanging on at the sides, instructing these young ones to become *groisa tzaddikim,* a great and righteous people. These young mothers, who have taken upon themselves the career of raising an army of offspring, are graduates of prep schools such as Bais Rachel. Here they are groomed to be discerning *balabustas,* home executives, who will meticulously uniform, conscientiously nourish, and lovingly discipline their young troops to uphold Torah values in a secular world. Graduating at age sixteen, they also receive cutting-edge bookkeeping, computer, and office management skills so that they may be well employed for a few years before they marry, and afterward as well if need be.

These women also showcase *tznius*—modesty, in dress, word, and deed. *Tznius* clothing is especially emphasized. Of course, every Torah community arrives at its own *tznius* look, reflecting the lives and lifestyles of their women. Crown Heights women, for example, tend toward a fast-paced, wash-and-wear wardrobe, reflecting the large *ba'alei t'shuvah* influx. These women favor easy-to-wear, familiar to the rest of the world clothing, and some suitable items might even be ferreted out from a Lands' End catalog. *Tznius,* sure. But it is possible to belong to this city and century and still be completely observant.

In Borough Park the outfits are more formal. A woman who wears a two-piece suit while grocery shopping on Thirteenth Avenue is probably from Borough Park. However, the most formal, regimented attire is found in Williamsburg.

Skirts are mid-calf. Sleeves are designed never to expose an elbow. Colors are subdued but pleasant, including not necessarily fashionable shades of navy, beige, blue, green, yellow, or brown. Girls braid their hair neatly, while married women carefully top their *sheitel* with a hat. Opaque stockings with clearly pronounced seams and well-crafted, functional shoes finish the ensemble. Women often design, cut, sew, and tailor their own wardrobes.

"*Kovod bas melech p'nima*"—the glory of the king's daughter is within, our sages tell us. *Tznius* is regal. *Tznius* attire liberates a woman from the dictates of fashion and allows her to externalize the standards that suit her soul. The soul requires majesty.

Rachel Rosenberg, a woman of ample height and girth with a warm, strong handshake and all-encompassing embrace, was a slightly enlarged version of the typical Williamsburg matron. A Renaissance-style woman, she gracefully modeled the Williamsburg standard—hat, *sheitel,* jacket, skirt, seamed stockings, right down to the well-crafted shoes. Her smile was tranquil, her eyes receptive. She was a woman who could give a lot. She and her husband came from fine *chasidishe* families, which carried weight in the community. However, it did not override the fact that the Rosenbergs ventured beyond the normal and the known, outside of their own community. Some people were cautious in dealing with the Rosenberg family.

Rachel, however, never had suspected that her life might be other than normal. As a girl she had simply hoped for a happy marriage. When she reached marriageable age she allowed her parents to select her husband for her, as was customary in her community. A girl has veto power, of course, but Rachel couldn't imagine using it. Her parents told her that the boy she would be meeting was a refined young man, a scholar, who was especially learned in Jewish law. Rachel felt very fortunate indeed.

Her parents, however, were aware that seeds of distinction

lay dormant in this particular *shidduch.* They approved and chose this for their daughter, and anticipated flourishing results. The details they couldn't yet explain to Rachel, but when the time came, she would understand herself. Meanwhile, they told their daughter of their pride in her, of their confidence that she was a God-fearing woman. This was to be a wonderful match.

And it was, even as Rachel perceived more clearly day by day the expansive and detailed world her marriage was sliding her into. A world in which many neighborhoods, villages, towns, and cities were increasingly discovering her phone number, keeping it ever handy, to call into her kitchen by day, and into her bedroom by night. Her husband was frequently and urgently needed. No, he had not become a medical specialist, nor did he direct some global operation. But he was increasingly recognized as a world-renowned authority on *mikvahs.*

A *mikvah,* in guidebook parlance, is a "pool for ritual immersion." More specifically, as any child in Williamsburg knew, a *mikvah* is a small pool where some Orthodox Jewish men customarily immerse themselves to sanctify themselves before *davening.* There are also ·smaller *mikvahs,* which resemble wells, and these are found in Hasidic household goods stores, for the convenient immersion to sanctify newly purchased pots, dishes, and utensils. (This *tevilah* has nothing to do with the dishes being *kosher,* which is an entirely different matter.) Other *mikvahs* are specifically for women, marked with the sign "Frauen" on their door. But when, why, and how a woman uses the *mikvah* is a subject not openly discussed. The most delicate *mikvah* matters are taught privately, from mentor to student, as part of the *kallah* (bridal) classes given to young brides during their engagement period. Here the young bride learns that after detailed preparation she will immerse herself in a *mikvah* before the night of her wedding. Thereafter, throughout her marriage, she, like all married women, will immerse herself in the *mikvah* at a specified time following her menstrual period. From the onset of her period until after her immersion, she and her husband will refrain from having marital relations, as well as from all physical contact. Because the night of the *mikvah* usually coincides with the time of ovulation, immersing at the proper time maximizes the possibility of conception. For this reason, among others, the night of the immersion ought not to be postponed.

Thus the *mikvah* is explained to the newly engaged young woman. She also is told something of what makes a *mikvah* a *mikvah*. Not just any body of water qualifies. A swimming pool, for example, or a lily pond, does not do. A qualified *mikvah* must meet exacting Torah specifications. One fundamental requirement is that the *mikvah* water must "kiss" or touch a source of natural water. Kabbalah explains that all natural waters are connected to the water that flows from the Garden of Eden, the home of Adam and Eve until they ate from the tree of knowledge.

When Sarah first mentioned the *mikvah*'s connection to the Garden of Eden, Rachel realized how much she still had to learn about *mikvahs*.

"Don't think," Sarah had explained, "that Adam and Eve had wrong intentions. They wanted to do what God wanted! Hasidic philosophy explains that they thought deeply into how they could best serve God. This led them to reason that if they ate from the tree of knowledge, they would know the difference between good and evil, and this knowledge would help them serve God better! And doesn't their reasoning makes sense?

"But Hasidus also explains their mistake. A *mitzvah* comes from a place that is higher than reason. It comes from the will of the master of the universe. In other words, *mitzvahs* are God's will! Of course a person's limited understanding can't begin to understand the will of the Creator. We learn all we can about the *mitzvahs,* but in the end, a *mitzvah* is to do, whether we understand it or not.

"What makes a *mitzvah* special," Sarah continued, "is that doing it brings its own reward. Our rabbis explain that when we do a *mitzvah,* we unite with God's will. That unity gives us a higher perspective, and now we can come to understand the *mitzvah* little by little. That's why, when the Jewish people received the Torah, they said *Na'aseh v'nishma!* We will do, and *then* we will understand: We do the *mitzvah* because it is God's will that we do it, and through doing it we will come to understand it better, through a kind of superexperiential wisdom. And this is one of the lessons of the *mikvah.* When we immerse in a *mikvah* and are covered completely, even over our heads, with the water which has its source in the Garden of Eden, we show that we are not making the same mistake that Adam and Eve made. We will totally submerge ourselves in God's holy will, and put His will and infinite wisdom before our own limited understanding."

Rachel had shared these insights with her husband, and he had appreciated them. He had taken upon himself to know everything—everything possible—about *mikvahs,* including the specifications of how to plan and build them, the technology to engineer and maintain them, and mechanics to fix them. Not to mention the myriad details needed to be sure that a *mikvah* was 100 percent kosher, 100 percent in accordance with Torah law. As a young man he had apprenticed himself to leading *mikvah* authorities, traveling with them at his own expense, to learn on site. To support his family, which, thank God, was growing, he began a business.

Both business and family expanded. Their first daughter

was followed by twins, two girls. Meanwhile, Rachel's husband began writing a *mikvah* column in Yiddish periodicals, alerting readers to conditions that could make *mikvahs* not kosher. He began to be summoned for *mikvah* consultations. Another daughter was born.

The little girls, his business, and his *mikvah* involvement grew. "*Mikvah*" was becoming more and more a household word.

"But you certainly don't say it out loud in front of the children?" an alarmed neighbor asked Rachel.

"Oh, they don't know what it means!" she replied, realizing that the reputation of her household was in question. Well, of course her daughters heard more about "*mikvah*" than other children did. They knew that "*mikvah*" was a *mitzvah*, which greatly involved their father. There was nothing wrong with that, but not everyone was going to understand. No matter. The One Above runs the world, and *mikvahs* must be built. Rachel continued to take emergency calls, did her part to help their business expand, and gave birth to another daughter.

Business prospered. Her husband could now realize his dream—to sell the business and devote himself entirely to his *mikvah* work. It was Rachel's dream, too. As much as their little ones were growing, a more spacious apartment was hardly necessary. Many of Rachel's friends lived harmoniously with twelve or more children in apartments no bigger than hers. She encouraged her husband to get a blessing from his *rebbe*, and soon the business was sold. With the proceeds of the sale safely invested, their only "business" now was the *mitzvah* of furthering the cause of *mikvahs*.

More frequently came the phone calls, more frequently did her husband travel to distant lands. As the children became older, she sometimes accompanied him. She would become friendly with women living in remote communities, women who hardly knew what a *mikvah* was for, women who were eager to learn such simple matters as the correct blessings to say before eating.

By then Rachel had become a regular at Sarah's table.

Conveniently, there is a shuttle bus that travels between Borough Park and Williamsburg. Because of the limited housing in Williamsburg, young families were moving to other communities, such as Borough Park. Women took the shuttle to go shopping, or to a doctor's appointment, or to a *sheitel-macher,* or for employment—but seldom for a *shiur.* Women of Williamsburg did not usually leave the community to learn. But Rachel enjoyed expanding her horizons. With her husband so often out of town, why not go for an occasional luncheon that happened also to provide food for thought? When her husband returned they would enjoy perusing the study sheets together. About this time, Rachel had her sixth child, thank God, another beautiful, healthy girl.

Amid the joy of this birth, friends and neighbors decided that they needed to *do* something to ensure a Rosenberg baby boy. This stemmed not from a preference for males, per se, but rather from the guidelines of Torah law: Despite their six delightful daughters, Rachel and her husband had yet to fulfill the *mitzvah* "to be fruitful and multiply"! In fact, even sixty girls without a boy, or sixty boys without a girl, would be insufficient. The *mitzvah* specified its quota: a minimum of one of each. And from the time the twins were born, the Rosenbergs had received plentiful advice on how to achieve a son. Everyone seemed to "know" the remedy. Some counseled on more intimate matters, others prescribed giving more *tzedakah,* or going to a *tzaddik,* a righteous man, for a blessing. When Rachel announced this sixth daughter, however, she was seriously advised to go to Meron, Israel.

"Go on Lag B'Omer," a neighbor said. "On the thirty-third day after the first night of Passover, the *yahrtzeit* of the *tzaddik*, Rabbi Shimon Bar Yohai, who is buried in Meron. Going to Meron on Lag B'Omer facilitates blessings, especially for the birth of a baby boy."

Rachel followed this advice and went with her husband to Meron. There she promised that if she had a son, she would name him after Rabbi Shimon. On the night that she returned from the *mikvah* her husband lit two candles. And within the year, her Shimon was born.

With this great *simchah* came a great question: What could she do to show her gratitude?

"How can we *not* show gratitude!" she recalled Sarah saying from time to time. "God doesn't need our gratitude. *We* need to show that we are grateful. Blessings come from God's infinity. It's not me and the strength of my hand—what are we if we rely only on ourselves? It's a training, and it's a fact: The more we are grateful to God, the more we have to be grateful for. And we need to show it, to teach ourselves, and to teach our kids! Our children need to see gratitude. If we don't show it, they won't know it."

There are many ways to show gratitude, Sarah went on to say. In the time of the Holy Temple in Jerusalem, one could bring a special thanksgiving offering. Now people often make a *kiddush*, a small celebration after *davening* on *Shabbos* morning to express gratitude for joyous events. It was also good to give charity. If God helps you, you should help others.

Yes, thought Rachel, this kind of gratitude is appropriate for events that seem to happen naturally. But what should one do for an event that seems to circumvent nature, an event that evidences exceptional divine intervention? A boy after six girls, and after some years, and after visiting Meron, was clearly beyond nature. It was a miracle. Of course there were greater miracles. Sarah our foremother, who gave birth when she was ninety, and our matriarch Rivka, who had to wait twenty years for her first child, both experienced miracles. Our forefathers were born miraculously, and bore a nation that throughout the millennia has miraculously survived. Shimon's birth also was above nature. Rachel wanted her son to know and appreciate that. She wanted him to join her in showing gratitude to the One Above in some way that would also heighten the honor of Rabbi Shimon.

Then came a thought, born at Sarah's table, but which Rachel could realize only in a place like Williamsburg. She resolved to celebrate the birth of her son with a party, in the unique Williamsburg style. Among Williamsburg women party-throwing is a passion, nearly a devotion, and Rachel could think of nothing more appropriate.

A party, of course, is not to be confused with a *simchah*. A *simchah* is a joyful celebration of a *mitzvah* milestone, such as a *bris*, or bar mitzvah, or wedding. A *simchah* is one thing—a family event, where friends join in on a wonderful occasion. But a party is different. A party as planned by the women of Williamsburg is actually an event where lemons become lemonade. Sunday afternoon is party time, and everyone is invited, and most attend. In fact, a party is typically not one party, but a party of parties. The ten or more party halls that line Bedford Avenue are booked solid each week for party-hopping guests, who try to attend as many of the gatherings as possible. Each hall is hired by a hostess, or group of hostesses, who set up an artistic and lavish table, then open the doors for guests to hop in. An open box graces the entrance, and each attendee leaves as generous a donation as possible at each stop. Ironically, the causes of the "celebration" may be a husband who is out of work, a child who is ill, a home in danger of foreclosure, parents at a loss to pay for a child's wedding, or various other difficul-

ties, which hostess and guests hope to alleviate, avert, or resolve
from the proceeds of the afternoon.

The proceeds of Rachel's party were to go to Meron. She
had seen that the annual Lag B'Omer journey is not an easy
one. On that day tens of thousands of men, women, and children from Israel and all over the world converge on this tiny
community to visit the gravesite of Rabbi Shimon, author of a
mystical kabbalistic work, the *Zohar,* to honor him on his
yahrtzeit. Traditionally, this day is celebrated with bonfires,
signifying the kabbalistic light that Reb Shimon brought to
the world. The holiness of this day is known to bring down
the blessings of children. Young boys who are three years old
are brought here for their first haircutting so that they also
should grow to be a light like Rabbi Shimon.

Travelers, exhausted from this arduous trip, whether jour-
neying from Jerusalem three hours away or from across the
ocean, need refreshment when they finally reach Meron. But
the few vendors that have brought supplies sell out quickly.

As an expression of gratitude, Rachel began her annual
refreshment table for the visitors to Meron. She oversees it
herself, with Shimon. And finances it with help from the partying women of Williamsburg.

Sarah was fond of saying, "It's ten percent how you take it, and
ninety percent how you make it." Last week Shaina had said
something to Rachel that Rachel didn't quite know how to
take. "What you and your husband do is one of the greatest
things I've ever heard." Shaina had been so enthusiastic. "I'm
thinking of you and your husband traveling around the
world, making sure women have *mikvahs.* I'm sure that when
you teach the laws of *mikvah* to the women everywhere, they
are very grateful."

Rachel didn't, couldn't, teach women the laws of *mikvah.*
The laws were detailed and sensitive. Only specially trained
women would dare to teach these laws. Yes, of course, she,
Rachel, was associated with *mikvah!* But a *kvater* is not a
mohel! An attendant isn't a surgeon! Gatekeepers don't launch
rockets.

And now it was Tuesday again. This week's parsha was
"Toldos." Rachel had just settled herself by her usual seat near
the kitchen, when Shaina came over again, this time clutching
papers.

"You won't believe it!" Shaina said. "This! This is a letter
from my mother. She faxed it to me this morning. You don't
have to know my mother. Just read and think about this the
next time you and your husband go on a *mikvah* trip."

"All right," said Rachel, her cheerful smile coming to her
aid. She read:

Dear Susan,

I hope this finds you as well as can be under your
circumstances. I must say that the children are looking better than they used to, or perhaps the photo you
recently sent us was touched up. Anyway, I found a
place for it in our back hallway gallery.

The reason I am writing now is to bring you up to
date about Lubavitch activities here in Akron. I still
find it hard to believe that there are Hasidim living in
our community, although Kaila and Mendy Sos-
sonkin are such a lovely couple that no one seems to
mind. They moved here some years ago, as *shluchim*
(I guess that means emissaries) of the Lubavitcher
Rebbe. Akron's Rabbi Liebtag, in fact, liked Mendy so
much that he turned the Orthodox shul over to him
when he retired. We don't belong to it, of course. Nev-

ertheless, Kaila invites us to participate in some of their activities, and sometimes we do. For example, we have gone to the brises of their sons, and I went once to a challah baking class. Kaila makes excellent challahs. And we did send a small contribution when they were fund-raising to build a *mikvah*.

A *mikvah* in Akron! Well, I guess Akron has changed over the years, although I still wouldn't call us a leader in multicultural happenings. Nonetheless, walking down Market Street today you'd think you've arrived at the World's Fair. We have Thai, Sicilian, Mexican, Korean, Indian, and Chinese restaurants, French manicures, a Russian grocery, African hair-braiding, and a Nordic spa. Apparently, today, anything can be anywhere. Therefore, it's not incongruous for even Akron to have a Hasidic *mikvah*. I'm sure Kaila finds it convenient, and you could use it, too, if you would ever care to visit. As I've mentioned before, you are always welcome if you can find someone to help with the children.

Anyway, they built their *mikvah*. We first heard it was open when we stopped in to buy some of Kaila's challahs. She actually makes enough to sell some—I think some of the women help her, but I don't know how she accomplishes *so* much. She has very bright children, too. Before her son Levi was even two, he could count to ten in three languages. Of course, she speaks English, Mendy is Israeli, and in their house they speak Yiddish, but the child didn't confuse any of the languages, not even the accents. I suppose Levi is doing calculus by now. Well, I guess Chana and Dovid are making progress in their own way.

Anyway, while we were there, Kaila invited me to

see the *mikvah*. Well, she couldn't have made it more attractive. Beautiful tile, crystal clear water—had they made it bigger and opened it for recreational purposes, they could put the swim clubs out of business.

Then Kaila asked me if I have ever been to a *mikvah*, and I replied yes, of course. I went to one, once, fifty years ago, before I was married. My grandmother took me. And I remember having my toenails cut there.

Kaila suggested that I go again!

When I told your father, he said they must be very hard up for customers. But I told him no, Mendy and Kaila have more sophisticated methods of fund-raising than rounding up seventy-five-year-old women to use their *mikvah*.

Anyway, I told Kaila that I was no longer in my child-bearing years, that I had bathed, showered, and even saunaed plenty of times since then, and how much difference could a dip in her little pool make?

She told me that spiritually it did make a difference, and that it was important for my marriage and for my children and grandchildren.

So I talked it over with Paula. "For my daughter and her children I should go skinny dipping?" I asked.

Paula replied that there was no use fighting a nice swim with spiritual benefits. So I called Kaila and told her I'd go for the splash, and that I could drive by within the hour. She said good, she'd give me the instructions.

What instructions? I can swim—do it twice a week at the JCC, to this day.

But she said there were a few other things I'd have to know.

A few! I won't go into detail here, I imagine you

know all the details. Kaila seemed very happy to sign me up. Well, she's a good girl and deserves a lot of happiness.

So I did what she said, all the details, and last night I went to the *mikvah*. Kaila said I should tell my friends about it, and I did. Paula already has her appointment. As Paula sees it, one dunk at our age gives us a *mitzvah* as long as we and our husbands are alive, until, as you Hasidim say, beyond 120. Which makes it a worthwhile swim.

With love,

Your mother,

Sylvia.

"May you have *Yiddishe naches* from your mother!" Rachel Rosenberg responded to the letter. "It's true that an older married woman who has not yet been to the *mikvah*, or who did not go regularly, can still benefit from it. We do sometimes see older women, but I had never thought . . ."

Reva came to look over the letter. "Eh!" she chuckled. "Well! Our sages do say that at whatever age a woman begins to keep the laws of family purity, it has a beneficial effect on her children and grandchildren. So your mom did a *mitzvah*, going to the *mikvah*. And one *mitzvah* leads to another. Children teaching their parents *mitzvahs*, you know, is a sign of Moshiach."

"It would take Moshiach himself to shlep *my* mom to the *mikvah*," Debra laughed.

"Sometimes I wish I had someone to help me get to the *mikvah*," said Iyelet. "My husband is always working late, so I have to try to find a sitter for three little kids! And when I finally find one, I can't even let her know where I'm really going!"

"What's the big secret?" asked Debra.

"*Tznius,* modesty," said Shifra. "There's a blessing on hidden things."

"So we all face the challenge of 'how to leave the house at night so that our children and everyone else will not know where we are going'!" put in Faygi.

"I just say I've got a meeting," said Erica Fine. "I always have meetings anyway. My daughter never thinks twice about it."

"My children would," mused Reva. "I once used the excuse that I had to visit a friend. So my son Judah had to know which friend. Yoni wanted to know if the friend had kids, and could he come. And Shoni started insisting that she come, too!"

"*Bikur cholim* is my best solution," said Esther. "Sometimes I just have to visit a sick person, who is not able to tolerate any visitor other than me!"

"Well, making up excuses for your children is one thing," said Yehudis. "But what do you say to your in-laws when *mikvah* night turns out to be the night they're supposed to come for dinner!"

"I couldn't deal with that!" said a newcomer. "I'd cancel and give them a rain check."

"Couldn't cancel! So I turned on some home videos of the kids and slipped out. I hope I wasn't missed."

"And what do you do when it's *Shabbos* and your whole house is full of guests?"

Shimona laughed. "Well, sometimes you can get a guest to baby-sit while you go to, as you say, '*daven* in shul.'"

"Once I did that. But my guest put two and two together when she saw a wet lock of hair sticking out from under my *sheitel!*"

"Sometimes it's not the easiest *mitzvah* to fulfill," agreed Reva, "but so what?"

"And what about the problem of married daughters and daughters-in-law!" put in Shifra. "With little children the trick is to get out—but with married children the problem is to get in! My three married daughters and my daughter-in-law use the same *mikvah* I do. We'd be very embarrassed to meet each other on the way in!"

"At least you won't meet them in the *mikvah* itself," said Nina. "Our new *mikvah* is designed to avoid such meetings. The planning committee arranged that every woman have private access in and out of her own private bathing room. No one has to know who else is there!"

"Levana, are you still giving classes on family purity to your congregants when they become engaged?" Tamar asked.

Levana nodded. "And we want them to understand the importance and beauty of the *mitzvah,* not only the details."

"Well, almost every article you read on family purity says how *mikvah* enhances a marriage," said Iyelet. "A guaranteed second honeymoon every month, they all say."

"Well, isn't it?" Faygi mused.

"Secular psychologists picked up on the advantages of periodic rest periods to enhance and recharge a marriage," said Sarah. "They arbitrarily prescribe time off to tone up the relationship. But they don't take into account the natural changes a woman goes through each month. And I wonder how many patients are so well disciplined that they follow the therapist's instructions. The laws of family purity, on the other hand, are God's commands, and are in sync with a woman's moods."

"And there are so many other aspects to *mikvah,*" added Yehudis. "The laws of family purity affect us and also our children, spiritually. Kabbalah tells us that *mikvah* helps bodies to be in tune with their souls."

"I think women intrinsically sense how important *mikvah* is," said Erica. "When we were traveling in Russia last summer, I heard amazing stories about the self-sacrifice women had to use the *mikvah*. Here in Brooklyn, with our plentiful, beautiful, even luxurious *mikvahs*, it's hard to imagine. But the communists closed all the *mikvahs* in Russia, and still, women found ways to keep this *mitzvah*! But what ways! The ordeals they went through!"

A new guest nodded. "Very true. When I was recently in Russia I saw a secret *mikvah* that Jews risked their lives to build at the height of the communist regime."

"Even though many *mikvahs* were closed," said Sarah, "the natural *mikvahs*, the ocean, lakes, and some rivers, springs, and sometime even wells, could be kosher *mikvahs* at the proper time and with proper preparation."

"I know of a woman from Russia who immersed in a well," said Yehudis. "In the middle of a Russian winter!

"We'll call her Shterna. She heard that a well 'nearby' could be used as a *mikvah*. On her *mikvah* night, in the middle of winter, she left her children with her husband and set out for this well.

"She arrived nearly frozen. The woman in charge of the *mikvah* lived in a cottage near the well. Shterna knocked on the window and waited for the woman inside to wake up. *"Ich cum."* The *mikvah* lady came to the door wearing a heavy fur coat and holding a cup of hot water. She motioned for Shterna to follow her to the well.

"Just then two other women also arrived to use the *mikvah*. So there was a little line up. But Shterna was first.

"When they reached the well, the *mikvah* lady poured the cup of hot water down the abyss.

"'To warm it?' Shterna wondered, as the *mikvah* attendant handed her a rope to lower herself down.

"She was already frozen. But as you know, there must be no intervening substance between the woman's body and the *mikvah* water! So Shterna somehow disrobed, grasped the

frozen rope, and lowered herself into the well. When she felt
the water, she thought she'd faint. She was already exhausted
and freezing, and if she lowered herself into that ice water, she
was sure she would not come out. Her husband would forgive
her if she didn't go in. He would understand. It wasn't his idea
that she go out on a night like this!

"But then she thought about the other women who had
also come to the well. What would they think if she didn't go
in? Maybe they would also decide that the water was too cold.
And suppose a soul, or maybe two or three souls, were destined to come down that night? Was she to be responsible for
stopping them?

"She went under. Deep under, so not one hair should float
above the surface.

"'How was it?' the women asked her when she came up.

"She managed to reply, 'You can do it.'

"They did. All three women immersed that night.

"But the story doesn't end here. Years later Shterna had a
private audience with the Lubavitcher Rebbe, who asked to
see a picture of her family. When she took out a picture, the
rebbe pointed to one of her daughters and said, 'This child has
a very high soul.'

"The *rebbe* was pointing to the daughter who was conceived the night she went to the *mikvah* in the well!"

As Yehudis concluded the women broke into enthusiastic
applause. Rachel remembered a trip she and her husband had
taken to Russia to supervise several *mikvahs* there. "You know,
today there are *mikvah* directories," she said, "to let people
know the nearest *mikvah*, wherever in the world they are."

"Bangor, Maine!" Reva exclaimed. "When Moshe and I
were first married we lived in Bangor, Maine. This is a story
you really have to hear! We were newlyweds, and one hot
August day Moshe came to tell me that the one *mikvah* in

Bangor was broken. It wouldn't be fixed for weeks. I looked at him and told him that my night to go to the *mikvah* was *that night!* We had to find a solution, and fast!

"'There's a *mikvah*, in Portland,' he told me, 'four and a half hours' drive. Now it won't be dark until after ten, since it's summer, but we could drive down there. . . . '

"'Moshe,' I said, 'I have an idea. I discovered something last week—and now's the time to show it to you. A lake! A gorgeous lake. Gillman Falls. Not even a mile from here. It's off a little road in the woods. Nobody goes there. It's a kosher *mikvah*, isn't it?'

"It was. It would be so simple, I thought, so exciting, to drive there, wait until sunset, take a quick dip and out. No need to shlep to Portland.

"So I made all the preparations, carefully, as I had been taught. Nails cut, hair combed, perfect cleanliness, the sweet aura of shared anticipation. And a new swimsuit. I had splurged—twenty-five dollars was a lot to spend on a suit, but I was a new bride, and it was okay!

"So I slipped a long terry beach robe over the swimsuit, went out to the car, sat in the front seat next to Moshe, and put my handbag on the seat between us, for then. Moshe smiled, turned on the engine. We were off. I showed Moshe the almost hidden road that wound through the woods to the lake. A little dirt road to a beautiful clear lake that seemed to be made just for us. Moshe pulled up to a parking spot near the water, which was already glistening dark blue and yellow as the sun began to set. A clear, warm, summer's night. It was perfect.

"When the sun hit the horizon I stepped out of the car to dip into the lake, just to get used to the water. I would have to wait for dark for the *mikvah* immersion; but meanwhile, the lake looked so inviting. Clear and pure. And pretty warm.

Heaven. It would soon be twilight, then totally dark; I'd take the plunge.

"Just then a car pulled into a parking spot not far from Moshe. Another couple had come to relish the setting sun! Then another car, with another couple. And another. And another. Let me tell you, these people were not here to use the 'mikvah.' My private place was turning out to be the most popular parking spot in town!"

"So I dog-paddled in the shadows, where no one would see, hoping they'd soon go away. No one was in a hurry. No one else, that is, but me. The warm water became tepid, became cool, became cold. The cars did not move. I began to wonder if I was doomed to spend the rest of my married life in this lake. The stars were partying in the sky that night, while the moon spotlighted the water. Strange noises wafted from the woods. I hadn't realized how dense the forest was. And then I remembered that foxes—wild cats—bears—were common to the woods of Maine.

"Finally the cars pulled out. Quickly I prepared myself, said the blessing, 'Blessed are you, Lord our God, king of the universe, who has sanctified us by his commandments, and has commanded us concerning the immersion!' I dunked under, three times, hoping to be blessed with wonderful children and a warm Torah home! Then I got out of that lake as fast as I could, hoping the strange noises from the forest weren't bears."

"From stories like these," said Sarah, "we see how important it is for every community to build a mikvah. In fact, the first obligation of any Jewish community is to build not a shul or a yeshiva, but a mikvah!"

"Easier to daven in a living room than immerse in a lake!" Reva agreed.

"Oh, I just love the idea of this mitzvah!" said Nurit, a

young woman who was new to the *shiur*. "I mean, *Shabbos*
and keeping kosher, of course, but *mikvah* was the first *mitzvah* I found really exciting! It was such a different idea to
me—to regulate intimacy—and I love it. I mean, who's always
in the mood, you know? I like having some time to myself,
and this way my husband isn't offended. It's a brilliant system:
two weeks of honeymoon, then two weeks of vacation, every
month! I'm glad I found out about it before I got married. I
have a friend who was married almost a year, and her rabbi
never told her about it. He explained *Shabbos*, and keeping
kosher, and all the holidays—but he left *mikvah* out! Why?
Because he didn't think she was the 'type' to keep it! But what
woman doesn't want to improve her marriage, her children,
and herself by doing things she'd like to do anyway? The rabbi
was probably thinking she wouldn't like the little details, but
women don't think like that. We're quite willing to do details.
Think about makeup, hydrating creams, facial nourishers, lip
balms, skin peels, cover-ups, foundations, powders, and
blush. And all that comes after facials and tweezing, bleach-
ing, waxing. For what? For a pretty face—which will last a few
hours, maybe, before you have to touch it up again! But we do
it—and it's even a *mitzvah* to do it, because we want to look
nice for our husbands. Did you know that when the Jews were
slaves in Egypt the women had copper mirrors so they could
beautify themselves for their husbands? So we multiplied even
in Egypt! Anyway, when I tell my unmarried friends about
mikvah, they all want to try it after they get married. A lot of
my married friends have started keeping it, too."

Sarah nodded. "Because the women used these mirrors
intending to build a holy nation, the mirrors were later used
to make holy vessels for the Tabernacle. This leads us to this
week's Parsha, 'Toldos,' which means 'offspring.' Does everyone have a copy?"

Rachel Rosenberg took a copy, but could hardly look at it. Perhaps she had been handed out enough at this *shiur*. It was one thing to come for uplifting tidbits, inspiring themes, beautiful stories—quite another when the afternoon presented an empty canvas, and she was left holding the paint and brush. Yes, she and her husband had been building, repairing, certifying *mikvahs*. But what good is building *mikvahs* where many women don't know how to use them? While she did informally instruct the women whom she met, the laws of *mikvah* were not among her lessons. She reiterated to herself that she didn't know how to approach these delicate matters. She didn't know what to say, or how to say it. Yet a strange feeling settled over her. If only she had been someone like Levana, who could teach about the *mikvah* so naturally . . .

"The question here," Sarah was saying, "is, why was Esau so very different from Jacob? The differences between Abraham's two sons, Ishmael and Isaac, we can understand—they had different birth mothers. But Jacob and Esau were born from the same parents, parents no less than Isaac and Rebecca, both models of righteousness. Not only that, but Jacob and Esau were twins, born at the same time. Same heredity—and same environment. Both were carefully and lovingly raised, both given the best possible education. How could they have become so different?"

"Rachel Rosenberg has twins," someone said.

"Oh!" replied Rachel, sitting suddenly straight. "Twins! Well, not all twins are alike. My twins look less like sisters than some of my other daughters. And very different personalities. But they do complement each other, unlike Jacob and Esau!"

The women smiled and looked into the photocopies, while Rachel drifted back into her thoughts. Yes, her twins did have different personalities. Suri was outgoing and friendly, while Esti was quieter and liked to stay home and bake. Esti baked their *Shabbos* challahs these days. And Suri would deliver the extra ones to neighbors who didn't have time to bake their own.

"So the question remains," continued Sarah, "how Isaac and Rebecca, two great and holy people, perfect in action, word, and thought, could have a son like Esau. We would think they would have only holy, Torah-loving children, like Jacob. How did they get an Esau?"

"Isaac didn't have a problem with it," Faygi replied. "Isaac loved Esau and wanted him to have the birthright. We would have said, 'God of our fathers, Abraham, Isaac, and Esau,' if he'd had his way."

"Rebecca knew better," said Tamar. "A mother has to be aware. She knew that the Jewish people could never come from Esau."

"I don't like the trick part. Jacob dressed up like Esau and craftily deceived his father," stated Mrs. Blisme.

"He didn't lie," insisted Faygi. "When Isaac asked, 'Who are you?' Jacob answered, 'It is I. Esau is your oldest son.' There was no actual lie there."

"But it is misleading," Sarah persisted. "And none of this answers my question: Why do we have an Esau? So let's look at our copies, please, friends," said Sarah, and Esther Springer began to read.

"What indeed did Isaac see in Esau? Peaceful Jacob and Esau the hunter fought even while they were in the womb. Yet Isaac clearly preferred Esau. How could he prefer the hunter?

"During his lifetime, Isaac endured several unique experiences. As a young man he was totally prepared to give his life to God at the *akeida* (altar). When he was not offered as a sacrifice, he went to learn for fourteen years in the tents of Shem and Ever—where he was entirely separated from the mundane. The Midrash says that at the *akeida* the tears of angels fell on his eyes and blinded him—blinded him, perhaps, to the physical world. However, his spiritual vision was twenty-twenty, especially regarding the spiritual roots of his offspring. He saw that his son Jacob's soul was rooted in the world of *tikkun,* the world of 'correction.' A lofty soul. But Esau's soul was even higher. His soul was rooted in a more elevated world, the world of *tohu,* 'desolation.' Esau had the greater spiritual potential. Were Esau able to serve God fully with *his* soul, his accomplishments would exceed his brother's. It often happens that what appears lower, grosser, more materialistic in this world originates from a higher place in the spiritual worlds. Isaac saw Esau's potential, and favored him.

"'Rebecca, however, knew that Esau was not a 'vessel' who would actually utilize his spiritual gifts. Yes, he *could* have used his prowess to elevate the physical world to become a Godly place. But he chose otherwise. He allowed the physical world to lower him. He utilized the physical world for its own sake, and his physical pursuits became a goal in themselves. His father and grandfather, Isaac and Abraham, were spiritually sensitive to the entire Torah and kept its laws long before God gave it to the Jewish people at Mount Sinai. Esau, however, didn't even observe the seven universal laws, the *mitzvahs* that were given to all mankind."

"Wait a minute," said a newcomer. "You mean ten laws—the ten commandments?"

"The seven universal laws are different," Sarah replied. "The Ten Commandments were given in the Torah at Mount Sinai, but the seven universal laws, which were given to the children of Noah, apply to all the nations of the world, even today."

Someone wanted to know what they were.

"These laws include the commandment not to worship idols or any power other than the one infinite Creator," Sarah replied. "They also include the commandments not to steal, not to murder, not to blaspheme God's name, to follow the laws of sexual morality, not to eat the flesh of a creature while it is still alive, and to set up courts of justice that uphold these laws. These seven laws may sound simple, but they are actually seven general categories with many components which require further study. In fact, the *rebbe* has often stressed how important it is for the world to learn and practice these laws now, in preparation for greeting Moshiach. Moshiach will not only teach Torah to the Jewish people, but he will also teach the details of the universal laws to all the nations of the world. At that time 'the earth will be full of the knowledge of God as water covers the seas,' as it says in Isaiah." She nodded for Esther to continue.

"Esau, despite his lofty soul-source, was known to steal and murder, to commit adultery, and he married women who worshiped idols. Rebecca, who was aware of Esau's failings, arranged that Jacob receive the blessings."

"So Esau wasn't a born loser," commented Esther. "He was a misdirected winner."

"This still doesn't answer why we *need* to have an Esau," said Shaina.

"Esau *is*," said Sarah, "and we need to recognize him. Esau represents the little force inside us that tries to get us involved in the physical world for its own sake. For example, we want to have a nice home so that our family will have a pleasant environment for learning Torah, for celebrating *Shabbos* and Yom Tov, and for welcoming guests. But to be involved in home decorating or lavish furnishings for their own sake—that's Esau!"

"True," said Erica thoughtfully. "Certain standards in home decorating become expected, and one could spend a whole day—even weeks—just thinking about window treatments! It is a challenge to keep everything in perspective. And I suppose one could say the same for clothing. We need nice clothing for *Shabbos* and Yom Tov, to show respect to our bodies, which are given to us by God, and even just to be part of society. Still, this is not an excuse to think constantly about clothes or go out and buy fifty outfits."

"Exactly," said Sarah. "And one way to keep our materialism in line is to be careful to give *ma'aser*—at least one tenth—of our earnings to charity. This elevates all the time we spent earning the money."

Mrs. Blisme sniffed. "Sarah, it's time to elevate that lasagna into lunch."

The women laughed, and Levana, Tamar, and Shifra got up to serve.

Rachel adjusted her chair to make room for the women going back and forth from the kitchen. Until now, she had always left Sarah's with a good word and a good feeling. But today she felt overwhelmed. The laws of *mikvah* certainly transformed a physical act into a *mitzvah*, a Godly act. And clearly, she could be teaching these laws to others. Yet she felt more comfortable as a hostess than as a teacher, and she did not see how she could possibly discuss laws that revolved around intimacy. She simply couldn't.

So what could she do?

As Faygi passed her a plate of lasagna, Rachel remembered Shifra's tape library. Perhaps there were tapes about the laws of *mikvah* that she could distribute to the women she met. And she could at least tell stories that showed the beauty and importance of the *mikvah*. She could also recommend books, for there were a number of fine books on this topic. She could make a book list and tell the women how to order them. She had even heard that there were *mikvah* directories on the Internet, and perhaps other pertinent pieces of information. Esther had a computer, and used the Internet a lot. She'd have to ask Esther. And maybe Shifra could recommend some tales.

Her plan of action mapped out, Rachel heartily enjoyed the lasagna. She could still be the hostess, still make blessings over cake and coffee, and then get the conversation around to the blessing women make when they immerse in the *mikvah.* Then she could explain the uniqueness of *mikvah,* how it elevates, benefits, rejuvenates a marriage. She already should be taking notes on her thoughts. No reason why "*mikvah*" shouldn't be a household word in a few households besides her own. She'd have a word with Esther, Levana, and Shifra to see how they would do it. Here was a challenge that rivaled raising funds for her hospitality stand in Meron!

Feeling no longer alone in her dilemma, Rachel enjoyed a cup of tea. Esther, Levana, and Shifra could become her allies in transforming one aspect of Esau into something that resembled Jacob. She would discuss it with them now.

5

Glicka: Exile of the Body, Homecoming of the Soul
Parshas Vayeitzei

Jacob left Be'er Sheva and headed toward Haran. He came to a familiar place and spent the night there, because the sun had already set. Taking some of the stones, he arranged them around his head, and lay down. He had a vision in a dream. A ladder was standing on the ground and its top reached up toward heaven. And angels of God were going up and down on it.
—Genesis 28:10–12

Jacob starts out on a journey away from his parents' home, at their bidding. He didn't just "go" to an unknown destination, as his grandfather Abraham did. He "leaves," "vayeitzei." His leaving left a void. As Rashi, the classic commentator, says, "When a righteous person leaves a place, his departure makes an imprint. As long as he is in the city, he is its glory and light and majesty. When he leaves, its glory, light, and majesty leave as well."

In leaving home, Jacob goes out into exile. Traditionally, the "place" where he stopped and rested is identified as Mt. Moriah, where his father, Isaac, had been bound as an offering. This place is also the future site of the Holy Temple. It is here in the dark of night that Jacob makes his unique connection with God, by initiating the ma'ariv, *evening prayer*, receiving in return God's promise to always be with him. His dream of the ladder, which stands on earth yet reaches to the heavens, contains a fundamental directive for divine service. On this ladder angels first go up, and then come down, demonstrating that whatever we do down here in the physical world is what ascends to the heavens. Here is where it counts.

Jacob was raised in a pure, safe home committed to divine service, and he is sensitive to his dream. He flees his brother's wrath, but he has received his father's blessing. Wherever he goes, his divine service will continue, and will ascend, and God's blessings will follow.

Sarah passed out the study sheets and asked Faygi to read.

"Sure." Faygi began: "For many years Jacob inhabited inner spaces. He learned at home with his father and grandfather, building his internal world of mind and spirit. For fourteen years more, he learned with Shem and Ever at their house of study. He was truly a 'man of the tent,' until his brother Esau, disinherited from the birthright, has thoughts of murder. Jacob flees for his life. That night he stops and dreams. When he awakes he describes the place as *Bet El*, the House of God. . . . "

Glicka slips into the room, and finds her seat in the back corner, behind chairs, babies, and books. In this cozy place she could see without being seen, watch without being watched, sit with others, yet remain alone. Or at least unknown. She felt relief to be in the company of others and not be recognized. At Sarah's she might make new friends. Meanwhile she found comfort in the study of Torah, which bridged the awesome gap between human beings and God.

Privately now, she could adjust to her present situation. Her past had given no hint of how her life would be today. The great change struck as suddenly as lightning, but before she had even sensed a storm. Like Jacob fleeing from Esau she and her family had to leave. And almost as abruptly they resettled. No, not re*settled*. She did not yet feel settled. But they were now in a very different place, under vastly different circumstances. All in a single moment, she was the same person, with a different life.

With a different life, *are* you the same?

As Sarah often says, life is time. Yet time can have such different characters. Some times hum quietly as a digital watch. During such times she could wake up not knowing which day it was. For example, those vacationing weeks spent in a cottage by the sea when her children were still little. She would watch them play on the beach during the long, warm, sea-spray days, building tall sand castles and digging deep water-filled moats. Those were weeks when days shifted like the sand instead of marching in orderly progression along a calendar. A time measured in the inches a child grows, in the T-shirts they outgrow, in the baby teeth they lose. Such days seemed very much the same.

And there are other days, rare landmark days that bong like the hours of a grandfather clock. These are the days that form the chapter titles of your life and tie boundaries around your being. For these days you grow, hope, work, and strive, and they mark a permanent change. Your wedding day, the birthday of the first baby, the day of moving into your own home. You are still yourself, but also a different self. You become also wife, also mother, also the builder of a home. These changes are the beautiful anticipated changes that mothers groom their daughters for. Her own mother, anticipating Rosh Hashanah, the Jewish new year, would sew new holiday dresses for each of her daughters, preparing them for change. "A beautiful new year, Glicka'le, and a beautiful new dress!" she would say. And she would add, "A bigger dress! See how you have grown!" Growing signified change and achievement. The bigger size is worn with pride.

Yes, her life had been a series of times of change, even all-encompassing changes, but these were filled with joy. Wearing the bigger dress, marrying a husband, bearing children. Each change was a challenge, and each offered joyous fulfillment. "What a beautiful home you have, Glicka!" Each change signified happy growth.

Then came this other change that signified—what? She, her husband, and her children had to leave their home, which was no longer theirs, flee to a foreign place, where they weren't known, and struggle with a new lifestyle. Now she worried each time a child needed shoes. This was a different kind of change. From such a change can you say that you have grown?

From such a change, must you say that you have shrunk?

The shock was over now. They had found an apartment to live in, a shul to *daven* in, a corner store to shop in, and a school for the children. Now was perhaps the aftershock. Adjusting to a new neighborhood. To a small apartment. To her husband being home every day, churning brain and *kishkes* that the wheel of fortune should turn up *again,* not for luxuries, or even for comforts—but only to have that peace of mind which comes when debts are paid. Now she needed to identify her new role. She needed wisdom to refocus her past, understand her present, and shape her future.

Wisdom came from Torah; Glicka grew up knowing that. She had been born into a warm Torah home on a boulevard of Milan, Italy, the only Torah home in Milan. Her mother, a woman of harmony and song, was giving birth to her first child when the doctors dutifully told her she was dying. Mrs. Brotman, however, gave herself another option, and vowed to the One Above that if He granted her life, she would devote herself to being a channel for souls to enter this world. She would give birth to however many the Almighty would send. Her prayer was answered, and her vow was kept. Glicka was born, followed by fourteen younger siblings.

Was there another apartment in Milan as sunny as theirs? As lively? As joyful? Which other sisters wore lookalike dresses

every *yom tov*, festival day, that their mother sewed herself—
with matching socks and bows? What other family had constant
guests passing through their house, for where else could you get
a kosher meal in Milan, if not in the home of the *shochet*,
chazan, mohel, and rabbi? In Milan, Glicka's father held all these
posts, and their home was open to all who passed through.

A home of warmth, love, siblings, action, and song. Glicka's
mother was always singing—early in the morning the children
heard her humming as she went about her work. Often she sang
original compositions to honor her husband and children. Her
home was joyful, always full of action. She planned it that way
so her children would be happy and not look for outside pleasures. Here everyone hummed, and everyone helped, and the
girls grew gracefully from one dress to the next.

Of the seventeen years Glicka lived in this home, three
special days stood out as life's landmarks.

Her first day of school in Ginnasio Akiba. A Jewish school,
but more modern than her parents would have liked. The
teacher, who required that all students have Hebrew names,
renamed Glicka "Maazel."

"At school I am called Maazel, Papa," Glicka duly
reported.

"At school," her father replied, his voice well controlled,
"you are to be called Glicka."

The next morning he visited her classroom. How distinguished he looked, Glicka had thought. Black hair, black hat,
black frock coat, red beard. "My daughter's name is Glicka," he
informed the teacher. "And that is what she should be called."

In a low voice her father explained. A name given in the
holy tongue—including Yiddish names, like Glicka, which are
also composed of the Hebrew letters—is not to be tampered
with. This name defines the individual, their function, their
purpose in the world, and is a conduit for their Godly energy,

their life force, which is channeled into the world through the letters of that name.

"'Glicka,'" her father informed the teacher, "is Yiddish for happiness and fortune. That is what we have named our daughter. And that is what she should be called."

"As wonderful as happiness!" thought young Glicka. Warmly and deeply the thought was imprinted in her memory. Her name was never challenged again.

The second remarkable day came years later, when she overheard her father and mother speaking in the kitchen. "It will be too hard on you," her father was saying. "She helps you with the other children. How will you manage without her? And it's too far away. Why should she be so far from home?"

Her mother would not be dissuaded. "A year at seminary is her chance for the future. She will learn to teach; she will get a certificate. Whether she uses it or not, such a thing is good to have."

And so Glicka learned for a year in Switzerland. For the first time in her life, she lived apart from her parents and siblings. During this different but beautiful year, she glimpsed into the depth of Torah and its wisdom. She learned to decipher the commentaries that surrounded the Torah text in the heavy volumes of the *Mikra Gedolah*—grand compilations of scriptural studies. For every mystery a Rashi, or Ramban, or Or Hachayim unravels, they open a hundred more, Glicka had once observed to her teacher. And her teacher replied that her observation was a sign of her growth in Torah. One learns more, only to realize how much more there is to learn.

That year passed quickly, and Glicka was soon home again, helping her mother with the busy, bustling household, not at all suspecting that another landmark, never-be-the-same-again day was about to happen. Had she known, she would not have answered the door wearing her housedress.

Had she known, she certainly would have put down her mop.

The rabbi and his attendant entered the foyer. They seemed pleased with what they saw, and greeted her parents warmly. Apparently her parents were expecting them. These guests were from Toronto, and apparently had business in Milan. Glicka herded the small children away from the salon so that her parents could speak with their guests.

These guests had come to discuss a *shidduch*. They represented a distinguished rabbi from Toronto who was interested in Glicka for his son. Many people passed through the Brotman home, and it was no secret that Avraham Brotman had a beautiful daughter of marriageable age, a girl who had attended seminary in Switzerland, a girl praised by her teachers as kind and refined with a good mind as well. When the offer was proposed to Glicka's father, Avraham Brotman looked into the young man. Excellent family. A good intellect. Nice looking, in good health, well situated. Fine. But the girl's father wanted something more.

"He's a considerate boy, known for his kind heart," confided the liaison.

"He is the one for my daughter," confirmed the man with the red beard.

Glicka's parents had found a *shidduch* for her. All that remained now was for the young couple themselves to meet and approve. They did.

Glicka was soon engaged. She and her husband were to live in Toronto.

True, in his country people spoke English, and in hers they spoke Italian. However, having grown up in a miniature international setting, Glicka understood several languages, including some schoolbook English. Her Italian, of course, was flawless. But neither Italian nor English would be the domestic language of this young couple. In their home, as in the homes of their parents, they would speak Yiddish.

Not that all Yiddish is the same. Accents and inflections vary, but a basic core vocabulary is common to all. True, Yiddish is a language of the road, and picks up vocabulary wherever it stops to chat. It inhales words from the land where it lives ("*Where is mine* cell phone?" is a question in Yiddish) and exhales its own vocabulary onto the land ("Come *kibbitz* and have a *knish!*"). It is the language of *chutzpa* and *oy gevalt,* of Bubby, Zayde, and *Yiddishe naches.* And it was the language that a boy from Toronto and a girl from Milan spoke together easily.

Glicka happily set up their first little flat. After their first baby, they moved to a larger flat, and soon to a large house. Glicka's husband learned Torah well, and learned business well. Exceptionally well. He became one of the most successful businessmen in Canada.

Business was her husband's domain. The home was Glicka's.

There is much a woman can do to make a home. She tried to make hers as warm, sunny, and open a house as her parents had in Milan.

She also tried to speak English. Glicka dearly desired to speak it correctly, but not bookishly, and with a proper accent. How she tried for that accent. She must speak more from the throat, not high on the palate, and greatly subdue her Italian lilt. She practiced, again and again, with mirrors and with tutors, but to project that broad tone and tenor was beyond her. She was nevertheless well accepted by her new community, and she devoted herself to her home and growing family. Collectors for needy causes came to her door, and she was able, and happy, to contribute generously. Everyone knew that her husband had an open hand and an open heart. Glicka felt fortunate to have a gracious home.

Just as she would not discuss with her husband the complexities of selecting window blinds for the parlor, the gardener's despair in taming the ivy, or her own preference for a particular pattern of china, so she did not expect him to share with her the intricacies of his business. She respected her husband's expertise in his domain; he respected her in hers. Her marriage and circumstances were as harmonious as one of her mother's songs.

There were some difficult times, of course. Her mischievous young son complained of headaches. When medications didn't help, the doctors ordered tests and detected a brain tumor. There seemed no choice but to operate. Thank God, the operation was successful, the tumor benign, and recovery complete.

There was the year her husband lost his father, who had been not only a loving parent, but also a wise and understanding mentor. She watched her husband suddenly age, as he took upon himself many of his father's responsibilities.

Yes, there had been difficult times, but thank God they had had positive resolutions. With their son's recovery came relief and joy. With her father-in-law's passing came the weighty comfort of a son assuming the responsibilities of his father, that his father's accomplishments should live on.

But in this third test, a resolution eluded them still.

That morning when her husband had called her into his office, not so long ago. She had never seen him looking as he did then—pale, deep furrows in his brow, white knuckles grasping the edge of his desk. Not worry, or grief, or pain— those emotions they had shared already. Before he spoke she was already feeling his feelings—shock, horror.

"Glicka, the business has turned bad. Very bad. We own nothing now, not even the clothing on our backs."

No, it was not exactly shock or horror either. Now, months later, as she sat in Sarah's dining room learning parshas Vayeitzei, she understood what it had been. What they had felt, what they had lived through, was the experience of being touched by a very close cousin of death.

Faygi was reading about how Jacob had fled from Esau.

"Eliphaz, Esau's son, overtook Jacob," she began. "And Eliphaz, who was also Jacob's nephew, was commanded to kill him! Ah—but Jacob was his favorite uncle, who had bounced him on his knee and gave him good, gentle advice. 'So what shall I do now, uncle!' he pleaded. 'I cannot kill you, yet my father says I must!'"

"'You need not kill me to honor your father,' coaches Jacob. 'Here, take all my possessions. A man who is destitute is like one dead.'"

Very true, and Glicka had learned this lesson well. What is death, after all? It's not nonexistence, but rather a different dimension of the soul. Here, in life, in this physical world, we can attach ourselves to God and God's infinity by using our physical bodies and the physical objects in this world to do *mitzvahs*. We offer guests a nice kosher meal, help support a yeshiva, buy a bridal ensemble for a needy bride. In the "next world," we reap the rewards for the *mitzvahs* we did here. We experience our hard-earned connection with the Almighty. But there we cannot add to our *mitzvahs!* Once the soul leaves the body, it can do *mitzvahs* no more.

When her husband would visit his father's gravesite, he would hide his *tzitzis,* the four specially knotted fringes that are attached to the small *tallis,* a four-cornered garment that men wear beneath their shirts. The *tzitzis* knots represent the *mitzvahs* in the Torah—which those beneath the ground can no longer do. Men hide their *tzitzis* so as not to embarrass the dead, who are no longer able to perform *mitzvahs.*

One who is destitute is also not able to perform *mitzvahs.* Without a home, one cannot welcome guests. Without food, one cannot share a meal. Without a bank account, one cannot support the poor. And Glicka, who had been accustomed to opening her lovely home to others, presenting fine meals, and giving fat donations, was suddenly now herself in need of all. How dreamlike it all seemed, but how awful and actual was the dream. Their house would be used to repay a small fraction of their debts—they must vacate tomorrow. They would stay no longer in Toronto, where their debts would hound them unmercifully. In the morning they would fly to New York.

She steadied herself and remained calm. She knew she could manage without the furniture. She had been permitted to keep her clothes. She was beholden for her very clothing! But she would miss the second drawer in her kitchen, the one that held the large bills for charities, which she had disbursed easily and graciously to all who asked.

Who would give to them now? And who would give to her?

Their younger children, who were not away at school, flew to New York with them. And questioned endlessly. Why were they leaving? When would they come back? Could their friends from Toronto come visit them and when could they go back to visit? Weren't they missing school? What kind of schools were there in New York? Where would they be staying? Was it all right to miss their dancing lessons? Would they be able to practice the piano? Her husband was uncharacteristically engulfed in his own "do not enter" world, and she had no ready answers She told the children that she was uncertain about the lessons, but she would teach them new songs, with wonderful harmonies. She would do as her mother had and make up one special melody for each child! And in New York, she assured them, there were many interesting places to go and things to do, although she couldn't remember just now exactly what they were. Meanwhile, the plane was flying through thick, dark clouds, and the children could see nothing through the windows. "Come," Glicka invited them. She would make up something to divert them; she would tell some wonderful story.

"It's in your pocket," her mother would call after Glicka and her siblings whenever they left the house. "Remember the *alef-bais*, the Hebrew alphabet. It's in your pocket." This was her mother's invention, a secret family code. *Alef* stood for *emunah*, faith, and *bais* for *bitachon*, trust. "Wherever you go, she would remind her children, have faith that God will help you, and trust in Him."

She looked at her own children, who seemed intent on pressing their noses to the window of the plane. Did they remember their *alef-bais*? And did she have hers? With nothing else in their pockets, they would surely need it now!

Glicka looked up. Tamar and Erica were setting out china for the entrée—Sarah's savory baked salmon. In Toronto she easily could serve salmon to a party of fifty, but how expensive this fish seemed now! Well, she would enjoy Sarah's treat, although every treat these days was also a painful reminder of what had once been commonplace.

Sarah's table. Tasty food, simply but elegantly prepared, Glicka's style exactly. She admired Sarah and would like to know her better. She had told Sarah a little about herself, where she was born, where she had gone to school, where her children were now going to yeshiva. Sarah's warmth as a hostess was rooted in her genuine interest in her guests.

Sarah was coming over to chat with Glicka now. Or perhaps not just to chat.

"Glicka," Sarah began, "I remember you telling me that you went to seminary in Switzerland."

Glicka nodded. Yes, twenty years ago she had learned in Switzerland. Sarah was bringing up the topic now as though

Glicka had the immediate knowledge of a fresh graduate.

"Would you be interested in teaching?" Sarah asked. "I have one opening. I need a scripture teacher, actually later prophets."

Sarah was offering her a job!

"I would have to look it over," Glicka replied. "It's been quite a while since I've studied that material."

"If you like, we could discuss the curriculum tomorrow afternoon," Sarah continued. "We could meet at my mother's restaurant."

Glicka nodded, while her mind raced. Could she teach a class now after so many years? She certainly would enjoy collaborating with Sarah. She could put up dinner early tomorrow morning, to have it ready for the children when they came back. Maybe split pea soup and tuna salad.

Sarah glanced into the kitchen. "Oh, I see there's a whole untouched tray of salmon," she observed. "What a shame, to waste it. I'll ask Mira to pack up some portions for your family."

An offer Glicka couldn't refuse.

During the remainder of the *shiur* Glicka imagined herself standing before a class. After so many years, how would she do it? Her mind leaped to discussing the curriculum with Sarah at the Resnicks' restaurant. She looked forward to meeting Sarah's mother, Mrs. Resnick. The restaurant, Kesser Cuisine, was apparently an extension of the family's successful kosher food-packing business. From what Glicka had heard, Mrs. Resnick, a woman in her seventies, arrived at the restaurant every morning and didn't leave until late evening. Amazing. To have a business was one thing, to actually work at it day and night was another. Why would the wife of one of the most successful businessmen in New York spend her days stirring cauldrons? Meanwhile, the *shiur* was continuing, Someone didn't understand why Esau was so upset over losing the blessing.

Sarah rephrased the question. "Why did Esau place so

much stock in his father's blessing? How important is a blessing from a *tzaddik,* a righteous person, or even from a simple, person? Actually, we do put a lot of confidence in a blessing, no matter who gives it, because a person's word is holy. In parsha B'reishis, when God created Adam 'God blew into his nostrils the soul of life.' We see from here that our breath, our word, comes from a high source. And even more so, if that word gives a blessing. When we bless another, we invoke God's blessing on ourselves as well. At the moment of blessing, there is a connection with holiness. The more that the one who blesses is connected with God, the greater the flow of energy from that blessing, and the greater the effect. Esau knew that. He also knew that the blessing bestowed great wealth. The blessing was everything."

"One thing to remember," said Tova, "is that not every blessing looks like a blessing. I heard a story which illustrates this.

"Once a man was shipwrecked on a desert island. After recovering from the initial shock, he gathered sticks and built a hut and found out where the coconuts grew. His main focus, however, was to get rescued. So every day he walked along the beach, scanning the shoreline for boats. As he did so one day, he noticed a cloud of smoke rising from the back of the beach. His hut was burning! Once again he had lost all of his possessions! He cried bitterly, losing himself in utter despair.

"He was still crying on the beach when suddenly a schooner pulled up and dropped anchor. Finally! He waved frantically, as he splashed through the water to greet the boat. The captain pulled him aboard and he was saved.

"Now he had a question to ask the captain. 'What made you decide to drop anchor here?'

"'I thought someone might be stranded,' said the captain. 'I came to see if I could help.'

"'But how did you know I was here?' the man persisted.

'I've been on this beach every day, and no one has seen me!'

"'We didn't see you either,' said the captain. 'We saw your smoke.'"

"It's very true!" said Ora, as the women nodded in agreement. "Sometimes what appears to be a disaster can save us."

"We need faith to realize that," said Reva, who was standing by the doorway, ready to take off. She wanted to get to the hospital. A seemingly minor cold suddenly had developed into pneumonia, and Moshe had been admitted again.

"Well, Jacob certainly had his ups and downs," Nina observed. "His fortunes changed like the spots of his sheep. First he's on top of the world, about to marry Rachel, the woman of his dreams—and the next morning he discovers that his father-in-law deceived him, and he is married to someone else. One day he's dealing with spotted sheep, the next day with unspotted sheep. He flees from his brother, then he's forgiven by his brother. He adores his son Joseph, and then his son is gone. And one day he has a home, and the next day he's in exile."

"What happens to the forefathers is a sign for us," added Tamar, thinking of the latest disappointing *shidduch* idea for her daughter. "Our lives are full of ups and downs And sometimes, in the midst of a predicament, it may seem like we'll never get out of it."

Sarah nodded. "We may not be able to get out of it, but we can rise above it by seeing our situation from a more elevated perspective."

"That reminds me about the story of Reb Zusya," said Ora. "Two Hasidim went to the Ba'al Shem Tov, wanting to understand suffering. He told them to visit Reb Zusya. After traveling for weeks, they finally arrived at Reb Zusya's town. They were directed to the outskirts of the village, where the road was no longer really a road, and there they found Reb

Zusya, in a hovel that looked ready to collapse. He lay on a bed which could hardly be called a bed, covered by tatters that were hardly blankets. The wind blew through the cracks in the walls and he had no fire in the fireplace. And no food in the house. Reb Zusya looked thin and weak, and he had sores all over his body.

"He tried to sit up, to welcome his guests. 'How can I help you?' he asked.

"They explained that the Ba'al Shem Tov had sent them to ask Reb Zusya to explain suffering. Baffled, Reb Zusya replied, 'The Ba'al Shem Tov must have meant someone else. I have never suffered in my life!'"

The women smiled. The story was well known, but it was good to hear it once again.

"To reach the point at which you don't feel difficulties is an awesome spiritual level," concluded Ora. "We can't always control our situation, but we can work at changing our perception of it."

Sarah smiled. "Just like the rock carrier did. You know, the man who spent his life carrying stones down from the mountain, always complaining bitterly with every step. One day, however, although his load seemed to be as weighty as ever, he didn't complain. In fact he was smiling, almost skipping, under that heavy load of stones.

"'What has happened to you?' asked his friends. 'Why are you skipping with your rocks today?'

"'Because today,' smiled the stone carrier, 'I am not carrying rocks. I am carrying diamonds, and they are mine!'

"Which just goes to show," Sarah continued, "how the way we perceive a situation determines our feelings. We would prefer that only obviously good things happen to us. But when a difficult thing happens, and we can do nothing about it, then we hope for a change in perspective—which we can achieve by *davening*. *Davening* is not the same as prayer. What's the difference? 'Prayer' means to ask, or petition. But how do we know what to ask for? We don't want our huts to burn down, yet perhaps there is a boat out there that will see the smoke. So what we do is to '*daven*,' which means to cling to the Divine. *Davening* isn't asking God to do things for us, but rather by clinging to God, we merge His will with ours, which raises us above our limited focus. As *Ethics of the Fathers* teaches, 'Make your will His will, so that He will make His will your will.' Similarly, we learn that a righteous person decrees, and God obeys. Not that anyone can tell God what to do, but when a righteous person *davens*, he merges with God, so there is no longer a difference between what he wants, and what God wants."

"Wouldn't it be nice," thought Glicka, "to see the world through God's eyes." She would have liked to know, rather than to guess, the reason for her poverty, and especially why her husband, who was suffering so much, had to endure this.

"I used to think I didn't have time to *daven*," commented Erica. "But then I realized that I don't have time not to *daven!*"

Sarah said, "We are all like Jacob. He was fleeing from his brother, but he made the time to say the evening prayer. The rabbis explain that when the Torah says, 'He arrived at a familiar place and rested because the sun was setting.' This means that Jacob said evening prayers. The stones around Jacob's head, some say, were not actual stones at all, but prayers that Jacob spoke to protect himself from Esau. You see," she concluded, "no matter what pressure Jacob was under, he made time to pray, and the prayers protected him."

The table turned to techniques the women could use to bring *davening* into their day.

"I've told my kids not to bother me when they see me *davening*," said Faygi.

"Mine don't bother me, but they use that time to bother everything else," said Iyelet.

"I get up half an hour earlier so that I can *daven* and then have my coffee," said Reva, "It helps to know that the coffee is waiting for me!"

"According to the Alter Rebbe," said Tamar, "it's better to eat something in order to *daven* rather than to rush through *davening* in order to eat! I find that having a glass of orange juice before I *daven* helps me to concentrate better."

"I find that learning something first helps me to concentrate better," said Yehudis.

"You're a true Hasid," said Sarah. "It's a Hasidic custom to learn before *davening*."

"Well, I'm going to start concentrating more on my *davening*," Shaina resolved. "No more excuses for me."

"Good luck with your youngsters," said Mrs. Blisme. "I saw you on the street with them the other day. I don't know how you even have time to even take a shower. And by the way, talking about babies, I have a new granddaughter."

The women exclaimed *mazel tov,* but Mrs. Blisme waved her arm, motioning for quiet. "Now you should know that this baby ought to have been named for my mother, may she rest in peace, Steesha Naami, of blessed memory! But my daughter-in-law named the poor thing after a vacuum cleaner—Ahuva!"

The women laughed, until Sarah added seriously, "Really, Mrs. Blisme, Ahuva is a beautiful, special name. It means 'one who is loved,' and, please God, that will be her destiny."

"She should have been named after my mother, her great-bubby!" insisted Mrs. Blisme. "My mother should have a grandchild named after her, to keep her blessed memory alive!"

"Names reflect the root of the soul," said Sarah. "Sometimes a new child does not have the same soul root as the deceased relative. Your granddaughter's mission in this universe must be connected with the capacity to love and be loved. Her name reflects this."

Faygi nodded. "The rabbis say that when parents choose a name for their baby, they actually have a moment of Divine inspiration, almost a prophetic vision. They were the channel for bringing this new soul into the world, and now they are given the capacity to name the new soul with exactly the most suitable name."

"Hmph," said Mrs. Blisme, obviously not satisfied. "I believe my youngest daughter is expecting—or I'm expecting that she will be expecting, God willing. Maybe her child . . . "

For a moment Glicka thought about her name—happiness, her father had said. As a child her parents had made her feel that she was a source of their happiness by being their precious daughter. As a married woman, her name reflected her material wealth and good fortune. Without that wealth, must she be less happy? Through teaching she could transmit what she realized now: that true happiness comes from within.

Sarah was looking at her. "Glicka, I know you have a beautiful voice, and that you love to sing. You have a musical gene—your mother's or father's gift of music, or perhaps from both."

"How do you know?" asked Glicka.

"I heard you humming. It sounded like a lullaby. Could you share it with us, Glicka?"

"Yes, please!" the women chimed in. Glicka hesitated.

"Sing! We want to hear!"

Glicka began to sing. Her mezzosoprano voice filling the living room transported Sarah's table to that Italian household, with the passionate, tender song of a woman determined to transcend the world's pain and temptations—with music.

The women began to say their good-byes, and even the stragglers were getting up to leave. Sarah nodded at Glicka. They would meet again tomorrow.

The sign over the Kesser Cuisine restaurant, once gilded, still had some trace of shine. More conspicuous were hand-lettered cardboard posters pasted to the windows announcing featured fare. Highlighted items included matzoh balls, borsht, kugels, and knishes at prices (three knishes for $2.25) that reflected a bygone era. Inside were chrome-and-vinyl chairs, not chic retro from the sixties but authentic survivors, some orange, some yellow, some green, none matching. Miscellaneous tables were uniform in their rich inner glow, achieved through elbow grease and age. Her mother's table had a similar luster, and Glicka felt comfortably at home. An older woman, wearing a red-and-white-striped T-shirt, denim skirt, and plastic apron, stood behind the cold-cut counter. Her face had a deep inner glow, similar to her tables. Glicka wondered at the elbow grease one must apply to the soul to achieve such a luminous face.

Sarah kissed her mother and introduced Glicka warmly. "A teacher—good," said Mrs. Resnick. "Come, sit, have a bite." She showed them to one of the tables near the front of the restaurant and served them bowls of steaming hot vegetable soup, which Sarah clearly appreciated.

"I'm glad to see you eat," said Glicka. "At the study group you never do."

Sarah shrugged. "It's okay—there's no time then. But I can always have something here."

A man, apparently a recent Russian immigrant, walked in, sat at the table in front of them, and pronounced his order: "*Mitbol!*"

"Ah, Mr. Zuskin!" said the waitress. "Good afternoon. Would you like a drink with it?" As she spoke she set up his place with pats of margarine, half a loaf of fresh, sliced rye bread, sugar, and nondairy creamer, and poured a glass of ice water. Mr. Zuskin shook his head. He didn't need any other drink.

The waitress returned with a platter boasting a melon-sized meatball garnished with vegetables and lavished with a thick meaty sauce. Mr. Zuskin washed his hands ritually and enjoyed his lunch, savoring the meatball, the sauce, the vegetables, and the bread. For $2.40 he enjoyed a lunch that would keep him satisfied for the rest of the day.

Next a woman walked in and made a beeline for the cold-cut counter. "A pound of sliced turkey, please," she ordered. As Mrs. Resnick rhythmically pushed turkey into the machine, as the paper-thin slices gracefully piled up, the woman began her story, speaking in high-pitched Yiddish. She was the grandmother. The mother was sick, the father had no work, and the boy, her grandson, was to be bar mitzvahed. Could Mrs. Resnick help?

Mrs. Resnick continued slicing turkey. Delicate slices, almost translucent, piling up on white waxed paper as the cutting machine, with its strong loud motor, set up its noisy wall of privacy. Even Glicka, seated just opposite the machine, could barely hear.

"Which shul?"

The woman told her.

Mrs. Resnick nodded. She knew the shul, its size, how many came on *Shabbos*.

"A simple *kiddush* . . . " the woman gestured.

"I'll tell my grandson. He'll deliver it Friday afternoon."

The woman nodded and paid four dollars for the turkey. No price was mentioned for the *kiddush*.

"Your mom does catering from here?" Glicka commented.

Sarah smiled. "Well, yes."

Glicka understood that the catering ran on a "sliding" scale. She looked around the room, observing the restaurant's other patrons. A well-groomed woman was sipping tea and enjoying a Danish. Some tables away was a woman who was known as a "regular" charity collector on Thirteenth Avenue. At a table for two, two teenaged girls giggled over hot dogs. Toward the back was an aged woman, surrounded by her wilted shopping bags. In the corner a crippled man wearing a mismatched suit ate bean salad and *shnitzel.* Glicka noticed that some of the customers stopped at the cash register before they left, while others simply enjoyed a cheerful good word from Mrs. Resnick and walked out. Of course. Sarah's mother had good reason to run this business. Here was her front to provide food for the needy.

The soup was delicious, the knishes very satisfying.

Glicka looked across the table at Sarah, who was outlining the prophets class that she envisioned for her eleventh-grade students. Glicka felt she could teach that class—more than that. She could feel the prophets coming alive in her mind. Haggai, Zecharia, Malachi, the last of the prophets, the last to experience this form of spiritual prowess until the gift of prophecy would return in the era that marked the dawn of the redemption. The lessons of the prophets were for all ages. And if people hadn't listened as they should have then, she and her students would delve into their words and heed them now. Just thinking about teaching gave Glicka energy. This class seemed designed for her.

Of course she would have to prepare. And how to present it? She wanted the girls to take the lessons to heart. She would *daven* each day before the class, asking for God's help.

"I feel you will be the right one for this class," Sarah was saying.

"I hope I will be worthy of it," said Glicka.

Sarah mentioned a salary, and Glicka nodded in agreement, just as she had agreed to the contents of the course. She didn't know what the going rates were for prophet teachers. But she knew that this salary would lighten her husband's burden.

Mrs. Resnick would not let them go without a generous package of knishes for the road. They had been at the restaurant only a short time, but Glicka felt wonderfully satisfied, in all ways. She remembered that a little of the challah of our foremother Sarah satisfied like a full meal.

If it was true of our mother Sarah, Glicka smiled to herself, should we expect less from Sarah's mother?

6

Levana: The Messenger of Peace
Parshas Vayishlach

And Jacob sent messengers ahead of him to Esau his brother, to the Land of Seir, the field of Edom.
—Genesis 31:53

The Hebrew word for messenger, mal'ach, *can also mean angel. Regarding this verse, some commentators say that Jacob sent actual angels as messengers to Esau. When he saw who Jacob's servants were, Esau realized that Jacob had remained constant in his service to the Almighty, had kept all the commandments, and therefore was worthy of the blessings he had received from his father. Esau would concede that he had no power over Jacob and would abandon his schemes to destroy him.*

Jacob's three-pronged plan for meeting with Esau became the prototype for approaching any enemy of the Jewish people: first, appease with messengers bearing gifts; second, prepare for war; third, pray.

The room was more crowded than usual today, and several newcomers were looking for places. One plump woman sat next to Mrs. Blisme, only to learn, of course, that she had taken Ethel's seat. She stood up in a huff and would have left had someone not graciously intervened. "Please, take my seat. It will be an honor."

The newcomer did so, while her rescuer smiled. "Let me get you some coffee," she offered, "and some cake." Gracefully, she served the newcomer. Then she made her way to the window seat and perched on its edge. Good. The view of Sarah was even better from here.

The hum of conversation died down, the clatter of dishes stopped, and finally all were seated and comfortable. Sarah passed around copy sheets of the weekly commentaries on the Torah, and the woman on the window seat took two sets. "The extra is for my mother," she whispered to Reva, who was sitting at the table nearby. "Sarah's teachings always cheer her up."

"Yes," Reva whispered back. "But who cheers you?"

Levana gave a small smile and shrugged. "When my mother feels better, I feel better, too." She didn't have to say much. Reva "knew." She had what Levana called "heightened antennas."

Levana is like her name, Reva thought. "Levana" is the biblical Hebrew word for moon. Like the moon that has no light of its own but reflects the light of the sun, Levana reflected the moods and feelings of those around her. When they were happy, she was happy. When they were not, which was often, then her face clouded. Yet, who felt sad when Levana was sad? Reva wondered. Who set their internal barometer by her feelings? Reva recognized a cloud on Levana's face, shut her eyes, and uttered a short prayer, asking God to give her friend strength.

As Sarah opened her *chumash*, bible, Levana also whispered a silent prayer. Maybe this would be the week. Mama refused to come to Sarah's table, but always enjoyed the tidbits Levana brought home for her—some tasty kasha salad, a cheerful Torah thought. Maybe this week's wisdom would provide such warmth, such resounding strength, that Mama would come out of herself. Her depression would lift like fog on a summer night, and the blinking stars and moon's cool light would bathe the world in wonder. Maybe today would be the day.

Maybe today. Maybe yesterday. Maybe tomorrow. Levana's life had been filled with the "maybes" of hope and prayer—and with the realities of effort and anguish. Her once cheerful mother, living upstairs, had withdrawn into her closed-door darkness; her daughters, Nava and Nomi, wrathful in their teenage righteousness, wooed, then scorned their mother's attention; her married children with their noisy toddlers turned her own small apartment into a three-ring circus. The little ones were adorable, but a handful! Just yesterday, Mindi was about to taste the dish soap while her brother Yossi climbed the living room bookcase, flinging books from their shelves until the entire bookcase was about to topple over. Their mother, Levana's daughter-in-law, was lying on the couch enjoying a book, oblivious to the pastimes of her children. Levana—only Levana—rescued the little ones just in time.

Almost as demanding as the toddlers were the congregants, the members of her husband's small shul. On the other hand, what was a *rebbitzin* for, anyway, if not to supply counsel, comfort, and kugels to needy congregants, including preparing the meal for mourners who return from the cemetery. Last week, there had been two deaths. And one of the deceased had an enormous family—seven children, all with spouses, children of their own, and even grandchildren. Levana had spent an entire night making egg salad, tuna fish, vegetable platters, and fruit bowls. She also had her hospital rounds, visiting and presenting chicken soup and cake to the hospitalized or homebound. And her classes, teaching the sacred laws of Jewish marriage to dewy-eyed brides. And her counseling, advising, comforting all those in distress.

And, most of all—most important of all—a *rebbitzin* was

a helpmate to her husband. The Jewish woman is called a *bayis*, a home, say the ancient Talmudic rabbis. If that is the case, then the *rebbitzin* is surely the home's foundation. And not only the foundation of the *mikdosh me'at*, the Temple in miniature that is every Jewish home, but the foundation of the shul. Surely the cornerstone of every shul is the *rebbitzin*.

Rabbi Aaron Kadesh, Levana's esteemed and illustrious husband, was tall, handsome, and eloquent. A man of oratory, of learning, of consequence. A man whose resounding sermons combined exhortations with scholarship. A man whose pulpit was a magnet, as scores of devoted Jews from all congregations, not only his own, streamed into his shul to hear his sermons. A man of fire. A man of fury.

And also a man of pain, and of sorrow. For all his success, for all the adulation of his congregants and the surrounding community, his attempts to find another congregation—a larger one, more worthy of a man of his intellect, background, and scholarship—had failed. Rabbi Kadesh was unhappy in Brooklyn, with its ready-made committed regulars hanging onto his words. He longed for Manhattan, where he envisioned young Jews listening earnestly to his sermons, changing their secular lives, and embracing Torah values. He was created for outreach, not for a well-saturated Brooklyn congregation. But he was turned down, again and again, each time he applied for a new position.

As a boy his shining elementary school grades had left him longing for high school honors. Why should his father pay attention to the accomplishments of a kid anyway? But being valedictorian wasn't enough, and Aaron looked forward to the day when his father would watch him graduate from Yeshiva College with the admiration and honors of all his rabbis. Ordination, postordination, his first little shul in Brooklyn Heights, and now this shul. . . . His father was old already, gumming his way through Ensure at a nursing home, but in Aaron's mind his hair was always black, his eyes flashing.

A shul in Manhattan would make Dad proud.

No such shul. Aaron was stuck here. In his humiliation and frustration he found fault—with his shul, with his family. His self-pitying mother-in-law. His rambunctious grandchildren. His self-involved teenaged daughters.

His beautiful, self-effacing wife. She was always trying to please him. "More tea, dear?" "Shall I get your warm slippers?" "Here are your shirts, just fresh from the laundry."

Her solicitude shamed and irritated him. He had let down his father, yes, but he was also letting down his wife by being stuck in this mid-sized shul. And she felt the brunt of his moodiness. Round and round it went, a vicious circle of self-hatred, moodiness, and more self-hatred. The more frustrated and guilty he felt, the more he took it out on the person who loved him and whom he loved the most: Levana.

Sarah was talking about messengers.

"And Jacob sent messengers to his brother, Esau," she was reading. "The Hebrew word for 'messengers' is the same as the Hebrew word for 'angels.' Some rabbis believe that Jacob sent human emissaries. But the commentator Rashi says that these were real angels sent to scare and impress Esau."

"I'd be scared," Tova said.

"Imagine," said Iyelet, snapping her fingers. "Excuse me, angel! Put up the spaghetti for dinner!"

"Wouldn't need a cleaning lady!" someone quipped.

How different life would be, thought Levana, if angels ran the household! One angel to watch the little ones. Another to cook dinner. A third to visit old Mrs. Hymanson in the hospital, if she, Levana, was too exhausted to go. And another to interface between herself and Aaron when he was out of sorts. That angel would have to be strong. Maybe Gabriel. Or maybe Uriel, who could bring Aaron light. Or Raphael, to heal him of his dark moments when, like an illness, they overtook him.

She would even be satisfied with a human angel. If she could only find another rabbi to whom she and Aaron could go for counseling. Someone she could turn to, pour out her heart to. Right now she could speak with no one. She dare not with friends. Or with family. And certainly not with congregants. She needed someone she trusted, and, even more important, someone Aaron could trust. An older mentor figure, a rabbi of scholarship and compassion, who could take Aaron under his wing, soothe his pain, and steer him through the turbulent congregational waters to an island of marital warmth and love. If Aaron could feel respected by this rabbi— maybe the rabbi could become a father figure for him, a surrogate for the man who had trampled through her husband's childhood and continued to raise his voice in her husband's private dreams and memories, even today.

Some people saw marriage counselors, doctors, psychologists, but these were not options for her. Aaron would never submit to a professional with "*goyish* values and corrupt ideas" who would use alien phrases to describe him. Levana, however, knew the phrases, and had even studied them. A librarian by profession and avocation, as well as a voracious reader, she worked a few hours twice a week in a branch library. There she searched the psychology and self-help books, looking for her husband's "diagnosis," trying to find the words that could convince him to go with her for help.

Secretly Levana wondered what impact Aaron's unpleasantness was having on their daughters. She could scarcely think it, even to herself, but could his behavior be contributing to the girls' problems? Nomi's poor grades and her constant hypochondria? Nava's angry face and uncooperative demeanor? Getting Nava to set the table was like trying soften pharaoh's heart! But Aaron would not accept help from a doctor. Yet, a rabbi could be like a doctor. If she could find one, would he go? Sometimes you have to stand exposed before a doctor so that you can be healed. Concealing your body only prevents the doctor from understanding what's wrong with you. If only there were a rabbi who could be a doctor to her marriage, she thought. If she could only find one he would go to.

Without one, could she stay? Could she handle more of this? She covered her face with her hands. A divorce was worse, wasn't it? A divorce was more shameful, more contemptuous, more humiliating than the words Aaron sometimes threw at her. To walk away from one's *bashert* rather than to stay and struggle together? No, divorce was another manifestation of the false values and self-orientation of modern times. And yet, Torah permitted divorce.

And what would it be like to be alone? To raise the girls alone? To bear the isolation, the failure, alone.

She was alone now. She often felt alone, but to actually be alone might be a haven. What message was this marriage giving her children?

What message would she give them if she left? That women were fickle? That they ran away when the going got tough? And there were also *shidduchim* to consider. Having divorced parents could injure the twins' chances of getting good matches when the time came. No—for her daughters' sakes, she had to stay.

Could she endure it? An angel, maybe, could endure it.

"We are all angels," she heard Sarah say. "Every time we fulfill the will of God, we rise to the level of the angels. You see," Sarah continued, "the Midrash explains that people were the

last creatures God created. Even angels were created before
human beings. Therefore, any time a person strays from the
correct path, God can say, 'You see? You are a lowly creature.
Lower than angels. Even a fly and a mosquito were created
before you!' But when human beings do God's bidding, then
they are even higher than the angels."

"Why is that?" Shimona asked. "I remember learning how
we're always *lower* than the angels. Only on Yom Kippur, when
we don't eat or drink all day and our sins are erased are we
allowed to be on par with the angels. That's why we say out
loud the words *boruch shem kavod malchuso l'olam va'ed,*
'Blessed is the glorified Name of His Kingdom forever and
ever.' Only the angels are permitted to say this phrase out
loud. When we recite it during our daily *davening,* we say it
quietly—but on Yom Kippur, when we are like the angels, we
say this line out loud."

Sarah smiled. "In a way, we're always higher than the
angels are. That's because we have freedom of choice, and
angels don't."

"They don't?" questioned Mrs. Blisme.

"Human beings, not angels, are told in the book of
Deuteronomy, 'Behold, I have given you this day life and
good, and death and evil, and you shall choose life so that you
may live.' But the rabbis explain that angels are each created
with a single mission and cannot choose to rebel. We, on the
other hand, have free choice in matters of God's commandments. To do, or not to do. Of course, many *mitzvahs* come
easily to us. But some do not. When we do these more difficult
mitzvahs, we are overcoming our evil inclination, which is
that part of us which says, 'I don't want to.' And that places us
on a very high level indeed."

So maybe an angel wouldn't do such a good job in the
house, Levana mused as Sarah continued her explanation of

angels and free choice. Would an angel know how to bring a smile to Mama's shadowed face? Or how to calm Yossi and Mindi? Or how to help Nava and Nomi with a school project or a new dress? Or how to soothe Aaron after one of his tantrums? Angels, Sarah was explaining, were static, incapable of depth, emotion, spiritual growth. How could they empathize with Aaron as she could? What did they know about being a curious little toddler, fascinated by everything, feeling like a windup toy? What did they know about being a beloved daughter who could stop Mama from sinking yet deeper into her depression. What could an angel do that she, Levana, couldn't do?

An angel could shut off the pain.

An angel could administer, however inadequately, without being torn apart.

An angel had wings to fly away from the struggle. She, Levana, had to stay.

Or did she?

"Maybe this is why the Torah left it ambiguous as to what kind of *mal'achim*, messengers, Jacob actually sent," Reva ventured. "Right before this section, we read that angels met Jacob on his way. He saw them and said, 'This is a camp of God.' There were angels all around him. But on the other hand, he had servants. He could have sent them. Maybe the Torah wants us to understand that we are all messengers. And angels."

Sarah smiled again. "Maybe we don't have to understand the idea of angels literally at all. Maybe an angel is a presence. A spiritual energy we carry within us and that surrounds us. Like the angels that accompany a man home from shul on Friday nights."

A chorus of voices broke out. "The good angel and the bad angel ..."

"And we greet them by singing 'Shalom Aleichem'—"

Sarah waited for the hubbub to die down and nodded. "Yes, two angels accompany a man home from shul each *Shabbos*. A good angel and a bad angel. If the man returns home to a lovely *Shabbos* table, a harmonious household, bright candles, and challah, the good angel says, 'May it be like this next week, too,' and the bad angel is forced to answer, 'Amen.' But if, God forbid, the house is disorderly, and not harmonious, and there is no *Shabbos* atmosphere, then the bad angel says, 'May it be like this next week, too,' and the good angel is forced to say, 'Amen.' So what does this mean?" She looked around her. "It means that we draw to us presences, or energies, that protect and support us in our chosen path. The rabbis say, 'One *mitzvah* leads to another.' The opposite is also true, God forbid. One negative deed can generate another. Every time we do a *mitzvah*, especially if it is difficult for us, we create an 'angel' to accompany us and support us, to encourage us to do the next *mitzvah*. No good deed goes unnoticed. We create angels."

Creating an angel. When Levana whispered a joke into Mama's ear, or brought her cake and readings from Sarah's table, she was creating an angel. An angel who would whisper in Mama's ear long after she, Levana, had to leave to comfort Hanna Stern, the shul president's wife, as she poured out her heart about her sick baby, or to console Aaron, carrying on about his unreasonable shul president. An angel created to bless everyone, as she, Levana, tried to.

"I think *you're* an angel, Sarah," someone called out. There were many nods and murmurs of agreement.

Sarah blushed and rushed to continue. "Jacob sent the angel, then sat down to do some heavy-duty planning. He had to deal with a brother who had wanted to kill him. God had told him to return to his home. But it was scary to return!

Who knew what Esau was planning? When Jacob got word that Esau was on his way over to meet him with several hundred men—a whole army—he must have been terrified." Sarah paused for a sip of tea. "But Jacob carried things out in a methodical way. He had a threefold plan of action. First, he sent gifts. He hoped that they would appease his angry brother. Then he divided his people into two camps, and planned strategies for war. Finally, he prayed."

"Imagine praying and loading guns at the same time!" Erica exclaimed.

"You can ask for God's help when you are doing anything," Sarah responded. "Making beds. Going to work. Picking up the kids. Cooking dinner. Preparing for whatever battle is going on in your life." She paused, then continued. "Then Jacob had a mysterious encounter with a man. An angel, actually. They fought, and he injured Jacob, but finally blessed him."

"I never understood that part," said Shaina. "When I was a child, a teacher once told us that story, but she wasn't stopping for any questions."

Sarah smiled. "There's plenty of time for questions here. Our sages say that Jacob went back to get some small vessels, dishes of some sort—maybe jugs—that he had left behind, and that's when he encountered this angelic figure. There are a number of ways to understand this. One interpretation is that Jacob lost sight of the real priority, which was to save his family and reconcile with his brother. He became distracted by material objects. Little jugs diverted his attention from his true purpose. That was when he met the mysterious stranger with whom he wrestled. The rabbis tell us that this stranger wasn't a human being at all. Actually, he was none other than the angelic protector of Esau. You see, every blade of grass has an angel standing over it, ordering it to grow. Every person has a sort of guardian angel in charge. So do nations. The person and the nation of Esau had a guardian angel who confronted Jacob that fateful night. Jacob was eventually victorious. But he was injured, and limped for the rest of his life."

This was a new angle on a story that Levana had heard, and even studied, many times. When you were selfish, when you thought of your own gratification, you were misplacing your priorities. You were chasing after little jugs, petty little pleasures and gratifications, ignoring your real soul's mission. That was when negative energies beset you. But if you strategized carefully, planning and fighting your battles through spiritual means, prayer, as well as through practical means, then you were staying focused on what was really important.

Levana remembered a conversation she had had the previous week with Reva.

"You're running yourself ragged," Reva had said. "You're spoiling everyone. It's as if the sun rises and sets with the desires of everyone except you. Your whole day is spent shopping, cooking, cleaning, and counseling. You're lucky you have the job in the library—at least for a few hours you have a break. When your mother wants a muffin, you'll get up at three in the morning to go to the bakery, never mind that you were up until midnight nursing a sick grandchild!"

"That's why I'm here. I want to be there for my family," Levana had replied. "To be a good parent, wife, daughter, and grandmother I have to be available."

She had struggled to explain it to Reva. Groped for the right words to express how she felt she had been created to serve. To make the lives of others better. How she had learned this from her own mother, who hadn't always been depressed, but had been loving, warm, and giving. Mama had raised her to understand that the role of the Jewish woman is to serve.

Her glory was that she kept her own needs and desires hidden, buried in the secret treasure chest of her heart. This is how Mama undertood the psalm "The glory of the king's daughter is within."

Now, after hearing Sarah's class, Levana thought she had clarified some of the choices and objectives of her life. More than anything else, she was committed to building a home for her family and she could focus on all the positive aspects of this. Her own hurt, her disappointment, her longing for more freedom, for a serene marriage, a more peaceful home—ultimately all of this was secondary. To say no to the wishes and needs of others, to refuse to be the buffer between the generations and the in-laws, for the sake of a harmonious home was unthinkable. It would be tantamount to going to the other side of the river in pursuit of little jugs—meaningless pieces of petty, insignificant crockery—and there, to meet the archangel of negativity and challenge, who would injure her and make her limp in her service of God.

Better to be a different kind of angel. An angel of giving and loving. An angel to protect those she cared for.

She now reconfirmed what she had always felt, that she and Aaron were each other's *bashert.* Soulmates. They were bound together for life, and she was created to care for this family. "For this have I been created." As she told her daughters, not every marriage goes smoothly, but if you keep *davening,* if you don't give up, you can achieve the harmony you're striving for. This was her life's work, her destiny for this lifetime—and it would be worthwhile.

The women were getting ready to leave. Reva observed Levana wrap up a portion of lasagna and tuck it into her shoulder bag. Their eyes met. "For Mama," said Levana.

She sounded tranquil. She looked softly luminous. Beautiful.

A pallor, a whitewash of pain, was the secret of Levana's beauty, thought Reva. Levana means white as well as moon. Like the moon, Levana's pure white light originated not from herself, but from a reflection—a reflection of the *or ein-sof*, the Divine Light Without End, which gives in proportion to one's giving. Levana's patient glow guided the three generations of her household through their growing pains. May they all continue to grow, please God, until they reach Levana's own level of selfless service.

7
Klara: Learning and Lawyering
Parshas Vayeshev

They [the brothers] pulled Joseph up from the pit. And sold Joseph to the Ismaelites for twenty pieces of silver. They brought Joseph to Egypt.
      —Genesis 37:28

God was with Joseph and extended kindness to him, granting him favor in the eyes of the prison chief.
      —Genesis 39:21

Even in Egypt, a decadent land unequaled in unholy practices, Joseph clung to the God of his fathers. In return, God was with him, protected him, and granted his descendants and the entire Jewish people the ability to hold fast to their belief in God and to the practice of His Torah, despite the darkness of long and deep exiles.

This year Chanukah, the Festival of Lights, spanned two of Sarah's sessions. The Tuesday of parshas *Vayeshev*, while not yet Chanukah, was *erev* Chanukah, the day before Chanukah's first night. On the Jewish calendar *erev* anything takes on the anticipation and most of the character of the thing itself. For example, there is *erev Shabbos*, a day so preempted by *Shabbos* preparations that a designation like "Friday" hardly does it

justice. Two other famous *erevs, erev* Pesach and *erev* Yom
Kippur, have acquired so many customs and activities of their
own that they have become honorary hallowed days in themselves. As for *erev* Chanukah, it surely has its own activities.
One must polish the menorah, the candelabra. One must
obtain candles, or olive oil and wicks. One must have the necessary supply of "gelt," money for the children; order an abundant supply of oil and potatoes for the traditional Chanukah
latkes, pancakes; and also buy jelly donuts and chocolate
coins. The *dreidel* (spinning top) must be dusted off and read-
ied for Chanukah games. At least eight stories should be prepared, one for each night of Chanukah. And if *erev* Chanukah
is on Tuesday, one must be sure to go to Sarah's. One tries to
attend every week, of course. But *erev* anythings at Sarah's are
special. Everybody makes sure to go.

"The first candle," Sarah was saying, "is the little bit of light that
takes away a lot of darkness. You can have a million lights shining, until the night is lit like day, adding light to light—and this
is what Chanukah is all about. But that first small candle is its
own statement. That first match struck in total darkness em-
bodies brilliance. To dare to bring light into some corner where
there is none, ladies, each of us in our own way has that opportunity and merit. Especially with our children. Make every holiday bright for them. Customs! This is what children
remember! The latkes, the *dreidels,* the menorahs, the candles,
the gelt! Chanukah is everyone's most memorable holiday! In
our family we have a family together sitdown meal for every
night of Chanukah! Customs, ladies! Play them to the hilt!"

Today was not destined to become a latke-recipe-sharing
session. "Friends," Sarah continued, "I have copies. Tonight is
the first night of Chanukah, but this week is the week of par-

shas "Vayeshev," when Joseph was sold into slavery in Egypt and was exiled from his family into one of the darkest, most unholy nations in history. What is remarkable about Joseph is that the *shmutz* down there had no effect on him. It didn't pull him down. He lit it up! He was the first candle in that darkness. He was the first lone pioneer who prepared the place so that his family could come down there and eventually turn that darkness into light."

As she spoke, Sarah looked around the room, noticing who had come. And who hadn't. She didn't see Klara. She hadn't seen Klara Kirsh in quite a few weeks. Klara, who personified the woman who could outwit exile. Where was she? If Klara didn't show up today, Sarah would give her a call.

Klara Kirsh did intend to come to Sarah's that day, and had not yet given up hope of spending *erev* Chanukah around Sarah's table. She had planned her morning schedule to allow several free hours for Sarah's *shiur,* and thought she would be there without delay, until her client called from her cellular phone to say that she was stalled by a pitiful traffic jam on the Belt Parkway. So again Sarah's *shiur* was in jeopardy. Bottom line: As much as Klara was self-employed and "chose" her hours, her profession had inevitable limitations.

Klara was a lawyer.

She looked outside. A dark, short winter's Tuesday, a day born with night nibbling around its edges, a day soon to yield to the first night of Chanukah. She had Chanukah ready. Menorah, wicks, olive oil, peeled potatoes floating in a bowl of water in the fridge. Just herself, her husband, and her youngest son Ari would be here tonight, and her second and third daughters with their husbands and children. She'd call her oldest daughter, now in Lakewood, later this evening and speak to the little ones. They were planning to come in for *Shabbos.*

Noon soon turned to a quarter after twelve. If her client would come *now* and stay only an hour, Klara would still catch a good hour and a half of Sarah's. But the client's estate was complex and might require a fat slice of time. Klara clicked onto a legal Web site to double-check the scope of a few relevant statutes. This law library at her fingertips wasn't even a dream when she was in law school.

There was also a time she wouldn't have dreamed of going to law school.

On the other hand, she had never imagined herself career-less. When she grew up in Russia in the fifties, women certainly had careers. Her mother, an educator and director of kindergartens, loved her profession, although she regretted its two drawbacks. The first disadvantage was a hazard particular to Soviet kindergarten directors: Her own children must do without toys, lest fellow citizens suspect them of playing with property stolen from the state. A second hazard, common to all working mothers, was that for much of the day she was cut off from her children. Even at ages four and five, her little ones had to manage without her from early morning until late at night. Klara and her younger brother had played, as other children did, near their cottage, which bordered the Carpathian forest. Forest children, they were. The forest was their playground, the trees their nursemaids. A poetic thought, but not to the maternal ear. Klara's mother dreamed of finding a grandmother, even a tiny, old grandmother, to watch her little ones. At work, educating other small children, she could not keep her mind off her own.

Klara remembered playing in the forest. She remembered toys she and her brother had crafted of twigs and leaves. She remembered the pretty bits of colored glass that they had collected. And she remembered also the gnarled, oh so old *bubichke,* ancient and ailing, whom her mother finally found to keep her little ones "safe."

Klara checked through the statutes and found everything in order, but her client had not yet arrived. More delay. In the distance, Sarah's beckoned.

"What goes up must go down," Sarah was quipping. "But spiritual progress is just the opposite. One must go down in order to go up. Hasidim call this process 'descent for the purpose of ascent.' We have to tumble into decadent lowlands in order to be catapulted to spiritual heights. That's what happened to Joseph in Egypt, and that's what happens in each and every exile, starting from the beginning of creation. Before creation, there existed only God, in His great Unity and Oneness. However, the Almighty, the epitome of goodness, desired something to be good to. Therefore He withdrew Himself and created a void, a canvas of seeming emptiness, where He could create the world. That was it. Descent for an ascent—an emptiness for the purpose of fulfillment."

Sarah saw that she was holding the women's attention. As always, the kabbalistic concepts that she mentioned had practical applications. So she continued:

"Adam's exile from Eden was another one. Did you know that the 'forbidden fruit,' the fruit of the Tree of Knowledge of Good and Evil, would have been permitted to Adam had he but waited a few more hours? Had he only waited until *Shabbos* he could have made the *kiddush* blessing on the fruit, elevating it, himself, and the entire world into the perfection of the messianic era. Adam himself would have been Moshiach. Of course, the service of his descendants would have been very different. We would be rising from great to even greater spiritual achievement, increasingly uniting with God and his infinity and power.

"However, Adam did eat. So instead of rising from height to height, he was exiled from Eden—an extreme descent. But even this was for a higher good, and, we are told, an even greater gain. Adam's job now is to elevate the entire universe by working the *eretz*, earth, literally, but related to the word '*ratzon*,' will. The service now is to unite with God by obeying God's will, even when it means setting aside our own. This is what Joseph did, and this is what kept him strong in exile."

With growing impatience, Klara wished she could be in two places at once. She couldn't desert her client, but she wanted to be at Sarah's. What would be the topic at Sarah's today? On *erev* Chanukah, they might be talking about miracles. Maybe Sarah would go around the table asking everyone to tell a miracle story of their own. Klara wouldn't know which of the miracles of her life to mention first. The miracle of how her family left Russia in the sixties, when almost no one escaped from communism's iron grip? The miracle of how she became observant while living in the Bronx? How she met her husband? Of course, all of those miracles had logical explanations. But that her parents survived the war and met each other was clearly beyond any natural likelihood. It was clearly miraculous.

Her parents were survivors. Miracle by miracle her father had survived the war, fighting in the Russian army. When he was enlisted he thought he was doomed, but the army, intolerable as it was, turned out to be a blessing in disguise. At the end of the war he found himself stationed in a remote Russian village, where peasants slyly peeked through his window, eager to catch their first glimpse of a Jew. Jews, they knew from newspaper pictures, had horns. This Jew, however, had none. He sat there, thanking God he was alive, yet not knowing the whereabouts of his family. It was not a joyful time.

Meanwhile, Klara's mother, a girl still in her teens, had

escaped the Polish borders and had arrived in that very same village. Her mother was blessed with a special aura and found favor wherever she went. Even the Russian peasant women took a liking to her and sheltered her. They protected her, and even decided to marry her off.

"*Bailishke!* One of yours is here! Yes, it is! One of yours! A *Jid.* Right here! You must meet him!"

Whenever her mother told this story she added that when a match is *bashert,* the One Above will find the matchmaker. Baila and Reuvain realized that their match was made in heaven, although it happened in a Russian town that wasn't even on the map. How far into exile her parents had had to go to meet each other. They stayed strong and perhaps passed their strength on to their children.

Klara got up and fixed herself a coffee. 12:25.

Sarah and the women were now perusing copies of an article that listed other exiles and redemptions. The next "descent," historically, was the flood. The first ten generations had failed continually in their Divine service, because of rampant theft and corruption. The earth required a total cleansing—a thorough inundation. The flood changed the nature of the world, but the service was the same. A rainbow of seven colors, symbolic of the seven universal laws, became a perpetual reminder for Noah and his children. These universal laws are also called the Noahide laws, after that righteous man who defied the whole world by obeying God's will.

Sarah continued to describe the postflood population, which enjoyed unparalleled unity. They spoke a single language, loshon hakodesh, the holy, original language of Torah and creation. Literally, "loshon hakodesh" means both the "holy tongue" and the language "set apart." In all other languages, where words are deemed "arbitrary," a rose by any other name could still be a rose. Only in the holy tongue is every word, letter, and even dot essential. Nothing is arbitrary, nothing superficial. In this original language each letter is much more than a symbolic representation of a sound. Each letter is an actual creative power, combined by the Creator to form "words"—created beings. This is why in loshon hakodesh the single word "*dovar*" means both "word" and "thing." The Creator's "word," a particular combination of creative energies, brings the thing into existence and sustains that existence.

Sarah gave a concrete example of this concept. "As kabbalah explains," she said, "God isn't like a carpenter, who takes an already created substance, like wood, and changes its form. When the carpenter has completed a chair his work is finished. To sustain creation, however, the Creator's creative energies continuously create the world, instant by instant, or all would revert to original nothingness."

"As you can imagine," Sarah continued, "speaking in loshon hakodesh was a privilege. Properly used, it would help people unite with God. What actually happened was something quite different. The people of that era unified not with God, but with themselves. This unity gave them the strength to feel that they could rebel against the Almighty. The Tower of Babel was an outgrowth of their plan to rebel. Therefore, the privilege of speaking the holy tongue was taken away from them. Instead of speaking words that expressed essence, their speech was reduced to 'babble.' From then on, only the descendants of Abraham, Isaac, and Jacob would speak loshon hakodesh."

Here Shaina had to make a comment. "You know," she began, "we do find some obvious vestiges of loshon hakodesh in other languages. Think, for example, of the 'magic' word 'abracadabra.' Abracadabra is rooted in the loshon hakodesh words meaning 'I will create what I speak.'"

"True," Sarah agreed. "Even an 'arbitrary' language is not in essence arbitrary, but rather more distantly removed from its source. The relevance of its words becomes more difficult to discern, but every language has its moment of clarity."

"Uh-huh," said Shaina eagerly, ready to interject additional examples of this clarity. "Look at some of the names of countries," she said. "The land God gave to Abraham, God himself calls '*Eretz*,' related, as you mentioned, Sarah, to *ratzon*, 'will.' This hints how this land runs to do the will of God. It deserves its reputation as a land that 'spits out its inhabitants,' for, as history has proven, those who live in *Eretz* Israel who do not do God's will are forced to 'run' (in Hebrew, *ratz*) into exile. Also look at the name of this country that we are living in—'America.' Did you ever think what that means in loshon hakodesh? 'America' means Nation (*Am*) Empty (*rek*) of God (*Kah*). Don't you think this could be a reference to a land where the name of God is minted on public currency, but muted in public schools?"

"Hey, you thought of that?" Reva elbowed Shaina. Shaina needed no more encouragement to continue. "'Russia' in loshon hakodesh literally means evil, which, I think you'll agree, is loshon hakodesh's view of atheism, the former official faith of that country. As our rabbis emphasize, even the best of doctrines must be backed by the Creator's laws or risk such pitfalls as KGB terrorism. And, one final example, Africa: 'Africa' becomes Anger (*Af*) Empty (*rek*) of God (*Kah*)—designating a continent caught in the throes of social and political unrest, with no end in sight!"

The women applauded; Shaina bowed and grinned. "Do you think this insight justifies my sojourn in the halls of academe?"

Sarah smiled. "Would you read from the handout, Shaina? You'll like what's coming up next."

"Like the descent from Eden," Shaina read, "the descent and diversity of languages is also a descent for the purpose of ascent. When people of all languages use their speech to do the Creator's will, and their voices to praise the Creator and the Creator's works, then even these more spiritually remote languages are being used to do the will of the Creator. This does more than rectify the Tower of Babel. It creates a forum which allows holiness to penetrate even the babbling languages themselves. The most far-flung areas, the most remote dialects, thus become a "dwelling place" for God. The Divine now dwells in the nethermost reaches, fulfilling the ultimate purpose of Creation."

"I'd like to add something to that," came a voice from the back of the portico.

"It's Margie Barris!" said Sarah, as she greeted an angular woman with glowing green eyes.

"I'm just back from '*Eretz*,'" said Margie, "and I can tell you that some of what's going on there is just terrible! This so-called 'peace' policy ought to be spelled p-i-e-c-e—they are giving our holy land away piece by piece and it doesn't take a genius to see that what this really spells is disaster! The *rebbe* has been crying out against it for years. Ladies, write your congressmen about it. Remember what Rashi says in the very beginning of the book of Beraishis (Genesis). Why does the Torah, the book of God's own wisdom, begin with 'In the Beginning, God created the heavens and the earth'? Says Rashi: 'Torah begins this way to declare the power of God's works to his people.' In other words, if the nations say to us, You are robbers, for you have taken this land by force, Israel can say, Look! All the world belongs to the Holy One, Blessed be He! He created it and gave it to whoever He saw fit! It was His will to give it to them and it was His will from the beginning, in the days of Joshua, to take it from them and give it to us.'"

"So here we are with the land God gave us in the Torah, the land God promised to the children of Abraham, Isaac, Jacob, and their descendants—the holy land for the people who keep the holy laws of the holy book! No one argues that! The land is ours, God-approved. How dare we give back an inch of it! Will we give Boston back to the English? Manhattan back to the Indians? Texas back to the Mexicans? Australia back to the Aborigines? Spain back to the Portuguese? But, if we think of *Eretz Yisrael* as a political piece of property to be a bargaining tool for 'peace,' then it's up for grabs. Our holy land becomes a free piece of cake. Any politician, any nation, can help himself. And what happens? For every piece we've given, they've gobbled us even more. Look into the Torah, ladies. It's our land because we have the deed—God gave it to us in the Torah!"

Some women applauded, as Margie sent around a petition for all to sign. "Margie, you're a Maccabee," said Mrs. Blisme.

"Margie, you're a leader in protecting our holy land," said Debra. "You even have the Maccabees' battle cry: All who are for the Almighty, follow me!"

"Do you ever get any sleep, Margie?" asked Reva. "I know you don't give the media any rest, catching them on every word."

"I can't sleep," said Margie. "How can I rest with the 10 o'clock news calling a terrorist an activist? Disputed territory, they call it? We're not disputing! It's ours! Ladies, e mail your senators, demand that your representatives represent you!"

Tamar shook her head. "We're all aware of what is happening there, Marge. It's already beyond politics. Our only hope is to appeal to God. There's no question that we have to increase our *Tehillim, tzedakah,* and acts of kindness to each other and pray that the Almighty will save our land."

Many women murmured assent.

Klara's mail thudded on her home-office floor. No sign of the client yet. Her eyes drifted to the mail pile, which was topped with a colorful brochure from the summer camp her son had attended last summer. Time to enroll him again—the camps fill up fast. There in the Catskills he would enjoy study sessions in the morning and swim, sail, and play ball in the afternoon. Quite a different experience from the one that Klara and her little brother "enjoyed" one summer before they left Russia.

Although that camp was organized by communists, campers were nevertheless invited to attend weekly church services. Klara, although she knew almost nothing about Jewish observance, still rebelled at the thought of attending church. "I'm not religious," she declared, demanding exemption from prayer services. The ploy succeeded for two weeks, until a fellow camper figured her out. Jew! Suddenly Klara was ostracized by the entire camp. "Come get me!" Klara wrote to her mother, "or I will kill myself!"

Her mother hastened to her rescue, and just in time to save not only her daughter, but also her son. She found him in the nearby boys' division, isolated in a sickroom where he was receiving no medical treatment. She hastily pulled both children out, and probably saved her son's life.

Klara knew that her parents longed to raise their children as Jews. Secretly, her brother had had a *bris*. And secretly her family watched, waiting, for an opportunity to leave Russia. When they had a chance to emigrate to Poland, they leaped for it.

Not to remain in Poland, of course. A less friendly place was hard to find. But from Poland they could, and did, finally emigrate to the United States.

In Russia, and more so in Poland, Klara had been singled out for being a Jew. Among Jews in America, however, she discovered that she was singled out for being a Russian. Her family was among the first Russian immigrants of the sixties, long before the first wave of immigrants arrived. Undaunted, Klara's father, born of a Lubavitcher Hasid, embraced the land of the free and the home of the brave, settled in Yonkers, found a shul, requested a bar mitzvah tutor for his son, and threw the shul into a quandary. How could they give bar mitzvah lessons to a child who hardly knew the *alef-bais?*

In the sixties, Russian immigrants were a novelty, but *ba'alei t'shuvah* were even more rare. Klara, strengthened by her previous experience in exile, had to spearhead both. And at that time, all roads for the newly observant seemed to lead to Lubavitch.

Klara pushed. She pushed herself to learn English and to excel in high school. She visited Crown Heights and began to spend *Shabbos* with the family of Rabbi Label Groner, the Lubavitcher Rebbe's secretary.

At the same time, a young Harvard astrophysics graduate took leave of his studies to learn Torah in Crown Heights. During this time he received a draft notice. He had *yechidus,* a private meeting, with the Lubavitcher Rebbe to ask what he should do.

"You might ask a different question," the *rebbe* responded. "You should ask about marriage."

The student repeated the *rebbe's* advice to his *Shabbos* family, who mentioned the situation to the Groners, and soon a match was arranged. Michael and Klara became happily married. And the army, cognizant of his science skills, awarded him a special position in California.

So in the land of flower children the young couple sojourned. And here Klara spearheaded another first. This was a land of beards and beads, but it had no kosher butchers or bakeries. Kosher meat had to be imported from New York, and challahs were baked at home. In Berkeley in 1967 the norm wasn't normal. But Hasidim? You must be kidding.

"You mean God cares what you eat?" a young woman with straight and flowing hip-length hair questioned Klara.

"God made us," thought Klara. "He knows what fuel we run on." But to the girl she only said, "Look, it tastes pretty good, you know. And I bake bread for *Shabbos*. Why don't you come join us for a meal?"

Klara's husband presided at their *Shabbos* gatherings. As a Hasid among scientists, he was an anomaly. His fellow graduate students believed that science and religion were mutually exclusive. You could only believe in one. The enlightened scientists, of course, chose science. This young, capable astrophysicist, who was also a Hasid, poked holes in their axioms.

"Science," Michael told his young wife, "is its own exile: the exile of knowledge from Godliness. The generation of the Tower of Babel used technology to reach and battle against the heavens. Today scientists aren't openly rebellious. But they are devious. While the Babel generation at least admitted that there was a Creator to rebel against, the believer in science uses knowledge to replace God. His creed becomes: Given enough time and manpower, all can be known and anything can be done."

"And isn't that belief unscientific?" he asked some fellow scientists over gefilte fish one *Shabbos*. "The first page of every high school science book states that science is based on theory! And that theory is based on the finite knowledge and observations of human beings! Anything that's eternal, that will not change, is beyond the realm of science! Want proof? Just look at the history of any field of science. Yesterday's scientific theory became today's giggle in history." He smiled at his guests. "Like the challah? How's the gefilte fish? Have some horseradish—but be careful. Klara made it herself, it's hot." He grinned and continued, "So you think our theories today will be any better tomorrow? It's obviously beyond the scope of science to dictate anything eternal, like, for example, a code of behavior for mankind. And that's how Torah comes in where science leaves off. You think it's based on faith? Not really. Actually, you'll see that Torah is more scientifically provable than science is itself. I'll soon explain. But now that we've finished the fish course, we have a tradition to make a *l'chaim,* on Russian vodka, in honor of my wife. No, it's not mixing drinks. We finished the wine a long time ago. *L'chaim*—to life. *L'chaim, l'chaim,* to life! Know the song? I'm married to Klara for three months and already can drink three shots of vodka and still sing straight. One gulp per glass. You *think* you can. *L'chaim!*"

As the vodka was passed around, Michael would continue, "Anyway, as I was saying, 'Torah,' which is the Infinite's knowledge encapsulated, means 'teaching.' The ultimate purpose of Torah is—hey, you did it! All in one gulp. Here, have a second—Torah's purpose isn't to give knowledge per se, but to teach us how to live to our fullest advantage, as individuals, and as members of a community. And as a matter of course it provides—I saw that! The second glass in one gulp! Klara, never denigrate an American—here, have a third, okay, show me. Yeah, Torah as a matter of course provides all the knowledge necessary to live—*L'chaim, l'chaim, l'chaim!* All you want. But we also have soup, matzah balls, chicken. . . . "

Proving an absolute God, with infinite knowledge, might be the topic of discussion a few *Shabboses* later. Torah, Michael would point out, was not the product of man, but divinely revealed at Sinai to millions—and this provided multiple evidence that had to be accepted, even on scientific grounds. That would be during the chicken course. And about the time Klara was passing out crème de menthe (nondairy) ice cream dessert, he would conclude by describing how God, the Creator of the Universe and of mankind, being Infinite, can, and does, stipulate a positive and absolute system of human conduct, which, when studied by all, will calm the emotions, harness the instincts, end the perplexities, and bring an era of harmony, goodwill, and world peace. Which was Klara's cue to bring in the Turkish coffee.

Many guests came back a second time. "They want more," said Michael. "No doubt," said Klara.

They seldom had leftovers.

California, then, was a time of teaching and self-discovery, as well as of parenthood. Klara and Michael had two daughters before they finally returned to New York. It was then that Klara discovered that her psychology degree was not a key to employment. She enjoyed working with people. What else could she do? "Try law school," suggested her brother, himself a recent law school graduate. "It's work with people. You'll be a counselor-at-law." With visions of Perry Mason, she enrolled.

In 1970, when she first appeared in moot court, the judge asked her, "Are you the secretary?" From then on she specifically wore a dark suit, a skirt, and a jacket and carried a black attaché case. There.

Who would watch her children? She found that she, like her mother, needed to leave someone, and not just anyone, at home to care for her little ones when she left home to work in the world. Fortunately, her mother volunteered. But on days when her mother couldn't come, Klara didn't go. She would rather miss her classes than leave her daughters with just any babysitter. Meanwhile, Michael realized that positions in astrophysics were closing down. As soon as Klara accepted her first law firm position, Michael began attending law school at night. His scientific background would prove useful in some technical international areas.

Helden, Hold and Keepe was the prestigious firm that employed Klara for most of a decade. She vividly remembers her first interview with W. Z. Hold, Jr.

W. Z. believed himself progressive, and if the candidate with the best credentials for an entry position at his law firm happened to be a woman, he would rise to the call of the moment. His original expectations that she might also do her own typing were laid to rest quickly when he saw how perfectly professional this young woman was. She wore a dark suit jacket, carried the requisite attaché case. She was all business. A Russian immigrant. They were reputed to be hard workers. He expected hard work. She was married, no problem, with two children. Hmm.

"We've never given maternity leave."

"If necessary, I shall use my sick leave. In general my health is good. On Fridays I must leave early for the Jewish Sabbath. I will make up the hours on Sunday."

She wasn't asking. She was making the conditions! A woman of principles. Now, how long would she last here? A small smile crossed the mouth of W. Z. He hired her.

W. Z. explained to the other attorneys on the floor that Ms. Kirsh observed the Jewish Sabbath, and therefore would be leaving the office early on Friday afternoons and make up the hours on Sunday. The announcement was less than well received. Most junior lawyers worked late on Friday and *also* came in on Sunday. Klara sensed resentment smoldering and retreated behind her caseload.

Every other week she presented her "billable hours" record to the bookkeeper, who eventually sent it up for W. Z.'s approval. He did not approve. Why were her billings so skimpy? A quick examination of her records revealed the "discrepancy." Ms. Kirsh's billable hours were computed incorrectly.

He had made it clear, he thought, but he would explain again. Clients were to be charged at six-minute intervals. Leftover minutes counted as if they were a full six minutes. Now here was a case where Klara had worked with a client for thirteen minutes. She should bill for eighteen, yet she had billed for only twelve. Here she had worked for thirty-five minutes and had billed for only thirty! Here she had researched for one half hour, and she needed that research for three different clients. She should have billed *each* client for *thirty* minutes, not ten! No wonder her billings were so slim.

"I'm not billing for work I didn't do," Klara stated. "How can I bill for eighteen minutes when I only worked thirteen! That would be stealing, wouldn't it?"

Stealing? Not at all stealing! It was the customary practice of law firms! Ms. Kirsh, however, would not adjust her records, and "billable hours" became a sore point in her relationship with the firm.

There were other irritations as well. The attorneys in the office were accustomed to expressing certain kinds of comments without inhibition, and the presence of a woman in the office put a damper on that. Although Ms. Kirsh did keep to her own corner and avoided the water cooler, there was unspoken (usually) resentment about this matter. In other matters she was simply an anomaly. She observed the Jewish law of having no physical contact with any man except her husband, to the point where she would not even shake hands with other men. She was pleasant about it, and few were offended, but all were surprised. Of course, one would not think of greeting Ms. Kirsh with a customary office kiss. Oh, she was smart. Shrewd. Astute. Discerning. And because of these fine traits, she was able to get the firm into, and out of, a fat mess on the Herringbone case.

Admittedly, W. Z. assigned Ms. Kirsh the most tedious, least interesting cases, ones that would not make news. Dr. Phillip T. Herringbone's case against an insurance company that we'll call The Cantaloupe Trust was the epitome of an uninspiring suit. Cantaloupe was known to hold back on its payments. Doctors always were suing Cantaloupe. W. Z. accepted the case and gave the file to Kirsh.

No one else would have noticed, no one besides Klara, how the patients' signatures didn't match up. Kirsh, in true form, brought the papers to W. Z.'s attention. "He's billing for unprovided services," said Kirsh. "Double billing."

W. Z. examined the documents. Yeah, he was.

"Anyone can see this," said Kirsh. "Certainly Cantaloupe will pick up on it. They could countersue big."

They could, yes. But it was not for their firm to make predictions.

W. Z. looked at her squarely. "Your job, counsel, is to represent the client." He emphasized an unspoken *period*.

The case was resolved by settling out of court. Deftly, Klara maneuvered for a settlement that was truly owed the doctor. Luckily, Cantaloupe agreed. No one seemed disappointed, but the stress of dealing with ethical issues such as these took its toll on Klara.

Klara stretched and stood up. These problems were history, now that she had her own practice. She could choose her clients and bill them as fairly, or as minimally, or even not at all, as she pleased. Another advantage of leaving the firm, so she had thought, was that she would be her own boss and have her own hours. It wasn't totally working out like that; she was still quite off the mark of satisfactorily scheduling her day. Still, being responsible to only her clients, herself, and

God was a big step away from being beholden to Helden, Hold and Keepe. She worked now with trusts, and also with immigration law. She actually was able to counsel people, which was what drew her to law in the first place.

Her client still hadn't come. Klara walked over to her library and pulled out a thick volume of the Five Books of Moses with commentaries. The parsha of this week was "Vayeitzei," the story of how Joseph was exiled to Egypt. Klara, like Joseph, had sojourned in many strange lands and persevered. She had learned that if you can't get what you want, look for another way to get what you want. Torah and its heritage grounded her, and never did she let any strange land, not communist Russia, the startling Bronx, flower-filled Berkeley, or the Manhattan isle of lawyers and legalese, lessen her attachment to Torah. In fact, in her own home law library, side by side with the thick, solid texts on property law and contracts, were volumes on the laws of *Shabbos*, the laws of the kosher kitchen, *midrashim*, *Me'am Lo'ez*, and other Torah commentaries. Also in her office was her private conference room, with its elegant mahogany table and cushioned armchairs. Today was another Tuesday afternoon that she might not spend with Sarah. However, she still had her Wednesday nights, when her law office received a special elevation. On Wednesday evenings a group of special women gathered in her conference room for a light dinner—and to learn Torah. An offshoot of Sarah's table.

Ah. There was Mrs. Grunwald at last.

Maybe she would get to Sarah's after all.

She arrived just before the entrée, in the midst of an expectant pause. Tamar was standing up, clearing her throat. "I get a *mazel tov!*" she announced.

Abigail? The room was about to split at the seams, waiting for the word—which didn't exactly come.

"Ephraim," said Tamar, whose smile doesn't flicker. "My son. To Bracha Milstein of Monsey."

"*Mazel tov!*" The congratulations are fast and furious, and near perfect. Ephraim, Abigail's younger brother, was engaged.

Nina Weinstein felt a wave of satisfaction. She had suggested this *shidduch*. It was so suitable, everyone felt that they got just what they wanted. Ephraim and Bracha knew practically from the first date that they were destined for each other. Yet the *shidduch* never would have happened if it were not for Abigail, who had given her younger brother her blessing to marry before her. In this merit she would certainly find a *shidduch* of her own.

Oh. There was Klara Kirsh! Her law practice, thought Nina, would no doubt introduce her to an extended circle of people. Perhaps she could also look out for Abigail. Maybe she would even have a *shidduch* suggestion now. Nina would make it a point to speak with her. Quite a woman, that Klara Kirsh.

Many women were in awe of Klara. Some even envied her: Torah, her family, her profession. It did seem like Klara had it all.

"Maybe I should be a lawyer?" Klara's third daughter once had contemplated, as she entered her senior year of college. Her brilliant third daughter. Yes, she could be a lawyer. She could have her pick of law firms.

By pushing. By juggling. By using all her wits. By appearing balanced when she felt stressed out.

"Of course you could," Klara had replied, "but perhaps consider education."

The suggestion was well taken, and her daugher became a

brilliant educator. Married a brilliant husband. Had four lovely small children.

So just now, Klara's daughter was a full-time mother. Her children needed her. Who could take her place? Only, maybe, a grandmother could fill in for an absent mother. But the grandmother of these children was busy being a lawyer.

A lawyer who perhaps would like to spend more time with her grandchildren.

But this lawyer had considerations, obligations. She and her husband helped to support three sons-in-law and their families while the young men continued to delve deeper and deeper in their rabbinic studies. She and her husband also contributed to a number of worthy organizations which depended on them.

"Exile," Sarah was saying, "like Joseph, like Judah Maccabee, we have to be strong to withstand the exile."

8

Erica: The Toil and the Oil
Parshas Mikeitz, Chanukah

Pharaoh said to Joseph, "I am Pharaoh. But without you, no man will lift his hand or foot in all Egypt."
—Genesis 41:44

These lights we kindle upon the miracles and upon the wonders and upon the salvations and upon the battles which you performed for our forefathers in those days at this time.
—Ancient song, sung as part of the ceremony of lighting the Chanukah candles.

Parsha "Mikeitz" usually occurs during Chanukah, the Festival of Lights. And there is a connection. Both Joseph, exiled to Egypt, and Judah Maccabee, who led the Jews against the Greeks, held tight to the Torah and mitzvahs and triumphed against overwhelming odds. In return, God performed wonders and miracles for them, and continues to do so in our time.

"Mikeitz" always falls out around Chanukah time, and so, Sarah asked, what is the connection between the parsha and Chanukah?

"If you don't stand for something, you fall for everything," Sarah answered her own question. "What Joseph and Judah the Maccabee had in common was that they both stood for everything—and fell for nothing.

"They each in their own way took exile—*galus*—head-on. Joseph, who held fast to Torah's teachings even in an Egyptian prison, became the most influential man in Egypt. Pharaoh himself decreed that without Joseph's approval no one had permission to lift his hand or foot. Joseph, through the power of his faith, became the ruler of the land.

"Judah wouldn't give an inch to exile either. The Greeks, by the way, were generous. They actually admired Torah and thought it was great literature. They didn't mind if everyone read it—so long as no one observed it! Read it, just don't do it, was the Greek way. Keep the literature, just delete your connection with God. But Judah and his followers knew that our connection with God is life itself. So they were ready to lay their life on the line to observe Torah. And with God's help they threw out the Greeks."

A cozy victory. A victory of light, and latkes, of remembering warm, cozy Chanukahs past. Glicka and Rachel had begun the *shiur* with lilting, haunting Yiddish melodies that they remembered their mothers singing. The melodies created an intense presence in the room, as though souls from the other world had come to have *naches* from their daughters. Sarah brought up another point.

"Chanukah is also the time of *pirsumei nisa,* of publicizing the miracle of Chanukah. For thousands of years we have placed our menorahs in windows and doorways, where passersby can see them."

"And now we light the 'world's biggest menorah' in downtown Manhattan where no one can miss it," said Shaina, who had braved the subway with Chana and Dovid so they could participate in the event.

"Not only Manhattan," said a new voice. "I'm visiting here from Milwaukee. We also have a public menorah lighting. And I believe there is one on the White House lawn as well.

Any town worth its place on the map has a menorah to light, these days, don't you think?"

Sarah smiled. "Yes. This is the true victory over the Greeks. Would you like to read our handout?"

The visitor from Milwaukee was more than happy to.

"Parsha 'Miketz' usually comes at Chanukah time, and Chanukah, the festival of rededication of the Holy Temple in Jerusalem, is also the festival of miracles. Not a clothed-in-nature miracle of palace politics and intrigue like Purim, but a truly above-nature, only-God-can-explain-it type miracle, which boggles the mind and justifies the soul. The tiny flask of pure oil that the Maccabees found in the desecrated temple should not have lasted for even one day, yet it burned for eight, until more pure oil could be obtained. An obvious miracle.

"What is not widely known is that the Maccabees didn't need to use pure oil at all. They didn't have to turn the Temple upside down to discover this one sealed flask. Under the circumstances, all they had to do was to light the menorah. Any oil would do.

"But it would not do for the Maccabees. The nature of their battle was unusual from the beginning. They had fought with all their might, but they had not been fighting for their lives per se. The Greeks were not a bloodthirsty people, and would have been delighted to settle their differences peacefully. They found much to admire in the Jews and their law. In fact, they admired the Torah so much that they gathered seventy sages of Israel to translate it into Greek. The Greeks, an intellectual, philosophical, artistic people, appreciated the nation's history, literature, and law. Indeed, keep this, they would have said. Just remove the part about God.

"On the other hand, one might point out that the Greeks had many gods. Why should they object if the Jews had one?

"However, the Greeks weren't concerned with quantity so much as quality. They were aware that the Almighty, the God of the Torah, also commanded the world at large. The Greeks knew about the seven universal Noahide laws, and a minority of Greeks actually followed them. The majority, on the other hand, preferred a different set of principles. Therefore, they devised deities that, far from being role models, were modeled after the Greeks themselves. Their gods were passionate, jealous, and openly immoral. Since such gods could demand no better of their followers, the Greeks could obtain divine approval to behave however they pleased."

"Either worship the God of creation, or create a god to worship," interjected Sarah. "Of course, any god created by mortals will suffer the same mortality as its worshipers. When, for example, was the most recent congregation to gather at the temple of Zeus?" The women laughed, and the woman from Milwaukee continued.

"Therefore, the deal the Greeks would have made with the Jews was: Keep your Torah, but let it become one of *our* books. Celebrate it as exquisite literature, written by gifted men. Leave out the Divinity, and live in peace."

"Extol the body, dump the soul," nodded Tamar.

"So the Maccabees fought for the survival of their souls. The soul, linked to Infinity, becomes Infinite, transcending nature. God fought on their side, and the Maccabean guerrilla troops ousted the Greek superpower.

"The Maccabees were fighting for the freedom to worship as they believed. They were fighting for the purity of their soul, so only pure oil would do.

"And God acknowledged the correctness of their deed with an eight-day miracle." The woman from Milwaukee sat down. "Thank you, Sarah. I never heard this aspect about Chanukah, but I like it!"

Sarah smiled. "There's more we could say about Chanukah," she added. "For example, Chanukah means dedication. You'll notice that the Greeks did not burn down the Holy Temple. They liked the building—the outward beauty of it. It was its holiness that they couldn't tolerate, so they defiled the altar. They couldn't handle Godliness, God's laws, or the Jews' connection with the Eternal. So the Greeks said, yes, read Torah. But don't observe the sabbath, or Rosh Chodesh, the hallowing of the beginning of each month of the Jewish calendar, or circumcision. They would have been happy to let us live had they been able to obliterate our Godly soul.

"Had they understood the nature of the Godly soul, it would have saved them a war. The Godly soul can be hidden even from us—but it's there, and no one can touch it. No matter how far we may seem from practicing our heritage, the Godly soul is part of us. How many Jews in the Holocaust died with the prayer *Shema Yisrael* on their lips, affirming their faith. Our Godly soul can never be squelched.

"So when we tell the story of Chanukah, how the few Maccabees defeated the world power that was Greece, we are telling the world that the Jewish soul, which our rabbis say is actually a part of God, can never be defeated. And ladies, when we tap into that Godly spark, we can overcome anything and do wonders."

"I heard a wonderful parable the other day," said Levana. "It doesn't really fit in with what we're talking about."

Sarah didn't mind. Speech leads to deed, deed leads to revelation of essence: feast the soul, famish the exile.

Levana continued, "We say the same prayers over and over every day, so we know them by heart. That could lead to mechanical *davening*. But here's another way to look at it. Our *davening* is like the score of an orchestra. Only when we know the score well can the feelings come out."

"A beautiful parable," said Sarah, as the doorbell rang. Two delivery men from Kemel's bakery entered with a blast of cold air, each carrying a boxed tray of jelly donuts. With best wishes for a happy Chanukah, compliments of Erica Fine. The women oohed and aahed at the donuts, with childish delight. Diets were forgotten as this abundance was piled high onto serving trays to be enjoyed by all.

"Where is Erica?" asked Sarah, looking around. Erica was often late, but should have been here by now.

"She's moving to Lawrence soon," said Esther. "I'm sure she plans to be here, but she might be caught up in some of the moving details."

Erica was on her way. She was, as Esther had suggested, detained by some last-minute packing. She and her family were moving from Borough Park to Lawrence, Long Island. Erica was looking forward to molding the spacious house they had just purchased into a gracious home. Most of her husband's colleagues lived in that area—it was a "good" place to live. A place where you weren't alone if you drove a Lexus. A place where her husband's sons would have room to run around.

They were not as close to a shul there, but there was one they could walk to—a mile and a half wasn't so far. The boys could have a hearty *Shabbos* walk with their father when they came for their biweekly visits. They would also have their own room and bathroom. Erica planned to set up their room with a navy carpet and coordinating plaid bedspreads. Dressers and closets and shelves—they would have space to stash whatever they liked. And then there was the whole enticing backyard—almost three quarters of an acre, not to mention unfinished space above the garage. Erica liked to leave some space unfinished. Unfinished space left room for the imagination, room for growth, room for trials and mistakes.

A stepmother, she had come to realize, needs room for trials and mistakes.

There are accolades, ballads, and praises for mothers, but stepmothers don't have the same image. And it's a harder role to fill. Raising any child is a challenge, but when the child is formed from your own body, for nine months growing from food you have eaten and air you have breathed, you have some innate knowledge about that child. She remembered the birth of her own daughter, born of her short-lived first marriage. At birth, her infant was taken from her, to be bathed and placed in a hospital nursery. That was the system then. As soon as she could, Erica went to the nursery window, saw thirty plastic cartons of babies, and noticed, in the far back corner, one little infant with her leg sticking up from her box. "That one is mine!" Erica knew. And it was. Later she called the nursery from her room and heard one baby crying. "That one is mine!" Erica was right again. "Yes," the nurse had confirmed. "Every mother knows her baby's cry."

Her first husband's sudden death after Malka's birth made Erica wonder if the whole purpose of that marriage was just to have the baby. Malka barely had seen her father, and didn't seem to miss him. Erica took comfort in believing that she could provide everything her infant needed. At first it seemed she could.

She kept her small Borough Park apartment, filled it with a crib, changing table, baby swing, playpen, high chair, infant tub, toys, and baby clothes—filled every corner so that nothing should be missing. Rabbinic law prescribes that a woman must not remarry until her child is two, and weaned. The demands of a new spouse should not take away from the needs of an infant—and a demanding infant shouldn't inter-

fere with the delicate adjustments of a new marriage. Erica
was blessed with a baby who enjoyed plentiful nursing, cooed
sweetly, and had just enough colic to keep her busy day and
night. The years flew.

Malka was almost three. Barbara, one of Erica's favorite
cousins, was visiting Brooklyn, and was spending the night at
Erica's. As she helped Barbara with her suitcases, Erica realized that this was the first time since her husband had died
that she'd be sharing the apartment with an adult. Malka
watched wide-eyed. "Mommy," she said at last, "is that a
daddy?"

"Maybe it's time to start thinking about getting one, huh,
Ric?" said Barbara.

"Maybe," Erica replied.

She already had received some offers. Borough Park was
fully equipped with women who "looked out" for singles and
would be happy to see a young widow with a child suitably
married. When Malka started preschool, Erica considered taking the offers seriously.

She needed a husband, yes, but a husband who was ready
and willing for instant fatherhood.

A number of men seemed ready and willing. One week
she had three dates and was offered a fourth. Barbara, in for
another visit, commented, "Seems that blondes do have more
fun."

Erica smiled, putting touch-ups on her makeup. "How do
I look?"

"Ravishing. Don't you ever give any of those guys a second
chance?"

"I'm not going to waste their time. The ones who weren't
married before seem immature. As for the widowers, it seems
they want to remarry just to drown out their sorrow. I feel
sorry for them, but I'm not getting married to be someone's

substitute. I need someone who has worked things through, who has resolved their grief the best they can. You need a kind of treasured corner room in your heart, filled with flowers and your past. And at special times you can visit there, and pay homage, and bring fresh flowers. But that little room must have a door, and you have to close it. If the scent from the flowers seeps under the door and makes the whole house fragrant, that's okay. A private, mysterious fragrance—but any perfume is offensive when overused."

"Erica!"

"Really. Well, according to Torah law, a widow need wait only three months if she isn't pregnant or left with a baby, before she can remarry. To me, now, remarrying means getting on with life. I'm not interested in a *shidduch* that's a grieving session. I've finished that, and I'm ready for something else."

"So?"

"So the right one will come, I guess. Maybe I'll cancel tonight."

"But you're already dressed!:"

"I know. But I did three already this week. More than met my quota."

"It's not a numbers game. Who's for tonight?"

"My girlfriend Hanna recommended this divorcé."

"Obviously with many redeeming features."

"Of course. Fine character, respected surgeon with established practice, good looking, and two little kids living with his ex-wife. The children would visit every other weekend."

"That's good?"

"That's reasonable. Don't forget, I have a daughter who needs a father. Someone coming in with children, even part-time children, may be more accommodating to the job."

Erica found Seth more than accommodating. Almost a

decade her senior and the father of two small boys, he was suitably mature. He respected her past, and told her briefly of his own. His was an "amicable" divorce, a marriage both he and his ex-wife had learned from, and both were determined that their sons suffer as little as possible from the disruption. Erica and Seth showed each other pictures of their children. Erica could find no resemblance between Seth and his little sons. But Seth said warmly of Malka, "She seems a miniature of you."

"It could be," thought Erica, "that this could work."

She didn't know that diamonds grew as large as the one on the engagement ring he bought her. When she lifted her hand, she felt its heft. She held it to the light, waved it gently, and watched sparkles of sunbeams scatter on the wall. The ring had energy, and so did the relationship. She realized that she felt very much alive with Seth. She went to Manhattan and invested a third of her savings in an outfit he would like. She looked in the mirror and admired what she saw. She felt strong and loving and generous. Not new feelings. Just feelings that had became enabled recently.

She met his friends, mostly medical colleagues. He met her parents, Hungarian survivors.

"So I will have a son," her father had said.

"And I will have a father," Seth responded generously. He had lost both parents about a decade before.

"So far so good," commented Barbara that evening.

"And Malka is all excited about having a father," said Erica. "As you can see, this dollhouse he bought for her is a tight fit for our living room. She can hardly believe it's real. He says there's a house in Flatbush with a little girl's room just perfect for the dollhouse, but he wants to show it to me before he buys it."

"Did you buy a gift for his boys?"

"They are practically babies. Not yet two, and not yet three. Somehow they looked older the way they were dressed in the picture I first saw of them. Seth has ordered a bunch of toys for them, to be delivered once we have a house with a playroom."

The house Seth had selected, a comfortable "detached" one-family, seemed very roomy to Erica. The kitchen had been remodeled recently, with convenient and separate areas for dairy and meat, which may not be cooked nor eaten together according to the rabbinic law.

Theirs was a small, intimate wedding, with a large, joyful reception, a honeymoon in a kosher resort in Aruba, and a blissful week "getting settled" in their new home. Malka took an extended vacation with Erica's parents.

Erica sensed something was bothering Seth. "I haven't seen the boys in almost a month," he said. "Do you think they could come this *Shabbos?*"

They had been advised to take things in "stages." To have his two very young sons as weekend guests on their first *Shabbos* together in their own home seemed to be skipping a stage.

"Sure," she said.

Looking back now, from the viewpoint of many years, she could reel off deftly the mistakes she made that *Shabbos.* First of all, she should have said that as much as she wanted the boys to come, to give them the proper attention she needed another week to get used to her own home. That not said, she should have realized that Seth's mind would be on his kids, not on her cooking, and she should have *bought* prepared *Shabbos* food, rather than making challahs, gefilte fish, soup, chicken, cholent, kugels, and cake from scratch, as her mother always did. We learn from our parents, but flexibility is also a virtue. Erica was an experienced cook, but the stress of working in a new kitchen, and pleasing a new husband, took its toll. Her challahs hardly rose, her cake sulked and sunk, she put too much sugar in the kugel and too much water in the soup. She scorched the first batch of fish, and had no time to put up more.

Years later she had insight into this *Shabbos*. In the midst of her volunteer work for a well-established charitable organization, the salaried director become ill, and Erica had agreed to fill in for the rest of the project. She gave it her best, and the project was so successful that the grateful organization insisted—*insisted*—that Erica accept a handsome payment for her efforts. Sheepishly, she brought the check home, and quickly recycled it to a charitable cause. From this experience she realized that to her success was not measured by a check from an office. Her pride was in what she could produce in her kitchen, and in how she ran her home.

That first *Shabbos* she did not feel that she was running her home particularly well. When the little ones arrived, tired, teary, and in need of tissues, things did not improve. Apparently, the boys had been awakened midnap to leave with their father. And they both needed diapering. "Are their diapers in their suitcase?" Erica asked Seth. The children had arrived with large suitcases.

The suitcases contained a zoo of stuffed animals, a set of giant Legos, a fleet of cars. A few articles of clothing. And two scanty diapers.

"I forgot about the diapers!" Seth exclaimed, bolting for the door. He had twenty minutes to go and come back before candle-lighting time.

The little boys were crying; their noses were running again. Were they really almost two and almost three? Malka was toilet trained by then. She had manners. She ate with a fork and spoon, as Erica remembered. She asked for permission before leaving the table. She put her own toys away, dressed herself, brushed her own hair. And if she wasn't doing those things then, she was certainly doing them now! Suddenly Erica realized that it had been years since she had had to deal with a baby. She didn't know which bawling, dirty-faced, runny-nosed, smelly little child to attend to first.

He ran out of the house for diapers. *She* should have run for the diapers. Suddenly she couldn't remember the boys' names. She was feeling delirious. When was Seth coming back?

He had been gone about two minutes. Time, Erica remembered reading somewhere, plays tricks on us when we are in a crisis.

She took a deep breath, asked the Compassionate One to help her have compassion on these two innocent babies who were in a sense half orphans for the weekend. She went to her linen closet and took a neatly folded, brand-new, embroidered soft white washcloth from the freshly painted shelf, dampened it with warm water, and gently wiped one dirty face. The child, still howling "Daddy!," was somewhat cried out by now and pushed her away with less than his original force. The older child, however, wouldn't let her touch him. Was he especially sensitive, she wondered, or had she gotten bad press? She chided herself for being suspicious. But what was she supposed to *do* with them? Their cries were loud enough to be heard on the street. What would passersby think? What if someone called public authorities, fearing child abuse? Seth had now been absent four minutes. For how long could children howl?

Erica escaped to the kitchen and poured each of them a glass of orange juice. They were still in the living room. If she brought the juice to them there, they might spill it on the carpet. "Please come and drink some juice," she suggested to them anxiously. They were beyond communication.

She drank the juice herself. Suddenly time flew and she had only minutes until *Shabbos*. She quickly arranged her *Shabbos* candlesticks, ornate, mirrorlike, sterling silver, large, and heavy to honor *Shabbos*. Near them she placed a smaller candlestick for Malka, according to the tradition that mothers light an additional candle for each child. Light is symbolic of spiritual light, and her Malka, she hoped, would increase the spiritual light in the world. A thought flew through her mind to light a candle for each of Seth's children, too. She had never read anything about this, but lighting a candle for them seemed like a nice gesture. Of course, their own mother no doubt lit candles for them herself. On the other hand, the children's father lived in this house, and they would be spending half of their childhood *Shabboses* here. How would they feel if Malka, and any other children that they might, please God, have, had a special candle lit for them, but these two had none? Erica recently had attended a *shiur* at Sarah Mandel's house and learned that light is symbolic of Torah. Women who are careful in lighting *Shabbos* lights will have children who are Torah scholars. Certainly, Seth would want that for his children. They also said that if you light *Shabbos* lights with a joyful heart, you'll be blessed with children who illuminate the world with the light of Torah, bring peace to Israel, and confer long life to everyone in the family. She wouldn't be able to light *Shabbos* candles with a completely joyful heart unless all of the children were included. Also, doing nice things for people makes you feel closer to them. In her breakfront was an extra pair of new candlesticks, a wedding gift from friends. She took them down and put two large candles securely inside, resolving to do as many nice things for the little boys as she could. She quickly put some coins into a *pushke*, a "charity box," which Seth had affixed to their living room wall, and lit her candles. How bright they were. She encircled them three times with her hands, covered her eyes, and said the blessing:

> *Boruch Atah Adonoy Eloheinu Melech Ha'olom asher Kidishonu b'mitzvosov v'tzivonu l'hadlik ner shel Shabbos Kodesh.*
>
> *Blessed are you, Lord our God, king of the universe, who has sanctified us with his commandments and has commanded us to light the shabbos lights.*

After saying the blessing over the *Shabbos* candles, she reached for her *techinah,* a book of heartfelt supplications that women have said throughout the ages at times of joy, stress, and devotion in general. After lighting *Shabbos* candles, Erica always read a special prayer from this book:

> *May it be Your will, my God and God of my fathers, that You should favor me, Erica, daughter of Leah, and my husband Seth, son of Zissel, and my daughter, Malka, daughter of Erica, and my husband's sons Hillel, son of Libby, and Jeremy, son of Libby, that you grant us and all of Israel a good and long life, that you remember us with blessing, salvation, and compassion, that You make our households complete, that You cause Your presence to dwell among us. Bless me to have wise and understanding children and grandchildren, who love and fear God. Help them to be people of truth, holy seed who cleave to God, who illuminate the world with Torah and good deeds, and who constantly serve the Creator.*
>
> *Please hear my prayer at this time, in the merit of Sarah, Rebecca, Rachel, and Leah, our mothers. Cause Your face to graciously shine so that we are saved, and illuminate our souls forever. Amen.*

Before closing the book, she flipped through it, and noticed toward the end a supplication for a stepmother:

> *Kind father.*
>
> *Your Holy Torah tells us that our mother Rachel was*
> *jealous of her sister Leah because Leah had children*
> *while she, Rachel, had none. You gave Rachel the inspi-*
> *ration to give her maidservant, Bilhah, to her husband*
> *Jacob, in order that she could raise Bilhah's children as*
> *her own. In the merit of bringing up her husband's chil-*
> *dren whom he had from another woman, Rachel was*
> *answered by having her own children.*
>
> *With this You showed us how great is the merit of*
> *bringing up stepchildren and treating them kindly. This*
> *merit is much greater than that of bringing up one's own*
> *children, because the attachment for one's own children*
> *is natural. Even animals have it. The hen raises her own*
> *chicks, but has no instinct to care for strange chicks, so*
> *she pecks at the stranger and chases it away.*
>
> *Raising stepchildren is a holy task. It shows a greater*
> *human feeling, higher than that of any other living crea-*
> *ture. The stepmother is likened to the ministering angel,*
> *and that is why her reward is so great. Therefore, You*
> *repay her with two great gifts. To Rachel You gave two*
> *righteous children, Joseph the Righteous, who sustained*
> *the tribes in Egypt, and Benjamin the Righteous, in*
> *whose portion was built the Holy Temple in the Land of*
> *Israel. She had naches, joy, without boundary in this*
> *world and in the next. So, kindhearted Father, purify my*
> *heart from all bad traits, especially anger and hatred,*
> *and plant in me goodheartedness and nobility. If my lot*
> *is to be that of a stepmother, at least let me be one of the*
> *good stepmothers that are a blessing to the world. Let me*

treat my stepchildren as my own children. Let me merit
to see from them and my own children much joy. Amen.

As Erica read the beautiful words of the *techinah*, she began
saying them with all her heart. It was a relief to know that she
wasn't alone in stepmotherhood. A relief to know that she
wasn't an evil person because she didn't feel instant natural
love for children another woman had given birth to. But she
could care for these children. With time and prayers, hopefully, she would come to love them.

They had fallen asleep on the floor, breathing heavily.
Otherwise the room was quiet. Erica looked up and saw Seth
standing in the doorway, holding a family-sized package of
Cuddles disposable diapers. Apparently, he was anticipating
many changes.

And he looked at her lovingly. "How good you are with
them. I see that they are sleeping."

Together they cleaned and changed the sleeping children
and tucked them into bed. How true it was that her natural
instincts, which had carried her through Malka's babyhood,
did not necessarily help her in attending to other children.

Over the weeks things did not improve. She and Malka
had been used to going out together on *Shabbos* day, and Saturday night had been her big, and usually only, night out with
Seth. Now every other weekend she could look forward to
staying home. Malka shared few interests with these little
boys, and was not happy to see them taking up so much of her
mother's time. And the boys seemed so unscheduled. They
insisted on staying up late, and then woke up in the middle of
the night at the most inopportune moments. They demanded
constant attention. If not from Seth, and often it was not from

Seth, for he would be at shul *davening*, then it all fell on her. Their toys did not stay in the toy room, and food also seemed to follow them everywhere. After they left, Erica would find their blocks, their Legos, their cookie crumbs and jelly stains in unlikely corners all week long. They left every bathroom they walked into a mess. Even *her* bathroom. She felt ashamed of herself, for she had never felt so possessive before. Although she would *never* have let Malka do these things, she couldn't set the same limits for someone else's children. To compete for her attention, Malka also was beginning to act like a baby. Well, Malka also had adjustments to make. She liked her new daddy very much. He left the house before she awoke, but returned just before her bedtime. He smiled at her, said she was so pretty, and gave her nice presents. He was a great addition to her life, he was the father she had always wanted. But these crybabies who were competing for her mother, and totally took over her new father, were something else. "If they have their own mother," Malka asked Erica, "why don't they stay with her?"

When the boys would finally leave, Erica was wiped out. It took her a good week to return to normal—and by then it was almost, again, *that Shabbos.*

After a number of weeks, Erica decided to visit Sarah's again. The week was parsha "Mikeitz," and she brought a few dozen jelly donuts with her to treat the group in honor of Chanukah. Sarah, needless to say, served latkes, the traditional potato pancakes, fried in oil. Mira, Sarah's kitchen helper, was frying them as the ladies walked in. Mira made delicious latkes. Sarah wasn't making these latkes, Mira was. And that in itself was the lesson that Erica learned from Sarah that week: It's okay to hire help.

Hire help! Why hadn't she thought of it before? She could hire someone to help in the kitchen and to clean up while she cared for the boys. Or better yet, since Erica enjoyed her kitchen, why not hire a *Shabbos* nanny for the boys!

A young woman from Russia who loved children turned out the be the answer to Erica's prayers. Bella romped with her charges, cooed to them, sang to them, cajoled them. She frolicked with them as though they were puppies, respected them as though they were kings. She kept them clean and neat and sweet and within boundaries. Every other week they tumbled into their father's house, boundless balls of energy in search of their new playmate. Erica could be relaxed and gracious, go visiting with Malka, and still have the pleasure of knowing that she was responsible for providing a delightful *Shabbos* for her husband's two small sons.

Erica looked around her. Most everything was packed now. She wasn't a person who held on to things. What was useful she used; what she could no longer use she gave away. If an item held fond memories, she'd snap a photo before finding it another home. Early on she had started special albums for Hillel and Jeremy. The boys loved perusing their own photo collections on rainy days. This helped them to feel at home in her home.

Yes, it did become easier as the boys grew. Easier, and also harder. Time and again she stepped back as Seth and Libby worked through "details" regarding the boys' educations. Which school. Which lessons. Which tutor. Which camp. Other problems arose. Should she or should she not accompany Seth to the boys' PTA meetings? What was her place at other functions where parents were invited to attend? To go, or not to go—she felt awkward either way. However, she decided from the beginning that it was not her comfort but Seth's that mattered most, and if he wanted her by his side, which he usually did, there she would be. She stood next to him, respecting his role as a father, quietly. She didn't involve herself. And it seemed to work that way.

Time flies. Years later now, parsha "Mikeitz" again. The boys have grown and need more space. A big backyard. A bigger bedroom. Room for their bikes and their workout equipment. They needed, Seth was certain, to move to the community of Lawrence, Long Island.

Erica wasn't so sure. Although there were a number of shuls in Lawrence, and religious people there, Lawrence was very much a land of exquisite houses and elite cars. Unlike Borough Park, every block did not house a yeshiva, little kosher food stores did not sprout at each corner, and Sarah's lunch and learn group was more than just minutes away. Lawrence had an upscale and admittedly secular pull. Home decorating, landscaping, entertaining could become overriding concerns. Most of Erica's volunteer work was here, in Brooklyn. As she wrapped up the last of her boxes, she realized that she was not entirely comfortable with this move. Was there really an advantage to leaving?

"A person's pleasure is his measure," Sarah continued, after giving Erica a warm greeting that week. "What we connect to shows us what we are, as we see from the story of Chanukah, and also from this week's parsha, 'Mikeitz,' which usually falls on Chanukah. You can be sure that if a parsha always comes during a particular special time, it has a deep connection with the events of that time as well.

"We discussed this relation last week, and this week we can take it a step further. We can ask, What were the odds that Joseph would come out of prison, that he would become prime minister and save the world from famine? What were the odds that the Maccabees would defeat the Greek super-power, and save the world from spiritual destruction? By nature, this was not a matter of odds—it was a clear impossibility! But Joseph and the Maccabees were connected to God—to his wisdom, infinity, and power, and this is what made them invincible and made them receptacles for His wonders.

"We also live in a time of wonders. A time when our land, *Eretz Yisrael,* has ironically been threatened with 'peace,' but we see again and again how our God protects us. This is all part of the 'birth pangs,' our sages tell us, of Moshiach.

"Because all Jews form one body, we all affect each other. Our *Tehillim,* our *mitzvahs,* our deeds of goodness and kindness affect Jews all over the world. Our spreading the Chanukah light here brings light to *Eretz Yisrael* as well.

"In fact, this is a lesson that we learn from the oil of Chanukah. The oil lasted for eight days, not only seven. What is the number eight? Six represents the physical world, which has six sides: north, south, east, west, up, and down. Seven, like *Shabbos,* represents the Godly within nature, the spiritual dimensions of our physical world. The physical world was created in six days, the seventh day is *Shabbos,* the day when our physically creative work is put aside and we rise to a higher level within the physical world. But eight is beyond nature. It is a miracle that has no natural explanation. The oil burned for eight days above the laws of nature. The number eight entirely transcends nature.

"During the eight days of Chanukah we remember that we also have the power to transcend nature. How? Chanukah is also related to the word '*chanukas,*' dedication, and '*chinuch*'—education. When we dedicate ourselves to a Godly education for ourselves and our children, we also unite with the power that transcends nature. Torah, by the way, is also compared to oil, which does not mix, but always rises to the top. When we saturate ourselves with Torah and its *mitzvahs*, we are above any opposition. We come out on top!"

Erica tried to think how this particular message applied to her. Not mixing in. That was something like her relationship with Seth's sons. She was there, near them, but also kept a respectful distance. She didn't mix in.

On the other hand, she realized, oil also saturates. By making sure that the boys' stay in her home was a pleasant one, she not only endeared herself to her husband, but she had become a part of the boys' lives as well. They asked for her, at times confided in her, introduced her to their friends. Like oil, she saturated; like oil, she came out on top.

She would stay on top in Lawrence as well, if she could only feel her sense of purpose there, something to hold on to that would help her to maintain—or better yet, increase—her spiritual strength. Meanwhile, she noticed Sarah's daughter Chana Leah approaching her. Chana Leah was probably in the midst of organizing the Chinese auction that funded the activities of her Inner Circle group.

"Mrs. Fine, we're putting together a brochure." Erica was familiar with the brochures, which were sent to thousands of homes. In the brochure each exquisite prize was so artfully pictured that you felt you already owned it. The brochures were a major factor in the success of the auction.

"We're looking for donors to help us cover our printing costs."

Erica nodded, whisked out her checkbook, and scribbled a check. Then she thought a minute, remembering several of her new acquaintances in Lawrence. "I think I know some women who can also help you with this."

As she spoke, a strange image filled Erica's mind. The many needy causes she was familiar with here in Brooklyn began to juxtapose themselves within the wide circle of new acquaintances who were welcoming her family to Lawrence. Two concentric circles, both urging her to join. She found herself between the two circles, not exactly part of either. Or, was she part of both? She seemed to be pairing off the members of one circle with members of the other—which was what her move to Lawrence could do. The move could enable her to be a liaison between the people of one community and the other. Yes, her involvement in charitable work could be even more powerful now, as she united with the very fine women she was meeting in Lawrence.

And wasn't this the ultimate victory over the Greeks? To take the beauty, sophistication, and abundance that was Greece, but to employ it for a Godly end. The time of Moshiach, she had learned, would be an era of great material wealth and comfort. These material blessings, however, would not be an end in themselves, but would rather give everyone the peace of mind needed to wholeheartedly serve their Maker. Now, as the messianic age dawns, it could be hastened by helping those who still lacked basic needs.

Erica helped herself to a serving of latkes, fried in oil. Oil, also symbolic of wealth, saturates all that it touches. Why not spread it to touch a little more? She began to think of other women she had met recently who would be interested in helping some very deserving groups that she knew.

It would be a good move.

9

Ora: Leadership with a Holy Vision
Parshas Vayigash

And Judah approached Joseph and said, "Please, your Highness, let me say something to you. Do not be angry with your servant for you are equal to Pharaoh. . . . Let your servant remain as a slave to my master instead of the lad."
—Genesis 44:18, 33

He [Jacob] sent Judah ahead of him . . . to prepare a house of study for Divine service. . . .
—Genesis 46:28

The discovery of Joseph's goblet "planted" in Benjamin's sack has stunned the brothers. They return to the palace, where Judah, in an emotional plea, asks to be accepted in Benjamin's stead, putting himself on the line to save his brother. His obvious repentance convinces Joseph that Judah bitterly regrets anguishing his father by allowing Joseph to be sold into slavery years before. He sees that all of the brothers regret their past and have reached the level of self-sacrifice to help each other.

Joseph can now reveal that he is their brother.

Later in the parsha, Jacob sends Judah to set up a house of learning in Egypt for when his brothers and their families arrive. Well aware that education is the foundation of Jewish life, Jacob would not transplant his family to Goshen until an educational system was already in place.

In high school, Ora Bloom had not been a serious student. She played her guitar, sang in the choir, wrote poetry—whatever allowed her heart to sing. A few years after graduation, however, she found herself searching. Some piece seemed missing from her life, and she felt that Brooklyn was an empty place.

She had remained close with Yael, her best friend from high school. In the midst of talking one day, Yael told her, "Do you remember my sister Batsheva? She moved to Far Rockaway. She gives classes there in a number of subjects, but her forte is psalms. So many people come to hear her, she can't believe it herself. Her place is packed." Ora did remember Yael's sister. Rebbitzin Batsheva Sofer had substituted in their class several times, and even from those few sessions she had left an indelible mark.

Ora resolved to visit Far Rockaway. On a bitter January morning she took the bus, in fact four buses, to sit in on Batsheva's class.

The class had just started when she walked in. "...sadness and depression," the *rebbitzin* was saying. "We can leave them behind. By means of song it's possible to open all the gates of heaven. Your life is a song, and everyone's song is unique. Let's sing the Twenty-third Psalm together before we go into the depth of the text."

She led them with a lilting melody. Ora didn't know what to make of this. Classes as she knew them revolved around straight textual readings and analysis. This "warm-up" kept her enraptured throughout the remainder of the session and inspired her to continue attending classes and further her own studies.

Rebbitzin Batsheva Sofer was the happiest person she had ever met. She hummed to herself as she did her chores. Ora witnessed this one Thursday afternoon when she had to drop a packet off at the *rebbitzin*'s home. She also observed that the *rebbitzin* enjoyed using her hands to prepare for *Shabbos*. She cut and chopped and diced and kneaded by hand, rather than by machine.

Through the *rebbitzin's* influence, Ora felt herself changing. She was beginning to access her soul through her intellect, and this intellectual connection opened channels to higher realms. Her learning satisfied her thirst for knowledge and gave spice to her life.

Sometimes she'd miss a bus and come to class so late that only ten or fifteen minutes of the session remained. No matter. To be there was still worthwhile. One day she decided to stay after the class, hoping to grab a word with the *rebbitzin*. She joined another student, who was also waiting to speak to her.

Ora noticed that before speaking with either girl, Rebbitzin Sofer went to a corner of her office to say a psalm. Later Ora learned that when the *rebbitzin* had to correct or reprimand a student, she first would say Psalm Fifty-one, imploring God to give her the right inspiration and words for the situation.

Rebbitzin Sofer became Ora's role model. She inspired Ora's daily reality check. Early in the morning or late at night, Ora would ask herself: Was she living up to the goal she had set for herself, to be a good wife, to do good for others, and to develop herself continually by being in a learning mode? With the *rebbitzin's* gentle face before her, she would plan strategies to guarantee that her answers to these questions would be "yes." It was a worthy thought, but not nearly so deep as the thoughts she would have a few years later, after a most significant event.

"I stand before You and thank You, eternal King, who has returned my soul to me. Great is Your faithfulness." Ora, now a mother and soon to be a grandmother, reached for the two-handled cup and poured water on her hands. Once. Twice.

Three times. As the cool water splashed over her fingertips she reflected, as she did every day, on the morning prayer she had just recited. According to the rabbis, sleep was a state of semi-death. You were physically alive, yes, but your soul wandered through other realms. With some of the soul transcending the body, you were not fully alive. And each morning, right after opening your eyes, before doing anything else, you thanked God for returning your complete soul to you and giving you life.

In childhood, Ora had rushed through these words in her haste to get the day going, rushing to breakfast, school, work, shul. After marriage, her destinations were different, but the pace wasn't. To work, to shop, to home, she rushed, a constant treadmill that gave no sign of slowing down, much less of stopping, to let her off and force her to face the great unknown.

Not so now. Now Ora took plenty of time in the mornings. The short phrase, the *modeh ani*, had become a meditation, an extended paean of gratitude—a celebration of her life that had been threatened years ago. That Tuesday morning she sat silently, coßntemplatively, before dressing slowly, preparing herself to leave for Sarah's.

Not a day went by when Ora didn't relive those traumatic moments that had set the spiritual—and physical—course for the rest of her life. She was twenty-seven, a carefree, new young mother, married just a little over a year, going about her daily life as a new being contentedly. Then all changed, literally overnight. She was transformed into a woman who never took anything, *anything*, for granted.

In the middle of the night she woke up, her body racked with pain, and vomiting, her clothing stained scarlet, a terrifying alert that this was no ordinary stomach flu. Something was wrong, terribly wrong. The family physician immediately took charge. He ordered an ambulance to rush her to the hospital, where a specialist in a green mask and gown awaited her in the emergency room.

Years later, Ora could remember each detail of that ambulance ride. Her worry for her baby. Their neighbor, Mrs. Kagen, a kindly aproned woman who had cared for six children of her own, was watching him, but how would the baby take to a stranger? Would the Kagen children be careful with him? He was still so young, and had never even seen a bottle. Would he drink from one now? Or would he fret and be hungry? And what about her husband, Benjamin, sitting so solemn and still beside her in the ambulance, a book of psalms open in his lap. Who would take care of him if something happened to her? And what about herself? She was afraid. She always had believed in God. She *davened,* of course, she accepted the teachings and principles of the Torah. Yet her belief had been distant and theoretical. She had never taken the time to develop a deeply personal relationship with the Almighty. But now—now perhaps she was standing before the divine throne, facing God Himself. What would that mean? Would God find her worthy? What lay beyond death?

The sirens wailed as her ambulance picked up speed. Ora closed her eyes. "Please," she prayed, "let me live. I will never take life for granted again. I will do something every minute to make my life a sanctification of Your Name."

She took the book of psalms from Benjamin and opened to Psalm 23. "What I am bringing upon you is not to destroy you but to educate you." Weakly she closed her eyes again and smiled. The verse was the answer to her prayer. She knew she could accept whatever was God's will. But somehow she also knew that she would live. And this experience educated her.

She now saw the world in new ways; her new purpose was to bring the presence of God into the world. Words from another psalm tumbled into her fading consciousness: "I will not die, but will live to tell of the works of God." She was not alone, and she would not die.

And so she lived.

She had nephritis, an abscess located directly on her right kidney, the doctor informed Benjamin as Ora was whisked off for surgery. The damage to the kidney was so extensive that it had to be removed. Even the other kidney had suffered. Another pregnancy could endanger Ora's life again. Ora was sent home to raise her child, and to rejoice in her second chance at life.

True to her resolve, Ora set about teaching Torah. She became an organizer. She arranged small classes throughout Borough Park, to teach young Russian Jews about their heritage. A basement here, a living room there became her classrooms. Once she even arranged for a group to meet in the cloakroom of a shul! She started by teaching these ignorant but eager young women how to light *Shabbos* candles. The pleasure on the faces of her students was palpable. "Taste and see that the Lord is good," said Ora to one class, quoting Psalm 119. "No one can explain with words how an apple tastes. Or how a chocolate bar tastes. You can say 'sweet.' But that doesn't explain why so many of us prefer chocolate to apples." There was a ripple of laughter as a few girls pinched their waistlines and giggled. "You have to try for yourself. No one can express in words how delicious *mitzvos* are. You just have to see."

Eagerly, her students "saw" for themselves. Ora invited them for *Shabbos* meals and also arranged for them to be invited to the homes of friends. Reva, Tamar, Tova, and Sarah all hosted "Ora's girls," as they became known. Eight already had married wonderful yeshiva students, with Ora and Benjamin looking on, their eyes brimming with tears and pride.

Yes, they were able to help some of the girls to establish fine Jewish homes. Yet Ora and the women who worked with her also assisted these women in other ways, directing them to the community services best able to meet their needs.

One of Ora's favorite success stories involved Bella Maslova and her "handicapped" daughter.

Bella was one of the women who showed up at Ora's *sukka* party during the intermediary days of the holiday of Sukkos. She was an attractive woman in her midthirties, although her face looked older than her years. What struck Ora immediately was that Bella was pushing a six-year-old child in a baby stroller. The child could neither speak nor walk.

"Mrs. Bloom, maybe you know someone who can help my daughter walk." She showed Ora a packet that she had brought with her from her former home in Tashkent, in Asian Russia, northeast of Afghanistan. The packet contained medical reports from Russian doctors, all claiming that the child would never be able to walk, that she should be institutionalized. America was Bella's one hope. Yet even here she couldn't find help. She couldn't even find a school to accept her daughter. All doors seemed closed.

Ora had replied, "I think I know some people who can help you." She immediately set in motion a team of concerned women who directed Bella to the special education that her daughter needed, as well as medical services.

The dedication of one woman particularly impressed Bella. Mrs. Fayerstein accompanied Bella to Mt. Sinai Hospital, then to another site for further tests. For the entire year Mrs. Fayerstein escorted Bella and her daughter for weekly therapies—and even picked up the tab for the car service.

"When I approached Mrs. Bloom that day I was feeling

hopeless. She seemed to be my last chance," Bella will tell anyone who will listen. Slowly but surely her daughter began to walk and talk. Now, seven years later, she's a junior high school student who walks home giggling with her friends.

Bella, ever wanting to help her child, worked ceaselessly to get a degree in occupational therapy. Always grateful, she credits Ora for giving her and her daughter life. But Ora wouldn't take the credit. "It was a group effort," she replied. "And God is the conductor."

As upbeat as Ora is about the progress of the women she works with, there are inevitable disappointments. There was, for example, the tragic day when a woman from the neighborhood was killed in a plane crash, leaving two school-age children. The father and children were helped as much as possible to cope with their loss. However, when Ora tried to convince the father to send his children to a Hebrew day school, he was not interested. As much as Ora stressed the smaller classes and personalized teaching of the day school, and assured the father that his son would not become a rabbi, but only learn about the history, culture, and traditions, as well as mastering the English language—for even religious subjects were taught in English—her arguments fell on deaf ears.

In her heart of hearts Ora knew that the children would thrive in the day school. She wanted the best for them. At the same time, she and the other women didn't diminish their other efforts on behalf of the family. It seemed in a sense that they were her children. Sometimes one sees fruit, and sometimes not, but just as a parent never gives up, Ora and her friends never stopped trying either.

These were Ora's spiritual children.

But Ora had another set of "children"—her poems.

Reva felt as though her head was filled with cotton wool. Her husband had been in pain last night, and she hadn't slept much. Fruitlessly she had tried to find the correct combination of pain medication, ice packs, and distraction to bring him some relief. At last, toward dawn, he had slipped into a fitful sleep—just minutes before she was scheduled to get up.

Bleary-eyed, she stumbled down the stairs and poured herself some coffee. Yes, she knew caffeine was unhealthy. In fact, she had battled with Moshe to give up *his* coffee. "If you know something is bad for you, why do it?" she had argued with him. She had cited chapter and verse to prove the nasty effects caffeine has on the stomach and heart. She had argued until she convinced herself. Reluctantly, she had given up her favorite coffee and cola.

But not today. A person had to live a little, feel a little energy, right? Tonight, God willing, she would sleep. She would pick up Moshe's prescriptions for a new painkiller and, hopefully, they'd both sleep. Tomorrow she wouldn't need the coffee. Today, she'd pour herself a second cup.

As she sipped, she thumbed through the mail. Three bills from the hospital, one from the anesthesiologist, another from the physical therapist, and also one from the insurance company. Why did she look through the mail at breakfast, she wondered, biting into a rice cake. It was a great way to grow ulcers.

Then her eyes fell on an envelope with familiar handwriting. A letter from Ora! She snatched it up, and slit it open with her knife.

Trust Ora to intuit when Reva needed cheering up. Trust Ora to reach out. She read Ora's latest poem:

But those obstacles were His *wishes.*
It's all in the great plan

> *As buffing produces diamonds*
> *So do obstacles polish a man.*

And the next lines, entitled "The Storm Will Bring Blessing."

> *And finally when the sun shines*
> *And the clouds are there no longer*
> *We see how He has blessed us*
> *And the storm has made us stronger.*

Reva taped the poem to her refrigerator. Dear Ora. Poems
flowed from her pen like water from the rock that Moses hit.
No, Reva thought. The poetry didn't flow from Ora's pen. It
flowed from the very depths of her soul, revealing the wisdom
of her *neshomah.*

Ora's poetry also flowed from her kidneys. Kidneys, according to the rabbis, were the source of advice. And her dis-
eased kidney certainly had given her wise advice! Gratitude,
love of life, love of God. All of that was expressed in her poetry.

Not everyone regarded Ora's poetry with the same rever-
ence that she, Reva, did. "Mixed metaphors," Shaina had said,
"that jingle like a greeting card."

Reva had objected. "You're looking for the esoteric and
murky writings of Shakespeare or Agnon," she said. "You've
been a student of literature. Maybe you have the soul of a *mis-
naged,* someone who—in the olden days—would have
opposed the simple fervor of the early Hasidim. But I believe
that the soul is something ultimately very pure. Like we say in
the morning prayer, the soul that God has given us is pure.
Purity is simpicity. It isn't complicated or complex and
doesn't require a Talmudic mind to unravel. It is like a sweet
melody played on a flute by a lowly shepherd."

Shaina had nodded, unconvinced. But Reva stood firm.

Ora's poetry came from a soul that shone and sparkled, having been cleansed and polished by pain. Ora, like her name: a light. A light for herself and for others.

Ora and Reva sat next to each other at Sarah's today. Ora gave her friend's hand a little squeeze as the women filled their plates and made their way to their seats. "Remember when we used to sit next to each other in school?" Ora whispered.

Reva nodded. "How could I forget?"

"You know, I couldn't believe it the day I saw you at Sarah's for the first time. Marvelous! After all those years to come across you again."

"And I couldn't believe your story! Your illness, and how your life had changed."

They both sat silent for a few moments, remembering, until Sarah cleared her throat and began.

"Can you imagine what it was like in that throne room as Jacob's sons faced the prime minister of Egypt? The recriminations! 'We shouldn't have sold him. We're paying for it now.' They spoke in Hebrew, not knowing that the prime minister was in fact their brother who understood every word," Sarah said. "Imagine you were Joseph's brothers. How do you feel? You know you've done something very wrong. You've betrayed your family. You've sold your brother into slavery because you were jealous of the attention your father gave him. Who could live with himself?"

"Aren't we told that the shame that they felt when Joseph finally reveals himself is exactly the same as the shame we all will feel when, after a hundred twenty years, our lives are played back for us, and we are confronted with our sins—like a video playback," said Faygi.

Sarah nodded. "Actually, the rabbis say that Jacob was

wrong to discriminate among his children. A person should never treat one child differently from the others. But, of course, that doesn't excuse the brothers. So, here they are, with their guilty consciences, facing the most powerful figure in all of Egypt, who seems to have a personal vendetta against them! They hadn't seen Joseph since he was a teenager being sold into slavery. They certainly don't recognize him now, an adult, bearded, and the viceroy of Egypt. Joseph gave no hint that he intended to benefit his brothers and heal the family. The brothers saw only a vengeful tyrant, and they thought they knew the reason. 'We are guilty because we heard our brother's cries for mercy and didn't listen to them,' they said to each other. They thought that their crime had caught up with them at last.

"And here," said Sarah, "is the part that every parent and teacher should pay attention to! When a child acts up or acts out, what should we do? What should we think? That this is a bad child, who should behave and be quiet? That's what the brothers thought about their younger brother, Joseph. He acted up. He made a big deal about his dreams. He was a tat-tletale. He made a point of combing his hair—and he flaunted his coat, which symbolized that he had been chosen to lead his brothers. What the brothers should have under-stood was that Joseph was motherless, and his father had to give him double attention. When a child acts up, there's a rea-son. He needs the attention for something! We'd better not ignore our acting-up kids, better not throw them in a pit. We need to figure out their real needs—or we'll be sorry too."

"Now, back to the brothers. They are remorseful, wishing they had listened to Joseph's cries and seen his pain, and they stand there, trembling before the tyrant—and suddenly he is smiling at them! He's saying all will be well if they'll only turn over Benjamin."

"It was a test," Ora said. "Joseph wanted to see if the brothers had learned anything about loyalty during the years since they sold him into slavery. He also wanted to know about Benjamin—who was Rachel's son, just like Joseph was. Were they mistreating Benjamin as badly as they had mistreated him? Would they be jealous of Benjamin, the way they were jealous of Joseph?"

"Whatever comes up in the Torah, we always find some way to call it a test," said Levana.

"That's because everything in the world is a test," said Tamar. "The universe is just a huge school, where every part of our education is accompanied by tests. The Torah is the textbook, and God is the great Teacher. Illness, sadness, even wealth and happiness—all of these are nothing but tests."

Sarah nodded. "True. In fact, one way of understanding the book of Genesis is that each of our ancestors was undergoing a series of challenges. How they handled these tests not only determined the rest of history, but also shows us how we can overcome difficult situations in our own lives."

"Well, the brothers sure were in a mess," Debra commented.

"They were quaking in their boots," agreed Sarah, "while the viceroy gives them a simple, cruel command. Joseph planted his personal silver goblet in Benjamin's luggage to frame Benjamin. Now Joseph claims he must detain the supposed thief, although the rest of the brothers can go home in peace. But to return without Benjamin would be devastating for their father, Jacob, who was still grieving the disappearance of Joseph. Judah has the solution. A leader, and true hero, Judah steps forward and offers himself instead of Benjamin."

"What groomed Judah to become such a leader?" Shaina asked.

"First of all," Sarah replied, "Judah had been through his

share of personal pain. His son, Er, died. Since Er was child-less, his younger brother Onan married Er's wife, Tamar, according to the commandment of *yebum*. This *mitzvah*, which requires that when a childless man dies, his widow marry his brother, was customary even before the Torah was given to the Jewish people. By fulfilling this *mitzvah*, the fam-ily name will be continued, and the *neshomah* of the deceased will reappear. Onan, however, wasn't interested in perpetuat-ing his deceased brother's family name, and refused to prop-erly consummate his marriage with Tamar. For this sin, God punished him and he also died. Now, twice widowed, Tamar was left waiting for the youngest son, Shelah, to grow up and marry her.

"Time passed," Sarah continued, "and Shelah became an adult, ready for marriage. Judah, however, made no move to arrange the wedding. Seeing no alternative, Tamar finally planned to bring her predicament to the attention of her father-in-law in an unheard-of way. She disguised herself as a prostitute and allowed Judah to sleep with her. She kept his staff. Later she revealed her pregnancy. Judah was outraged. For being intimate with a man outside the bonds of wedlock, his daughter-in-law, bound by the laws of *yebum*, deserved to die.

"At the risk of her life, Tamar would not embarrass Judah. She sent the staff to him, with the message that the owner of that staff was the father of her child. Judah recognized the staff. Could he judge her? He had neglected his responsibility toward her! And he admitted it. Owning up to shortcomings and accepting responsibility are major aspects of leadership."

Ora was silent. Before her illness she, too, had had her shortcomings, which had become obvious to her during that terrifying ambulance ride to the hospital. Until then, she had taken so much for granted—her own health, the people that she loved. She had not led a sinful life, but she had led an unthinking life. Like Judah, she had been wrapped up in herself. Judah had been engrossed in his own life and business. After all, the story with Tamar occurred during the season for shearing sheep—perhaps that was why he neglected his widowed daughter-in-law, a yearning, bereaved lonely woman who depended on him. He probably feared for Shelah as well. After all, he didn't want to lose his third son. But Tamar's pregnancy had been Judah's wake-up call, just like Ora's illness had been her own catalyst for change.

And, like Judah, she had been catapulted into a position of leadership.

"T'shuva—turning, returning, is what we are talking about here," Sarah concluded.

Klara said, "Maybe this is why the kingship was given to Judah. It was from his tribe that King David descended."

"Exactly," Sarah said. "Later in the story, when Jacob was bringing his entire family to Egypt, he sent Judah ahead. Why? To establish the houses of learning. On his deathbed, Jacob described Judah as a 'lion.' He said, 'the rod'—meaning the scepter of leadership—'shall never depart from Judah.' It was a prophetic statement, indicating that the kingship was destined to come from the tribe of Judah."

Ora had a sudden inspiration. "Maybe that's why we always read the Torah sections dealing with the story of Judah around the time of Chanukah. Chanukah is also about leadership—and the hero of Chanukah was also a Judah—Judah Maccabee. His courage and vision saved the Jewish people from the Greeks. He was willing not only to fight, but to lead. His battle cry was 'Whoever is for God should follow me!'"

"That's your battle cry, too," Reva commented to Ora. "You with your outreach groups."

"There's a fire out there," said Ora. "I know I'm not a fireman, but I do think of myself as a lamplighter. We can't just sit. We have to do something." Ora blushed. "Anyway, that's what the Alter Rebbe said. We should all be lamplighters."

"You're just being modest," said Reva, tapping her friend on the arm.

Ora mused that Chanukah, the Festival of Lights, celebrated the small flask of oil that miraculously burned for eight days. The *rebbe* stressed how Chanukah showed us the importance of increasing light, as when we light an additional light on the the menorah for every night of Chanukah. Ora also had started small. When she encouraged the young women in her learning groups to light *Shabbos* candles, they enjoyed a simple, pleasurable *mitzvah*. In the soothing glow of the candles, they sensed their souls; as our sages tell us, the soul is likened to a candle of God. They came back for more.

Light creates energy. This inspires another *mitzvah*, which creates more energy and light. So the sages say "one *mitzvah* leads to another."

"Moshiach, the messiah, will come from the tribe of Judah," Yehudis said.

"That's right," Sarah nodded. "But do you know who will lead the people at the time of Moshiach?"

Ora glanced up at a burnished copper wall-hanging of Miriam, the prophetess, Moshe's sister, leading a group of women in a dance. The faces of the women shone like gold as they held their tambourines. "Yes," Ora smiled. "The women. The rabbis say that it was the women in Egypt who kept the faith and insisted on having babies, even though the situation seemed hopeless. Had it been up to the men, the Jewish people would have died out. And at Mount Sinai, it was the women who refused to participate in the sin of the golden calf."

The women concurred with affirmatory nods, and a few "you bets."

"We give birth to the kids," said Yehudis.

"We diaper them, too!" This from Iyelet.

"We work, we clean, we cook, we comfort," Reva finished. "We do all that because we have faith. The future is in our hands."

"And it was Miriam who led the women in a celebratory dance after the splitting of the Red Sea," Sarah said.

"You know," Ora mused, unable to let go of the Judah story. "This goes right back to the story of Tamar. Her desire to marry Shelah and bear children wasn't only because she was lonely and wanted male companionship. This was *her* vision for the future. Her knowledge of the importance of continuing the family of Judah. And if she hadn't—if she had let Judah continue to be oblivious to her predicament—she never would have given birth to the ancestor of King David, who was the ancestor of Moshiach. This woman saved the day!"

There was a pause in the action while everyone took in this point.

"And look what happened to her," Glicka said, a sudden darkness in her voice. "Tamar risked her life. Judah wanted to have her killed. And then, when she was giving birth, she actually did die."

Another silence.

"Tamar had courage," Reva said. "Women are willing to do whatever it takes in the name of our vision to fulfill our role and destiny."

Ora thought again of that night in the ambulance. She had been scared, yes. She had wanted to live. But she knew now—it came to her in a rush of insight—that if it had been her time to die, God forbid, she would have gone willingly. The willingness to die for God had given her the clarity and courage to live for God. And that was the secret of Judah Maccabee.

Without planning, without even thinking about it, Ora began to sing. Rachel joined in. Then Glicka, Levana, Klara, and even Mrs. Blisme began to sing. Sarah, Reva, and all the others joined in a soulful melody that seemed to break through barriers of time and space.

Torah reports that at Mount Sinai the Jewish people "saw the sounds." Ora understood that now. You could see the light of Chanukah in the song of the women.

10

Sarah: The Ingathering, the Life, the Blessings
Parshas Vayechi

May the angel who has redeemed me from all evil bless these lads, and let them be called in my name, and in the name of my forefathers, Abraham, Isaac, and Jacob, and may they multiply in the land.
> —Genesis 48:15

And Jacob called his sons and said, "Gather together and I shall tell you what will happen to you at the end of days. . . ."
> —Genesis 49:1

Throughout the ages, it has been a sacred custom to bless one's children on Shabbos evening. As the father places his hands on the child's head, he pronounces a blessing reminiscent of parshas "Vayechi": "May God make of you as Ephraim and Menashe," he blesses his sons. "May you be as Sarah, Rebecca, Rachel, and Leah," he blesses his daughters.

Jacob was about to reveal to his children the time of the redemption, the time when the exile would end, when suddenly prophecy was concealed from him. Why? Perhaps because, at that time, his children would be discouraged by the length of the exile. In our generation, however, the signs of immediate redemption are obvious: the overnight fall of the Soviet Union, the ingathering of more than a million exiles to the holy land, the *throngs of Jews returning to their roots in Torah, as well as an increase in serious spiritual questing among non-Jews. As the Lubavitcher Rebbe has quoted, "The time of your redemption has arrived."*

For us it is not a question of how long will this exile last, but how soon will redemption come.

It was Tuesday.

They were all gathered around her table. Her "regulars," she called them. She could not see them as her students. After all, who was she to consider herself their teacher? They had taught her so much more than she could ever teach them. Often she recalled the phrase from *Ethics of the Fathers:* "I have learned more from my students than from anyone else. From all my students I have gained wisdom."

So who were these women? They were her teachers, then? Her friends. A constellation of stars, a network of precious souls with whom she was privileged to share the holy words and teachings of the Torah. All these friends, their bright eyes shining like *Shabbos* candles, fixed upon her. Sarah. Waiting for her to speak.

Had someone told Sarah when she was a teenager that one day she would be regarded as a leader in the community of women, that people would whisper about how she was a *tzaddekes*, a righteous woman, an angel, an *eyshes chayil*, a woman of valor, she would have laughed. "Why, me?" She would have waved her hand dismissively—a gesture that would have been graceful, even elegant, as all of Sarah's physical gestures were. She would have laughed and changed the subject.

And not from modesty either. Sarah had been neither scholarly nor community-minded. In fact, she always had been a private person. She was closest with her younger sister,

Leah, who lives now in Rochester, and her older sister, who lives in Safed, Israel. They still talk every day. "The middlest" child, she used to call herself—number five of nine children— Sarah spent her childhood summers wandering in the Catskill woods near her summer house as often as she could escape from the seemingly endless household activities and chores. She had found a little spot all her own—a tiny thicket that, in her child imagination, she had named "the Garden of Eden." A blessed little spot, surrounded by arching willows, a tiny brook babbling its way along.

A place to *daven*. A place to sing quietly. A place to meet God, Who lived here more vividly than in the classroom, or in the dining room where her father, a staunch and passionate Lubavitcher Hasid, shared Torah insights with his family. She felt closer to God here—even more so than in shul, although she had never admitted this to anyone. She imagined herself growing up and marrying someone who learned Torah and loved the outdoors as she did. Who knew? She would find some place where religious men worked the land and also learned. She would till the soil, too, and gather berries in the woods with her own children one day.

As she grew older and people began to suggest *shidduchim*, Sarah cringed. Every time someone mentioned a "fine yeshiva fellow" from a good family, she didn't want to know the details, and would answer, "God willing, at the right time." At her older sister's wedding, her aunts had clucked, *"God willing by you"*—their wishes that God would also soon send her a nice young man. She shrugged and fell silent.

But God had something—someone—in store for her. Sometimes, with a little smile, she would tell her friends that "God had a trick up His divine sleeve." And He did, although she didn't suspect it when it happened. She had anticipated no more than an ordinary plane trip. She and her mother had

gone to a Lubavitch women's midwinter convention in
Florida, and they also had visited with her classmate, Aliza,
and her family. Aliza's mother drove them to the airport for
the return flight. Every detail of this trip remained etched in
Sarah's memory. How a bored, mechanical-voiced ticket
agent announced that their flight was delayed. How Aliza's
mother waited with them in the airport. And how Aliza's
mother had spotted the handsome young man with the
yarmulke.

"Maybe you'll get to meet him," she said to Sarah. "You're
going on the same plane."

"I'm sitting next to my mother," Sarah had replied. They
were waiting in avocado-colored armchairs until the flight
attendant announced boarding time. Then the handle of her
carry-on broke, and she had to hoist the bag over her shoulder like a giant, misshapen baby. The aisle in the plane was
narrow. She made her way through, hoping to find room in
the overhead compartment for her luggage. Soon, she told
herself, she would be sitting in the window seat she had
requested, watching the earth disappear as she flew into a
world of clouds. She always looked forward to that part of the
trip. She stumbled down the aisle, looking for her seat.

Her window seat was not to be. A mix-up landed her in
the center aisle, while her mother was sitting two rows up. An
apologetic stewardess explained that the plane was packed,
and she couldn't switch the seat. Sarah swallowed her disappointment and decided not to make a fuss. Although she had
a right to demand the window seat, to make a nasty scene
would be a desecration of God's name. It would show an
observant person in a bad light.

She stashed her bag, pulled out her book of *Tehillim*, and
was about to open it, when she saw the young man with the
yarmulke standing next to her, checking his ticket. His seat

was next to hers. "Giving up the window seat took a lot of self-control," he remarked. "You look like someone who would enjoy the view when you fly. You probably didn't want to give it up." Then he quoted from *Ethics of the Fathers* in Hebrew: "Who is strong? Someone who conquers himself."

Sarah stared as the young man sat beside her. She noticed his fine, handsome face: high cheekbones, an ebony beard, kindly brown eyes. When he smiled his teeth were as white as the flour she used to bake challah. A tiny dimple played by the corner of his mouth, half hidden by his beard. His yarmulke was large, black.

He introduced himself. "I'm Daniel Mandel."

Sarah had been brought up not to speak to boys or men. There were no social mixers in her circles. Men and women met for marriage through *shidduchim* meetings, which were usually arranged by mutual friends or, occasionally, by match-makers. But there was something about this man that mysteriously called to her. Something that caused her to feel immediately at home in his presence.

"I'm Sarah," she said. "And you're right. I do love to look out the window. It was hard for me to give up that seat."

"I love looking out as well," he told her. "I look at the vast blue sky, endless and clear. Then I look at the land beneath. The little squares, no bigger than a pocket-sized prayerbook, which are really plots of farm land. The little dots that represent houses. Then, as the plane climbs higher, and everything gets even smaller, you see patches of brown and green with lines of blue running through them. Miles of land and rivers that look so small. Makes you think of how God sees us. How great and tiny the world is at the same time."

Could this yeshiva boy really feel the same as she did about nature? About natural beauty and scenery? "I feel that when I fly," she said. "I also feel that sometimes in the woods. I look at the great sky above, with all its clouds, and then at the tiny ants crawling around my feet. And I think, the same God made both of these."

They continued to talk until the plane landed. He told her about himself. Daniel—whose mother still called him by his secular name, Martin—came from St. Louis. He was attending Yeshiva Torah V'Daas in Brooklyn, and had been sent to Miami as a speaker representing the yeshiva. He would have stayed longer, but when the weather changed, he changed his plans, and was happy to get this flight back.

Sarah also told Daniel about her family. Her noisy, squabbling, loving siblings. Her serious and learned father, whose bylaw was that "being a Hasid is not only a privilege, but a responsibility." She told him about her mother, whose kitchen was always open to the hungry. "I can close my eyes and envision my mother ladling gigantic helpings of soup into the bowls for homeless people," Sarah said musingly. "Some of these people scared me when I was a child. They were all over our kitchen. Some of them were dirty, with holes in their clothing, and some had no teeth. But my mother always told me that no one will be hurt doing a *mitzvah*. On the contrary, we would be protected."

"Don't feel bad," Daniel comforted her. "I've heard that the great rabbi Hayyim Soloveichik, of blessed memory, allowed indigent and homeless people to sleep in his house. There were always unkempt people lying on the floor, under the kitchen table, even on the kitchen table. His grandson, Rabbi Joseph Soloveichik, of blessed memory, said that even he was scared of the characters he saw at his grandfather's house."

Sarah even found herself telling this stranger (who did not seem like a stranger at all) about her special spot in the woods. He responded by telling her how the Ba'al Shem Tov, the founder of Hasidism, spent many hours in the woods instead of at *cheder,* the children's school. "There is room for spiritual connection through nature," he told her.

Amazing. This man, steeped in his studies of Gemara, and not even from a Hasidic family, understood. He understood her, and he seemed to understand the heart of Hasidism—the immediacy of connection with God, the presence of God in everything, and Torah as a bridge between human beings and their Creator rather than as an end in itself.

As they stood next to the revolving luggage carousel, looking out for each other's suitcases, they knew their meeting was not mere happenstance. No coincidence. This was *bashert.*

Sarah left the airport with her luggage in her hand and Daniel in her heart.

When her father heard about the romance he was beside himself. Who ever heard of such a thing? That a girl from their family should meet a young man on an airplane and fall in love? Like any American? A *shanda!* Sarah was frantic. Daniel was the right one for her—she knew that—but she didn't want to bring pain to her father. Her fondest dream was to bring *naches* and joy to her parents, not grief!

It seemed an impossible situation. Tensions were mounting, with Sarah torn between her inner knowledge that Daniel was the right one for her, and her father's stern determination to see his daughter marry the sort of man he always had envisioned for her—and someone she would be introduced to in the proper manner.

Finally, Sarah's mother resolved the matter by suggesting a call to the Lubavitcher Rebbe. Distraught and prayerful, her father placed the call.

And here was the second miracle, Sarah always thought. Additional proof (as if she needed it) that Daniel was truly her *bashert,* her intended match. The *rebbe* said, "Let the *shidduch* be and accept it. I will double their blessings."

Sarah's father acquiesced and blessed the union of Sarah and Daniel—a marriage, Sarah knew, that was surely made in heaven.

Sarah smiled, remembering how quickly the *rebbe*'s blessings followed not only for her and her husband, but also for her parents. An abandoned factory in Brookfield, Pennsylvania, turned out to be an unexpected treasure trove. The little postwar boomtown that employed a handful of locals was otherwise deserted, and this factory was for sale. Sarah's father put down money ("a ridiculously tiny sum," he always said) and turned the old place into a thriving glatt kosher operation. It rapidly became one of the largest kosher food manufacturing plants in the world.

As the business prospered, Sarah's parents expanded their home to accommodate extended family as well as anyone else seeking lodging. The house was a palace, many remarked, complete with marble entry hall, beautiful carpets, and a magnificent library of Jewish books. But the only piece of artwork in the entire house was a life-size picture of the Lubavitcher Rebbe. No knickknacks. The house was beautiful in its austere simplicity.

Best of all, at least to Sarah's mother, were the many wonderful bedrooms where the homeless and the travelers could sleep in cozy, soft beds and awake to delicious breakfasts. The Resnicks already had opened Kesser Cuisine, a landmark restaurant among the hungry or lonely, who felt at home dropping in for an "on the house" after-hours meal. A cauldron of thick beef soup always simmered on the stove, and bread, freshly baked on the premises, was always abundant.

In their home every Saturday night, Sarah's parents hosted a *melaveh malkah,* a feast to bid farewell to the Sabbath Queen and escort her out of the house until the next week. Sarah and her siblings would light two candles as her mother would lay out bagels, lox, salads, and kugels. With warmth and love, they sang songs late into the night, bidding adieu to the sabbath bride.

Sarah married Daniel, and found him to be everything she had hoped for. Truly a soulmate. He was compassionate, kind, and committed to the same values that she held dear. He understood her and learned Torah with her. For the first time, Sarah felt no conflict between the natural beauty of the woods and the scholarly beauty of biblical commentators. She grew in learning and depth of understanding.

Her family was growing, too. Daniel was offered a position in Atlanta, and there Sarah had one child after another until her brood included five little ones under the age of six. A challenge! Especially since Daniel, fastidiously neat by nature, appreciated an orderly, elegant home. Sarah met that challenge by envisioning her home as a *mikdash me'at,* a miniature Holy Temple. When she cleaned, she imagined herself shining the menorah, the candelabrum in the Holy Temple, or dusting off the special altar. She pretended to be a high priestess and saw her children as assistants, their babbling, squabbling, and giggling all music of praise to their Creator. And in between diaper changes she snatched a few moments to read a short *midrash,* a rabbinic explanation of Torah episodes. She also learned *Hayom Yom,* a book of daily Torah thoughts compiled by the Lubavitcher Rebbe. Each day after *davening,* Sarah would connect with the energy of that day by reading that day's particular thought. As a time-oriented person, this gave her life daily focus.

So the children grew in a whirlwind of spiritual and physical activity, until Daniel accepted a job in Brooklyn. He was going to be the principal of the Beth Jacob School for Girls. Sarah was especially pleased that her husband would be involved professionally in the education of young Jewish women. At times she had wondered what her own childhood would have been like had she had a school principal like Daniel, with his depth, compassion, and commitment to women's study. His students would be lucky indeed.

The move to New York brought new challenges. A larger home, new social obligations, and, wonderfully, new children. Daniel became involved in the local and national Republican party. Sarah became well versed not only in Torah, nature, and parenting, but also in politics. She entertained her husband's colleagues and friends, throwing lavish dinners as well as parlor meetings.

A constant whirlwind. Exciting, yes, and sometimes fulfilling, but more and more, Sarah felt herself tired and lonely. Daniel was gone often. They had little time to learn together, and she had no time to be alone and just think. More and more she craved the solitude and silence of her wooded spot. She stepped out to visit a little "park" near her house, which boasted a patch of scuffy earth bordered by sparse, bare trees. Here sooty sparrows huddled near a dilapidated bench where young mothers paused to jiggle squeaking baby carriages as their toddlers poked sticks into the dirt. Sarah felt her energy level dropping.

Suddenly, things that she ordinarily did joyously seemed flat and dull, burdensome. She found herself snapping at her children. She pricked her finger when she sewed; she burned the rice and chicken. Once she actually dozed off during one of her husband's speeches to the Republican party. Fortunately, no one noticed.

Sarah realized that she was in a spiritual crisis. She tried to talk to Daniel, but the phone kept ringing, the children kept interrupting, and she gave up. Somehow she would have to find the answer—if there was an answer—inside herself. But how?

She hired a babysitter for the day and decided to find a

quiet spot to sit and think. Suddenly she remembered the botanical gardens.

Why not? Winter was edging into spring. The snowdrops were drooping already as bold crocuses and impetuous forsythia insisted that the world prepare for brighter times. Here she found what she needed to know: Silence is internal, a perspective that can be maintained even among the noisy. She remembered Nachmanides's commentary on the words in Deuteronomy: "Those of you who cling to God are alive today." To "cling to God," he explained, was an internal process. Precisely among others, in the marketplace, where there is commotion and bustle, one carries around that private connection with God. Like a secret, she understood. Like being in love, where the more difficult your outer world, the more rich and special your inner world.

But now she saw that this wasn't enough. While phones rang and babies cried and pots bubbled on the stove and toddlers fought with one another—under these conditions, to maintain serenity and hold that spiritual focus was hard. She needed an external support system. But what? And how? Then it came to her.

She was determined to share her idea with Daniel. "I want to take a day just to ourselves," she said that night. "I don't want to wait until the summer, when we take our walks in the Catskills. We need a recharge now."

Daniel noticed the determination—even anxiety—in her voice. He agreed to cancel his commitments for the next day and accompany her to the botanical gardens.

There they had one of the most important conversations of their lives.

"I hadn't realized how much of a toll my busy lifestyle has been having on you," he said thoughtfully. "I guess I didn't want to admit it, even to myself. I'm sorry."

Sarah nodded. "I need some more personal spiritual connection and interaction," she said. "Yes, *d'veikus,* clinging to
God, is an inner state. But it's easier when you're in a con-
ducive environment with others. You know, Tamar and I
sometimes learn together. We both have big families and
responsibilities, and learning gives us both a spiritual booster
shot. There must be other women like us. I was thinking of
starting a women's learning group. I'm going to write to the
rebbe for a blessing."

"What a wonderful idea," he answered.

"I like it, too."

And so the Tuesday learning group was conceived. And,
like her household, it grew and kept growing.

Now, so many years later, Sarah sat facing the upturned
faces of her learning group. The women here felt like her
mothers, her daughters, her friends, her angels.

"The rabbis tell us that when Jacob gathered all his sons
around him and said he wanted to tell them about the end of
days, he really wanted to tell them what life would be like during the time of the Moshiach, during the messianic era," she
began. "But God wasn't ready to have this type of information
revealed, so as Jacob was about to speak, the Spirit of God, the
Shechina, departed from him and he lost his gift of prophecy.
Instead he spoke to his sons about themselves, their personalities, their lives, and their destiny, with only veiled hints of
messianic times."

Sarah looked at the women gathered around her. What,
indeed, had Jacob felt, watching the expectant faces of his
sons? What was it like to know their fate and future, yet to be
unable to share it with them? Fortunately she, Sarah, was not
a prophetess. She knew no more than any other mortal about
the future. But she did understand what it felt like to have no
easy answers, to have a group of eager faces just waiting for

solutions to the greatest problems, and to have nothing to offer but, perhaps, advice.

"I often ask myself why God didn't permit Jacob to reveal the future," Sarah continued.

"I'll tell you what my six-year-old daughter said," commented Iyelet. "She came home from school one day and announced, 'I want to be a *neviah*, a prophetess, when I grow up!' She made it sound like a normal career option, like being a doctor or a lawyer." A ripple of laughter passed through the room. When it died down, Iyelet continued. "Then she became serious. 'But it might not be such a good idea,' she said, 'because then there wouldn't be any surprises. And what would I do on my birthday?'"

Sarah smiled, then picked up on a serious vein. "Your daughter has a point. When we don't know the future, all possibilities are open. Everything that lies ahead is one great big surprise. We are asked to trust God, without really knowing what He has in mind for us. If we knew everything, there would be no challenge, no mystery."

"But imagine if we could know just what it would be like when Moshiach comes," said Levana wistfully.

"Imagine that we knew *when* he would be here already!" said Ora.

"We have to believe he's here, any minute," Reva added, "and at the same time we have to do all that we can to improve our current situation. And that's hard. I mean, when we know a situation is temporary, do we really try as hard to fix it? Imagine I knew for *sure* that my husband would be well next week. Would I work on myself as hard as I do now to understand him? To take care of his needs? I've grown so much because of his illness. Would that growth have taken place if someone, even God himself, had patted me on the head and reassured me that this was just for a few more days?"

"If I knew that Chana and Dovid would run and talk and think like other children by next week, or even next year," added Shaina, "I wouldn't be making sure they had so much therapy now."

Sarah nodded. "It's really true. The work we have to do to bring Moshiach is difficult. We'd likely do less if we knew that we'd be greeting Moshiach on such and such a day, no matter what we left undone."

"How could we face Moshiach knowing we left work undone?" asked Faygi.

"What work undone?" grumbled Mrs. Blisme. "If that work involves doing goodness and kindness, we're surely doing that, did that, done that, and Moshiach should be here right now, from yesterday!"

Sarah nodded. "Yet we don't see that Moshiach is here. There must be something more we have to do. Let me tell you a story, though some of you already know it, which took place at the time of the second temple. There were two bitter enemies. One was named Kamza, and the other's name isn't mentioned in the Gemara, so we'll just call him Mr. Party, because he threw a big party. He had a friend named Bar Kamza, whom he invited, but the invitation by mistake was delivered to his archenemy, Kamza. because, well, their names were very similar.

"I guess the post office messed up the mail even back then," someone said.

"I know about that," commented Mrs. Blisme's friend Ida. "We're always getting the mail of the other Goldmans who live upstairs. He's Nathan Goldman, only one 'n'. My late husband's name was Nathan Goldmann, of blessed memory. Two 'n's."

"Kamza was overjoyed to receive the invitation," Sarah continued. "He thought that Mr. Party was ready to make up with him. He came to the party, very happy. But Mr. Party was not happy to see him. He was angry, and demanded that Kamza leave."

"Poor Kamza," someone said.

"Yes, and Kamza begged to be allowed to stay, but Mr. Party refused. Kamza pleaded, 'Please, don't embarrass me in front of all these guests. I know many of them. And there are also important rabbis present. Please don't make me leave. I'll even pay for the drinks!' Mr. Party refused. 'I'll pay for half the party!' begged Kamza. 'I'll pay for the whole party!' Mr. Party refused and pointed to the door."

"Do we even know what they were fighting about?" asked Erica.

Sarah shook her head. "That's the thing about fights. We remember the bad feelings, but often we don't even remember what started it."

Many of the women nodded. "Nathan and I had fights like that," mused Ida Goldmann.

Sarah wanted to get back to the story. "Kamza looked around and saw that none of the other guests, including the important rabbis, had stepped forward to stand up for him. No one told Mr. Party that embarrassing someone in public is considered as bad as killing him. No one said, 'Please, let this man stay.' So Kamza became embittered and vindictive. He went to the Romans and gave them information that ultimately led to the destruction of the Holy Temple in Jerusalem and to exile.

"So it was causeless hatred that led to the destruction of the Temple," said Sarah. "And only causeless love, unconditional love, will lead to its reconstruction. I know that the *rebbe* said that the road that will take us to greet Moshiach is paved by acts of unconditional love."

"But how do we find strength to do that?" Levana asked.

"How do we find the strength to love someone who has hurt or betrayed you? Or a person who has injured someone you love?"

"We have to tap in," Sarah replied. "Everything, everyone, is ultimately an agent of God. When God wants to speak to us, he does so through the agency of natural phenomena. Sometimes these are events that happen in the material world, such as rain, or sunshine, a car accident, or a financial setback. People are God's agents."

"You mean the mailman isn't responsible for delivering the letter to the wrong address?" asked Ida.

Sarah gave a short laugh. "Yes, but you wouldn't blame the mailman for the contents of the letter, right? So we can't blame others for their actions. They are simple messengers of God. Not only should we not blame them, but we should even be grateful to them!"

Mrs. Blisme's eyebrows shot up. "We should be grateful when someone isn't nice to us? We should be grateful for their ingratitude? When my daughter-in-law doesn't thank me for putting aside my whole evening to babysit for her children, I'm supposed to be grateful for her ungratefulness?"

"Exactly," Sarah nodded vigorously. "Because your daugher-in-law is God's messenger. Maybe she's there to remind you to be grateful to God, to remind you how it feels when someone isn't so grateful. Maybe she's there to inspire you to do a good deed, without hope of recompense."

Sarah paused as she saw the front door swing open. There was Sheila, who hadn't been to the group for months. Her husband had passed away a few weeks ago. Sarah stopped everything, ran to Sheila, and enveloped her in a huge, warm embrace. The women made a place for Sheila to sit near Sarah, and Sarah asked her to read.

"You're pushing me, Sarah," said Sheila.

"I know," Sarah replied. "Here. It's a beautiful story about the Ba'al Shem Tov."

"One year," Sheila began, "weather conditions destroyed the *esrog* crop. Jews couldn't find a citron anywhere to perform the commandment of reciting the blessing on the four species during the holiday of *Sukkos*—Tabernacles. Some students of the Ba'al Shem Tov managed to track down a gorgeous *esrog*. Of course they asked to buy it for their *rebbe*, but the owner refused. They pleaded, offering more and more money, but the man wouldn't sell. Finally he said, 'Okay. I'll sell it. But not for money. I want the reward that the Ba'al Shem Tov would have gotten for performing this *mitzvah*. I want his share in the world to come.' The students were outraged. But the Ba'al Shem Tov was delighted. 'Just what I always wanted,' he said. 'To do *mitzvahs* for their own sake, and not for the sake of earning a reward!' So you see," Sheila concluded, "the highest level of doing things for others is to act without expecting any thanks."

"That is the path to Moshiach!" Sarah concluded.

There was a lull in the room as the women pondered this thought.

Reva thought of how she cooked macrobiotic dishes before dawn, and coaxed her recalcitrant husband to eat them. How many foods had he pushed away in a dismal attempt to deny the severity of his illness and his need for a specialized diet? Had that cooking been in vain? Or had it been an act of unconditional love, precisely because she never knew how it would be received? Who knew how long this caretaking arrangement would have to continue. It could be that Moshe might never, God forbid, really recover, and that her new role in life was to be his nurse—that she would be called upon to continue to pour forth love, and she prayed that she would be strong enough to fulfill this role, if need be.

Levana thought of her husband, scowling and impatient, and how she brought him tea and slippers, speaking softly and hoping he would respond to her love. Was it not the highest form of love, to give and give, never knowing how he would respond?

Ora thought of the students in her outreach groups. Sure, some brought her immense satisfaction by becoming religiously observant, starting to keep *Shabbos,* eating only kosher food, and marrying fine, upstanding Jewish young men. But others appeared impervious to her attempts to reach them. Were these the most real students of all? Those who didn't come with an apparent reward attached, but who reminded her that all she could do was try to reach out— since success and failure lay in the hands of God. She could take no credit for the "successes" any more than she could blame herself for the "failures."

Glicka thought of the evanescent fortune. The money she had lost, and all that she had learned since. Could the people who had betrayed her husband and plunged her family into hideous debt and ignominy be well-disguised angels of God? Bearers of spiritual gifts and blessings rather than curses? She thought of her own upcoming move to Monroe, New York, where the rent was more reasonable. She would commute to work. Maybe some new mission awaited her there. Instead of dreading the move, maybe she could embrace it and celebrate it, and bless the landlord who had sold the apartment building where they had been living, leaving them no choice but to move. Maybe God had things He wanted her to do in Monroe.

Rachel pictured South Africa, for the first time without a lump in her throat. She and her husband were planning an extensive visit, and, yes, she would miss her friends even temporarily. She would miss Brooklyn. She especially would miss

Sarah's table. But she clearly had a contribution to make on the other side of the globe. Her carefully planned explanations of the *mikvah* and its use were important to the women in the communities they would visit. With that in mind, her future looked shiny and holy.

And Shaina considered her Chana and Dovid. They didn't stop. She coaxed, she chased, she shlepped, she plotted, through sleepless nights and endless days—would her incessant "early intervention" pay off? Would they ever talk, become toilet trained, learn to read and write and swim, and someday mature to become independent adults? Would she have *naches* from them? But did she do this for *naches*? She was doing it for them! And, please God, of course they would become independent adults! In the meantime, they also had a right to be children. Just now, they weren't even three!

"The answer," Sarah was saying, "lies not in changing other people, but in changing ourselves. In changing our perspectives and attitudes. The world is as the world is, but think of how different it looks when we put on different lenses."

"Do you do that in your life, Sarah?" asked Glicka.

"I try," Sarah replied modestly. "It's a daily battle for me, just as it is for everyone else. I just had a wonderful trip to Toronto, visiting my daughter. Her children kept us hopping nonstop. Then the plane was delayed on our return trip, and by the time we got home I was falling off my feet. I hadn't even unpacked yet, when a woman called me up for advice. I asked her to call back later, but she wouldn't stop talking. She was absorbed completely in her own story and showed no consideration for how I was feeling, even though I explained to her several times that I had just returned from a major trip and it wasn't the best time to speak."

"I couldn't have handled that," someone said. "I think I would have just hung up."

"Believe me, I was tempted," Sarah said. "But then I thought of the lenses. Literally, I closed my eyes and envisioned putting on a pair of lenses that would enable me to see the pain in this woman's heart. I pretended to put on a hearing aid that would filter the externals, the clutter, from her words and strip them down to the following message: 'Hello, this is God speaking to you through the mouth of Mrs. So-and-so. Your job here is to learn patience and compassion. Sure, you're tired. But you're tired because you just got back from enjoying your wonderful grandchildren. Think of this poor, lonely woman, who has no one and who's tired from shlepping groceries with her arthritic hands and back because she has no husband, children, or grandchildren to help her.' By the end of the conversation, I had invited her for *Shabbos,* even though I had been looking forward to a quiet *Shabbos* after the noise and commotion of all the children. But this was more important. And it's related to the redemption. The first redemption, as you probably know, was from Egypt, which in Hebrew is *Mitzroyim.* The root of the word *Mitzroyim* is *tzar,* meaning narrow. The real redemption involves freeing ourselves from our own little *Mitzroyim,* our own narrowness and constraints. Pushing ourselves beyond our tight comfort zone into something more difficult."

Sarah spoke casually, as if this heroic inner battle was something everyone did all the time. But the women were filled with admiration and awe. Reva remembered how often Sarah said, "If you're feeling down or tired, just do something nice for someone else." Sarah lived by her words.

"It's hard to do," Tamar commented, reaching for a cracker. "I find inconsiderate people intolerable. But I'm beginning to get a handle on it."

"This is the hardest life battle," Sarah replied. "But you know, no one is 'intolerable.' We are all an integral part of

God's plan, even those who seem unpleasant. We know this from the letters in the Torah scroll. Even if one letter is smudged, damaged or written incorrectly, the entire Torah scroll is invalid and can't be used for ritual purposes. And why?" She paused, then went on to answer her own question. "Because we are an organic whole. We are an inseparable entity. Each is precious, no one is to be discarded. Even a damaged individual must be respected."

"That's the symbolism of the four species on *Sukkos*," Faygi said. "We're supposed to bless a palm branch, an *esrog*, a myrtle, and a willow. The *esrog* smells sweet and is edible. The palm tree has edible fruit, but no aroma. The myrtle has a nice smell, but no fruit. And the willow has no smell, and no fruit. This symbolizes different types of people. Some do good deeds and are scholarly—they have fruit and aroma. Some have one or the other, and some have nothing. But we hold all of them together and bless them."

Sarah nodded approvingly. "Exactly. And here's another metaphor. You know that at the end of prayer services, we recite a seemingly strange paragraph about a service in the Bais Hamikdash called the incense." A few women nodded.

"Right," Esther said. "It comes right at the end of the *davening*."

"Among all the ingredients that made up this incense sacrifice was one called *chelbanah* (frankincense). It was quite foul-smelling. Yet it was included in the sacrifice to show that even people who appear to be 'foul-smelling'—who are difficult or unsavory—are still to be welcomed into the community and embraced."

"This sounds like a deodorant commercial," someone commented.

After the laughter had subsided, Sarah said, "This is our life's work. Everything else we do is window dressing. Our most important work is the day-to-day, minute-by-minute adjustment and readjustment of our attitude to feel love instead of rejecting people. It doesn't matter what their crimes were, what their level of religious observance is, or how they treat us. The only thing that matters is how we treat them."

"This goes back to what you were saying about the comfort zone and about *Mitzroyim*," Tamar observed. "Many times we have a narrowness of vision. We might judge the way a person is dressed, and not look for the soul beneath those externals. We need to broaden our vision."

"Everyone needs to broaden their vision," agreed Shaina.

Sarah picked up on the thought. "And the more we do, the more is done for us. The less we judge, the less we will be judged when our time comes. This isn't a simplistic tit-for-tat arrangement. We can see it in more mystical terms. The Ba'al Shem Tov explains that God is really our shadow. He mirrors what we do. Every time we act lovingly, we create a channel through which love flows. That channel is the conduit through which God's love reaches us."

Sarah looked around the room again. Glicka would be moving to Monroe. Rachel was taking an extended trip to South Africa. Reva might become less available as her time increasingly would be taken by her ailing husband and her publishing work, her children, and her grandchildren. This nexus of friends and soulmates—what would happen to them?

She felt her eyes blur, then her vision swam back into focus as she knew the answer.

They were soulmates, all of them. They were together to teach each other and then to carry those lessons over to their independent lives. They always would be linked by their love, by their memories, and by the spiritual teachings that had tied them together. And each time Rachel would teach a South African woman about being a Jewish wife, each time Ora would teach a Russian immigrant about *Shabbos,* each time Glicka would excite her students, each time Reva would juggle her home life with her publishing, Sarah and all those who gathered around her table would be with them.

And so each woman would follow her individual steps, in a giant choreographed dance. The dance of Miriam and the women after the splitting of the Red Sea. The dance of sisterhood and soul. And one day, they would join hands as their souls lofted them above Jerusalem, a circle of redemption, the dance of Moshiach.

Afterword

Someone sits down in Ethel's seat before Mrs. Blisme arrives.

"Uh-oh," thinks Levana.

"I'm really sorry," Shaina approaches the newcomer. "But this seat is always saved for someone. Won't you please join us over here?"

"Oh, this seat is fine," replies the newcomer. She is a refined, agile woman in her seventies. She seems relaxed, and quite at home for a first-timer, as she pours herself a glass of seltzer.

"Um, you don't understand," ventures Glicka. "This is the seat that one of our ladies always saves for her friend. You could sit anywhere else."

"Thank you," says the woman. "You are very kind, but it's hardly necessary."

"Oh, you'll see exactly how necessary," thinks Tamar, anticipating fireworks.

Suddenly Mrs. Blisme stands in the doorway. She eyes the seat, she eyes the newcomer. Her face seems frozen in disbelief.

"We're in for it now," thinks Ora.

"Ethel!" exclaims Mrs. Blisme. "You came!"

The room breaks into applause.

"Why, thank you very much," says Ethel. "I'm so happy to

be here at last. I've heard so much about what you ladies do, and I think it's just extraordinary that you meet like this every Tuesday. I do believe that your gatherings must be just as delightful as the lunch and discussion group that Mabel Blisme leads every Wednesday afternoon, when we sit around Mabel's table."

"I learned it all from Sarah," says Mrs. Blisme, modestly.

"In Monroe we're making a table Sunday morning brunch," says Glicka.

"My Wednesday night group is still going strong," adds Klara.

"Monday lunch is a good time for us in Lawrence," says Erica.

"Mondays might also work for us in Williamsburg," puts in Rachel thoughtfully.

"Well, Sarah," says Tamar. "The wellsprings have really spread out."

"Yes, but on Tuesdays they flow back in," said Mrs. Blisme. "On Tuesdays, Sarah, don't forget to set a place for me."

Glossary of Hebrew and Yiddish Words

akeres habayis. Foundation of the home, the wife

alef-bais, or alef-bet. The Hebrew alphabet

avodah. Holy service

Ba'al Shem Tov. Rabbi Israel Ba'al Shem Tov, founder of the Hasidic movement

ba'al t'shuva. One who "returns" to Torah-observant Judaism

Bais Hamikdash. The Holy Temple in Jerusalem

balabusta. Homemaker

bashert. (adj.) destined; (n.) one's soulmate

Boruch Hashem!. Blessed be God, a frequent Hasidic exclamation

bris. Circumcision, lit. "covenant"

chillul Hashem. Desecration of God's name

cholent. Traditional *Shabbos*-day stew, cooked slowly overnight

daven. To pray

esrog. Citron, lemonlike fruit, used during the *Sukkos* festival

farbrengen. Get-together for spiritual inspiration

frum. Yiddish word meaning "religious"

gematria. The numerical value of Hebrew alef-bet (alphabet) letters. The value of the first letter, alef, is one, the second letter, bais, two, etc.

Gemara. Also known as "Talmud," the "oral" tradition of the Torah, also Divinely revealed at Sinai

gevalt!. Yiddish expression of woe

halachah. Torah law

Hashem. lit. "The Name," referring to God

Hashiveynu. lit. "return us"; the name of an outreach organization

Hasidus. The mystical depths of Torah, along with its practical application, as revealed to the Ba'al Shem Tov and his students

Havdalah. Ceremony separating *Shabbos* from the rest of the week

hesed. Kindness

Kabbalah. Mystical Torah teachings

kavanah. Intent

kiddush. Usually refers to the blessing over wine that inaugurates the *Shabbos* or holiday meal. May also refer to refreshments following the *Shabbos* services

leibedik. Lively

loshon hakodesh. The holy tongue, referring to Hebrew

Lubavitch. Hasidic movement founded by Rabbi Schneur Zalman of Liadi, a grand-student of the Ba'al Shem Tov

Lubavitcher Rebbe. Menachem Mendel Schneerson, most recent leader of the worldwide Hasidic movement

Melaveh Malkeh. Farewell to the *Shabbos*

machatin. Father of the bride or of the groom

machatonim. Relationship formed between the families of the bride and groom

mezuzah. Hand-printed parchment scroll required by Torah to be on the doorpost of every Jewish home

Midrash. A compilation of anecdotes from the Torah

mikvah. Ritualarium; special pool of water used for immersion

mitzvah. One of 613 commandments of the Torah

mohel. One who performs circumcision according to Torah law

morah. Teacher

Moshiach. Messiah

na'aseh v'nishma. "We will do and we will listen," as declared by the Jewish people when they received the Torah at Mount Sinai

naches. Joy, satisfaction

past nisht. Not suitable

rebbitzin. Rabbi's wife

shaliach. Emissary, messenger

Shechinah. God's hovering presence

sheitel. Yiddish for "wig"

Shema Yisrael. Hear, O' Israel. Hebrew prayer that affirms the Jewish faith

shidduch. Match with matrimonial potential

shiur. Hebrew for "lesson" or class of Torah study; plural: *shiurim*

shochet. One who slaughters animals according to Torah law

Sholom Aleichem. Traditional greeting, meaning "may you have peace"

Sholom bayis. Household peace, harmony

Shulchan Oruch. Code of Torah law

simchah. Happiness; a joyful event

Tanya. Seminal text of Chabad Hasidic philosophy, written by the "Alter Rebbe"

tzaddik. Righteous man

tzedakah. Charity

yahrtzeit. Anniversary of a passing

zivvug. Soulmate

Zohar. Kabbalistic source

Suggested Reading

Chasidism, Its Development, Theology, and Practice by Nosson Gurary. Northvale, N.J.: Jason Aronson, 1997.

In the Garden of the Torah, Insights of the Lubavitcher Rebbe, Rabbi Menachem M. Schneerson on the Weekly Torah Readings. 2 vols. Brooklyn, N.Y.: Sichos in English, 1994–95.

The Ladder Up—Secret Steps to Jewish Happiness by R.L. Kremnizer. Brooklyn, N.Y.: S.I.E Publications, 1994.

The Living Torah: The Five Books of Moses by Aryeh Kaplan. Brooklyn, N.Y.: Maznaim Publishing, 1981.

The Seven Colors of the Rainbow by Yirmeyahu Bindman. San Jose, Calif.: Resource Publications, 1995.

Techina: A Voice from the Heart by Rivka Zakutinsky. Brooklyn, N.Y.: Aura Press, 1992.

Toward a Meaningful Life by Simon Jacobson. New York: William Morrow, 1995

Waters of Eden: An Explanation of the Concept of Mikvah by Aryeh Kaplan. New York: National Conference of Synagogue Youth, 1976.